Pilgrims
&
Politics

Rod And Staff Bookstore
Quality Christian Literature
Crockett, KY 41413
(606) 522-4348

Pilgrims
&
Politics

A Pilgrim's View of the Political World

ARUNDEL PRESS
Mazeppa, Minnesota, USA

© 2012 by Michael S. Martin

Published by Arundel Press
43265 County Road 83
Mazeppa, Minnesota 55956
USA
(507) 843-3020
For trade discounts or quantity purchases, contact the publisher.

Printed in the United States of America.

All rights reserved. No part of this publication may be reproduced, stored in a retrieval system, or transmitted in any form or by any means—for example, electronic, photocopy, recording—without the prior written permission of the publisher. The only exception is brief quotations in printed reviews.

ISBN 978-0-9883120-0-5
Scripture quotations are taken from The Holy Bible, Authorized King James Version.

Photo credits: U.S. Capitol and crowds at inauguration of Barack Obama,
  ©Ryan Beiler /Dreamstime.com
  Ignatius before the lions, *Martyrs Mirror*
  All other photographs and artwork courtesy of Library of Congress

Cover Design: Brenda S. Martin

Typesetting and Printing: Silverline Publishing, Lititz, Pa.

Editor: Marvin Eicher

Copyeditor: Mary Hursh

Reviewers: Jerry F. Martin   Omer P. Miller
  John Paul Raber   Brendon Halteman
  Melvin G. Horst   Dennis Torkelson
  David L. Martin   Bradley Eberly
  Merle Ruth   Steven K. Horst
  Lester Showalter   Dallas Witmer
  Virgil Schrock   John D. Kurtz
  William T. Child   Stephen Russell
  James L. Boll   Donald White
  Joseph Stoll   Samuel Coon
  Randall Plett   Grant B. Martin

First Printing, 2012
Second Printing, 2016

Dedicated to the memory of the late

James L. Boll

*A close friend, mentor, and coworker.
He encouraged the writing of this book
and contributed to it in numerous ways.*

Contents

Foreword
Introduction

Part One
The Bible and Nations **14**

   1. Why There Are Nations 17
   2. Why Nations Fall 27
   3. How God Influences Nations: An Old Testament Survey ... 45
   4. How God Influences Nations: A New Testament Survey ... 57
   5. Are There Godly Nations? 75

Part Two
Early America—a Christian Nation? **86**

   6. Religion in Puritan New England 89
   7. Religion in the Middle Colonies and in the South; the Great Awakening 115
   8. A Righteous Revolution? 135
   9. The Religious Views of the Founding Fathers 153
  10. American Protestantism in the 1800s 183
  11. American Social and Moral Issues in the 1800s 199

Part Three
A Christian View of Modern Politics **224**

  12. Understanding Civil Religion 227
  13. A Christian View of Civil Government 253
  14. A Christian View of Officials 275
  15. A Christian View of Laws 293
  16. A Christian View of Culture 315
  17. A Christian View of Foreign Cultures 345
  18. A Christian View of Political Action: Part 1 367
  19. A Christian View of Political Action: Part 2 395
  20. A Christian View of War 423

For Further Reading 457

Foreword

Were you ever accused of being a second-rate citizen or a parasite? Were you ever told that we ought to try to Christianize our government? Whether or not you have yet had such an experience, you need to read this book. This book will fortify you against the intimidations that will inevitably come your way.

You can dip into this book at any place and read with profit. However, it will pay you to start at the beginning. We must understand how God relates to nations in order to understand how Christians should relate to nations.

One of the unique features of *Pilgrims and Politics* is that it interprets history from a conservative Anabaptist viewpoint. Because of that, it does not reflect the narrow nationalistic viewpoint that is so characteristic of the typical American history book. This book may lead you to rethink some long-held assumptions.

In order to arrive at correct conclusions, a writer must begin with the correct assumptions. The author has built his arguments on a very solid foundation—the indisputable fact that the New Testament is permeated with a two-kingdom worldview. Without this basis, Christian thinking about pilgrims and politics becomes practically impossible.

Rather than glorify the American way of life, the author employs God's plumb line to show how crooked that way of life has been. However, unlike some writers who display an anti-government spirit, he infuses an almost profound respect for government, laws, and officials.

Contrary to popular opinion, we learn here that the birth of America was not as glorious as we have been led to believe that it was. In fact, most Mennonites and Amish of the Revolutionary era viewed the so-called war for independence as rebellion. From then until now, there has been a seemingly irrevocable tension between the American government and its nonresistant citizens. The author shows that this is precisely what should be expected.

Chapter 12 is an excellent and much-needed explanation of the difference between civil religion and true religion. Many professing Christians have failed to recognize this difference.

Wrong conditioning has likewise given many professing Christians a mistaken view of patriotism. In this book we discover a disturbing truth: patriotism, as popularly conceived, is in fact a form of idolatry.

As you read this book you will learn that when Christians yield to the temptation to enter the political world, they inevitably get involved in non-Christian methods and activities. Further, trying to improve public morality by means of political action has repeatedly proven to be a very disappointing venture. This book will leave you with the understanding that the Christian can make his greatest contribution to the world by serving as an ambassador for Jesus Christ who alone can change the human heart.

Parents, schoolteachers, and ministers will find here a gold mine of material with which to correctly indoctrinate the rising generations.

Merle Ruth
Annville, Pennsylvania
May 2011

Introduction

An air of uneasiness prevailed in the days before William Clinton's election as 42nd President of the United States, and it continued as various scandals erupted during his administration. Christians sat in church on Sundays, singing "Maker of All Things," "The Lord My Shepherd Is," and "A Mighty Fortress"—songs that describe the cheerful hope of the soul stayed on God and the fact that we need not tremble before the prince of darkness, because "one little word will fell him." Yet in many private conversations between Christians the rest of the week, apprehension and culture-trust showed up.

"Our society is going to ruin," people said. "Whatever will happen to us now? How difficult it is to raise families in such an age, when even persons in high office sin with little fear."

I felt that fear. I was in McBride, British Columbia, attending a youth Bible study, when news reached us that Mr. Clinton had won the election. "I have to go back to the United States," I told my friends, "to rescue the young lady I am courting from Clinton's reign."

"And I," announced one of my fellow Americans, "am not going back at all. I will stay here in Canada."

But at the end of the week, we went back to the United States, and we rescued no one.

In the years that followed a question kept nagging at my mind: Why were some of us Christians singing so calmly in church about our trust in God no matter what rages about us, but elsewhere we were so set-jawed about the conditions in the world? Why does the Bible present such a positive picture of the victory of God's kingdom, when here on earth it looks as if His kingdom is hardly making headway? The difference between what I felt and what the Bible said sent me on the journey of research that inspired this book.

Pilgrims and Politics has three parts. Part One includes five chapters discussing how the Bible depicts nations and how God talks about nations. This is the foundation for the rest of the book. We need to understand nations from God's viewpoint if we will relate to politics in a godly way.

Part Two contains six chapters discussing American history from an Anabaptist perspective. The main purpose of this part is to point out that the oft-recommended return to "the way America was" is full of misconceptions and is not the call of the Gospel. Christians in America need to understand this country's history from a Biblical perspective if we are to be an effective witness today.

Part Three discusses a Christian view of modern politics. How a Christian should relate to civil officials, laws, culture, foreigners, political action, war, and more are discussed in nine chapters.

For readers who are not familiar with the term Anabaptists, these people were the third wing of the Reformation—a group who did not agree with the Catholics or the Reformers. They believed that Jesus taught nonresistance to evil, and that the kingdom of Christ and the kingdom of this world were two distinct kingdoms struggling for the allegiance of the human heart. They believed the New Testament taught that government and politics belong to the kingdom of this world. Descendants of the Anabaptists are called Amish and Mennonites, and in this book I often refer to them as Anabaptists for the sake of conciseness. I am one of them, and am grateful for their contributions to my life.

In this work, I have quoted from many authors. I am thankful to the publishers and authors who granted permission for the longer quotes. A selected bibliography is included for those who wish to do further research.

I am deeply grateful for the help of God and the assistance of others. The advice of the editor and those who offered critical reviews of the manuscript were invaluable; their names are listed after the title page. I am especially grateful for the extensive help provided by Brother Lester Showalter of Greencastle, Pennsylvania.

No one provided more help than my wife in listening and in suggesting improvements for the manuscript. Thank you, Brenda.

For me, the ten years of research leading up to the writing of this book was filled with learning, and I still have far to go. Writing this book does not mean that I fully understand my subject; and reading it will not answer every question you might raise about the Christian and politics. I only hope that it will be a step in the right direction for both of us. I write not so much to teach as to comprehend myself what Jesus means when He says "Follow me." I write not so much to share anything new as to clarify the Bible principles and history that we already know. May God be praised if there is any truth on these pages that can lead someone to a closer walk with Him.

Michael S. Martin
Mazeppa, Minnesota
May 2011

Part One

The Bible and Nations

Introduction

Why are there nations? How does God control the nations? The Bible is written specifically to teach people the way to personal salvation through Jesus Christ, but it also answers basic questions about civil government. The Old Testament stories of the early centuries of the world, as well as the history of Israel and mighty nations such as Assyria and Babylonia, tell us about the character of nations and their leaders since the beginning of time.

Understanding nations from a Biblical viewpoint is important because it is the key to knowing how God looks at nations. This understanding helps us to trust God and His work in the world, and it helps us avoid common errors in the way we think about politics.

Chapters
1. Why There Are Nations
2. Why Nations Fall
3. How God Influences Nations: An Old Testament Survey
4. How God Influences Nations: A New Testament Survey
5. Are There Godly Nations?

And the Lord said,
> Behold, the people is one,
> and they have all one language;
> and this they begin to do:
> and now nothing will be restrained from them,
> which they have imagined to do.

Go to, let us go down,
> and there confound their language . . .

So the Lord scattered them abroad
> from thence upon the face of all the earth.

Genesis 11:6-8

1

Why There Are Nations

After God sentenced Cain to be a fugitive, Cain moved to the land of Nod on the east side of Eden. There his family multiplied, and there he built a city. At the same time, Adam's other children populated other areas. Before the time of Babel, many towns and cities rose.

Mighty men led early civilization. It appears that most of these "men of renown" were proud, violent, and corrupt chieftains.[1] None of them were godly, because Genesis 6 tells us that Noah and his family were the only righteous people left.

There are nations because men want to rule.

The Flood destroyed the wicked civilization of the early world. But after the Flood, the "mighty man" culture of

---

1. Genesis 6:5, 11-13

pre-Flood times quickly rose again. Genesis 10 describes how Cush's son Nimrod became mighty in the earth—"a mighty hunter before the Lord."

Nimrod's kingdom began with Babel, situated in the rich, silted plain of Shinar between the Euphrates and Tigris rivers, north of the Persian Gulf. This land was overrun with wild animals, but Nimrod's hunting skills proved equal to the task.[2]

Nimrod set up the kingdom of Babylon with four cities, the first such organization mentioned in the Bible. He had more political power than anyone else in the early Biblical record. Old Jewish records say that he was "a hunter of the sons of men" and that he convinced people to despise God's law and to follow his own judgment.

Assyrian and Roman histories describe Cush, Nimrod's father, and Nimrod as influential in turning people toward idolatry. *Nimrod* means "one who rebelled" or "let us rebel." Some language scholars believe that in the phrase "a mighty hunter before the Lord," *before* actually means "against." In building Babel, apparently a temple of idolatrous worship, and in the desire to "make us a name," Nimrod exalted himself.[3] He was deified after his death, if not before.

Ancient history also calls Nimrod the father of battle. The earth was violent long before Nimrod's time, but he may be the first one who carried on the organized violence of war. He had a fierce, ambitious disposition, and he gathered other

---

2. Ancient records indicate that wild animals were a problem for a number of civilizations for the first several thousand years of world history. In Exodus 23:29, 30, God told the Israelites that He would drive the Canaanites out slowly so that wild beasts would not take over the land. He also warned them that wild beasts would decimate their population if they did not follow His laws (Leviticus 26:22).

3. Genesis 11:4

strong young men with similar personalities. This group of men are said to have conquered many tribes who were yet unacquainted with war.

Nimrod's example influenced Asshur, another mighty man, who became the father of the Assyrians. Asshur set up a rival kingdom with another four cities.[4] Nimrod and Asshur wanted to preserve their names and ensure that their kingdoms were supreme. They paid any price to do it, because they wanted to rule.

The desire to rule people has been part of worldly authority all through history. Pharaoh told Moses, "Who is the Lord, that I should obey his voice to let Israel go? I know not the Lord, neither will I let Israel go."[5] With that he pursued an even more ambitious plan of city and monument building. Solomon became so drunk with power and wealth that

The desire to rule is in human nature, and it will always be a part of worldly government.

he oppressed the people he was called to serve. Jesus described it this way: "Ye know that they which are accounted to rule over the Gentiles exercise lordship over them; and their great ones exercise authority upon them."[6]

Carnal men love greatness, and they will sacrifice moral principles to become great and stay great. That is one of the reasons both the Old and New Testaments refer to nations as beasts. The desire to rule dulls normal human sensitivities. National leaders often act savagely, destroying people

---

4. Genesis 10:11, 12
5. Exodus 5:2
6. Mark 10:42

and natural resources with little regard for the helpless individuals caught in the crossfire. Men who do not go that far will lie, defame others, and compromise to gain their ends. The desire to rule is in human nature, and it will always be a part of worldly government.

There are nations because of the Babel dispersion.

As the tower of Babel rose, Nimrod and his fellows drew much of the population after them. The godly remnant was apparently so small that as the Lord looked on the scene, He said, "The people is one."[7] To stop this destructive unity, God simply gave those people a number of different languages, a masterful stroke that eventually scattered "them abroad upon the face of all the earth."[8]

God's judgment at Babel meant much more than giving mankind some new languages. By this action God created diversity among people on earth. He checked the "one empire" spirit and stopped the political unity that would lead the world back to the rampant pre-Flood wickedness.

The Babel dispersion showed men that God ruled in their kingdoms. It created a situation where God could judge segments of the world's population without destroying mankind completely, as the Flood had nearly done. The different peoples and political ideas that produced the wars of Genesis 14 show how effective this dispersion was.

There are nations to keep civil order.

The social and spiritual judgment that God imposed on Cain after he murdered Abel is the first Biblical record of civil

---

7. "The people is one" indicates that Nimrod's rival Asshur did not establish his kingdom before the Babel dispersion.

8. Genesis 11:5-9

order. Cain became a vagabond—a man that society did not want to have around. God had created people with a deep respect for human life, and Cain fully expected to suffer capital punishment for violating that respect. He was saved from that fate only by God's intervention: "And the Lord set a mark upon Cain, lest any finding him should kill him."[9]

Five generations later, vengeance and civil justice lived on. When Lamech killed another man or two in alleged self-defense, he expected other people to take revenge on him for it. "If Cain shall be avenged sevenfold," he said, "truly Lamech seventy and sevenfold."[10]

After the Flood, God further described civil order to Noah.

> And surely your blood of your lives will I require; at the hand of every beast will I require it, and at the hand of man; at the hand of every man's brother will I require the life of man. Whoso sheddeth man's blood, by man shall his blood be shed: for in the image of God made he man (Genesis 9:5, 6).

In most places, throughout most of history, civil law upholds basic order because of the ideals of fairness and morality that God put into everyone. But because of man's dark, fallen mind, every government has some regulations that are inconsistent with God's laws.

There are nations to protect the godly remnant.

When Joseph was cruelly sold into Egypt and later had the chance to repay his brothers for their wrong, he said, "Now therefore be not grieved, nor angry with yourselves, that ye sold

---

9. Genesis 4:15
10. Genesis 4:23, 24

me hither: for God did send me before you to preserve life. . . . and to save your lives by a great deliverance. So now it was not you that sent me hither, but God."[11] God told Jacob not to fear going down to Egypt, for there he would become a great nation.

Later in the Israelites' history, God wanted to punish most of them for their sin, while preserving the faithful remnant through whom His Son would come. So He used Babylon as both a scourge and a shelter. He told the Israelites to settle down in Babylon and pray for the city, so that they could live in peace as captives.[12]

When Elijah thought the godly line had been swallowed up by Ahab and Jezebel's idolatry, God told him that there were yet seven thousand souls who had not bowed to Baal. Even though Israel as a whole was not the godly remnant, it contained and sheltered that remnant.

When Rome spread her wings, she authorized certain religions and selected certain buildings in which people could worship. None of these approved religions were allowed to claim superiority over any of the other approved religions. Christianity appeared to have no chance to survive in that situation.

Yet God said He sent His Son into the world in the "fulness of the time."[13] God allowed the Roman Empire to become so gigantic and to have so many different cultures that she could not closely control all her subjects. In this setting, Christianity flourished. It came at the right time to provide an answer for the terrible Roman morals. It came at the right time to spread because of the advances in travel and economy and the absence of major wars.

---

11. Genesis 45:5, 7, 8
12. Jeremiah 29:1-7
13. Galatians 4:4

The church apostatized in its first several hundred years, and most of it became the Catholic church, which began to fiercely persecute true believers. Yet all through the Dark and Middle Ages, God protected His remnant. Sometimes He sheltered them in remote regions where the long Catholic arm barely reached. Other times He protected them in cities with lenient governments, or in rural areas where local officials flouted Catholic rule as much as they dared. Even though in these times many believers died for their faith, a remnant survived because God sheltered them.

> **Within nations, God has provided a niche for His people all through history.**

Beginning in the 1500s, God used the Reformation and military struggles to weaken the Catholic dominance and provide the remnant with more opportunities to grow. In that time Europeans discovered North and South America, which eventually became havens for persecuted believers.

Within nations, God has provided a niche for His people all through history.

There are nations to punish other nations.

God promised Noah that there would never again be a worldwide flood to punish mankind for their sin, but He did not say there would be *no* earthly punishments for sin. Universal punishments such as guilt and the law of sowing and reaping help to control wickedness. The Book of Revelation shows that God may judge sin with harsh weather, plagues, and geological catastrophes such as volcanoes and earthquakes.[14] The furnace of Sodom is a sobering reminder of divine wrath.

But the most common judgment in the Bible against sinful nations was destruction or deportation by other sinful peoples. When the Israelites came to Canaan, God used them to punish the terrible iniquity of the Canaanites, and at the same time gain a homeland. But when the Israelites, in turn, needed to be punished for their sin, God moved the Assyrians to deport them.

It is impossible to create an ideal society through civil government.

The Assyrians had no idea that God was using them, and their deportation of Israel was but a small part of their conquests. When God was finished using them, they fell to wicked Babylon, God's next major tool on earth. There are many other examples stating God's intention to punish one nation by another.

There are nations to show man the weakness of earthly institutions.

Some nations have lasted only fifty years while others endured a thousand years or more. But no nation has ever stood permanently.

No nation has ever brought lasting satisfaction to men's souls, stopped their downward moral slide, or been able to abolish war. None of them have been able to erase despotism, grinding poverty, or ill-gained riches from their own people, let alone the whole world.

Nations cannot meet man's greatest needs. They cannot change his selfish heart. That is why, even though civil

---

14. However, this does not mean that such catastrophes are necessarily a punishment for sin.

government fills a vital role, it is impossible to create an ideal society through civil government. When nations fall, it reminds men that there is a higher calling for humanity, and that trust in nations is always disappointed.

As Isaac Watts stated in the song "Joy to the World," God uses the sinfulness and impotence of nations to prove the beauty of the true church.

> He rules the world with truth and grace,
> > And makes the nations prove
>
> The glories of His righteousness,
> > And wonders of His love.

In Daniel 2 God revealed to King Nebuchadnezzar that He would set up a kingdom "which shall never be destroyed: . . . but it shall break in pieces and consume all these [worldly] kingdoms, and it shall stand for ever." The only lasting improvement for mankind comes through Jesus Christ.

Oh, where are kings and empires now
    Of old that went and came?
But, Lord, Thy church is praying yet,
    A thousand years the same. . . .
For not like kingdoms of the world
    Thy holy church, O God!
Though earthquake shocks are threatening her
    And tempests are abroad;
Unshaken as eternal hills,
    Immovable she stands;
A mountain that shall fill the earth,
    A house not made with hands.

—A. C. Coxe, 1839

2

Why Nations Fall

The Bible gives four basic reasons why nations fall. They fall because of pride, because of moral corruption, because God's purpose for using them is eventually fulfilled, and because they are destined to fall.

Nations fall because of pride.
Pride in power. When God warned Israel about the consequences of unfaithfulness, He said, "And I will break the pride of your power."[1] Israel was a special nation to God, and He gave her special commands, promises, and assistance. Yet He

---
1. Leviticus 26:19

recognized that she would tend to be proud of her power just like any other nation.

The Moabites, descendants of Lot's oldest daughter, rose and fell in prosperity and power for hundreds of years before Christ. Around 760 B.C., Isaiah said that they were "laid waste" and "brought to silence."[2]

"We have heard of the pride of Moab," Isaiah testified; "he is very proud: even of his haughtiness, and his pride, and his wrath: but his lies shall not be so. . . . Surely they are stricken."[3]

Jeremiah recorded a similar humiliation 140 years later. "The horn of Moab is cut off, and his arm is broken, saith the Lord. . . he magnified himself against the Lord. . . . How hath Moab turned the back with shame! so shall Moab be a derision and a dismaying to all them about him."[4]

Jeremiah 49 records the pride of Esau's descendants, the Edomites, in their ability to conquer. Their own strength deceived them, so God promised to make them small among the nations.[5]

Ancient Egypt, isolated by desert and sea, grew into a powerful and proud nation. About 595 B.C., God promised through Ezekiel to send a sword upon them. Egypt and her allies would fall, and the pride of their power would be broken. They would become a desolate and wasted place. "And they shall know that I am the Lord," Ezekiel prophesied, "when I have set a fire in Egypt, and when all her helpers shall be destroyed."[6]

Nebuchadnezzar is one of the best examples of God's judgment on the pride of power. A bold and brilliant man,

---

2. Isaiah 15:1
3. Isaiah 16:6, 7
4. Jeremiah 48:25, 26, 39
5. Jeremiah 49:15, 16
6. Ezekiel 30:4, 6-8

2 • Why Nations Fall

Nebuchadnezzar rose to power in 605 B.C. as Assyria was falling. He allied Babylonia with the Medes, drove the Egyptians out of Syria and Palestine, and in twenty years gained a massive empire. He built and beautified temples and palaces and made Babylon an international center, and while he did it "his heart was lifted up, and his mind hardened in pride."[7] When he looked at all his work and told himself how he had done it all by his own might, calamity struck. He was sent into the fields to live as an animal, until he would learn that "the most High ruleth in the kingdom of men, and giveth it to whomsoever he will."[8]

Eventually God cripples or destroys self-confident, boastful nations because they obscure the true Source of power.

God might tolerate a nation's pride in power for a long time, but eventually He cripples or destroys self-confident, boastful nations because they obscure the true Source of power.

Pride in commerce. Tyre was an old seaport city, situated partly on the mainland and partly on a well-protected island just off the Mediterranean coast of Phoenicia. Having few natural resources, the Tyrians sailed to all parts of the known world and became famous traders. The prophet Isaiah called them a marketplace of nations.[9] Secular history shows that their greatest affluence was between 1100 and 573 B.C.

The Tyrians did business with everyone and in everything. Fine clothing, wood, ivory, spices, gems, gold, and lesser

---

7. Daniel 5:20
8. Daniel 4:32
9. Isaiah 23:3

metals passed through their markets. They traded agricultural products such as wheat, honey, wine, horses, sheep, goats, and wool. They bought and sold slaves. Their ships were built of the highest quality wood, sported ivory benches on the decks, and unfurled sails of embroidered fine linen. Their trademark was extravagant quality and beauty. To protect themselves and the stability of their markets, they lined up mercenary soldiers on their walls.

Tyre's organized trading enriched her business partners, and a sense of secure prosperity grew among them. Tyre claimed she was perfect; her economic prowess was the envy of other nations. She was so proud that she called herself a god, and claimed that she sat "in the seat of God." She believed that her wisdom and her commerce were unconquerable. But in Ezekiel 27 and 28, God sent an entirely different message to this opulent city, before He allowed Nebuchadnezzar II to sack her in 573 B.C.

"O thou that art situate at the entry of the sea, which art a merchant of the people for many isles . . . ," Ezekiel cried. "All the inhabitants of the isles shall be astonished at thee, and their kings shall be sore afraid. . . .

Man does not control the markets, and he is not the source of economic stability.

Therefore thus saith the Lord God; Because thou hast set thine heart as the heart of God; behold, therefore I will bring strangers upon thee, the terrible of the nations: and they shall draw their swords against the beauty of thy wisdom, and they shall defile thy brightness. . . . Wilt thou yet say before him that slayeth thee, I am God? but thou shalt be a man, and no God, in the hand of him that slayeth thee."[10]

"Who hath taken this counsel against Tyre?" asked Isaiah. He answered in the same breath, "The Lord of hosts hath purposed it, to stain the pride of all glory, and to bring into contempt all the honourable of the earth."[11] Certainly God cared that some people suffered physically due to the sudden collapse of the world's economic jugular. But it was far more important to Him to stain the pride of glory and bring the honorable of the earth into contempt, than it was to keep a stable economy. Tyre had mocked other nations as they fell; now it was her turn to be mocked.[12] By destroying Tyre, God reinforced in man's mind that he was only human. Man did not control the markets, and he was not the source of economic stability.

Revelation 18 records a typical scene that has happened over and over in world history. As finances seem secure and trade increases, men tend to push off their spiritual needs and find satisfaction in earthly comfort. Prosperity enables scientific discoveries and intellectual achievements that tend to pull people away from God. But when God allows great economic centers to collapse or decay, people are reminded of their need for their Creator and Saviour.

Pride in security. Between two mountain ranges south of the Dead Sea there once lay the territory of Esau's descendants, the Edomites. To the north, sea and mountains made access to the area difficult, and to the south lay a vast desert. Mountains to the west cast up massive, rocky faces about two thousand

---

10. Ezekiel 27:3, 35; 28:6, 7, 9
11. Isaiah 23:8, 9
12. Ezekiel 26:2

feet above sea level, punctuated by broken ridges, cliffs, and deep ravines. To the east lay an unbroken limestone ridge, rising about three thousand feet above sea level. Edom was a wild, rugged, and almost inaccessible land. But it had some fertile interior plateaus and valleys that the Edomites farmed and pastured. Genesis records that they possessed these rocky holds long before Israel became a nation.[13]

After successfully defending their mountain stronghold for hundreds of years, the Edomites thought they could never be overthrown. But God had a different message for them.

> Thus saith the Lord God concerning Edom, ... The pride of thine heart hath deceived thee, thou that dwellest in the clefts of the rock, whose habitation is high; that saith in his heart, Who shall bring me down to the ground? Though thou exalt thyself as the eagle, and though thou set thy nest among the stars, thence will I bring thee down, saith the Lord (Obadiah 1, 3, 4).[14]

Jeremiah declared that these proud, secure people would be made "small among the heathen, and despised among men," and that the earth would be moved at the noise of Edom's fall.[15] When men think that they are invincible, they are ripe to become an example to the rest of the world. God restrains boastful mankind by sinking the unsinkable and conquering the unconquerable, often by surprisingly simple means.

Pride in reaction. Proud nations will usually not admit defeat until they have practically nothing left. After Edom was but

---

13. Genesis 36; see also Deuteronomy 2:1-5.
14. See also Jeremiah 49:7-22; Ezekiel 25:12-14.
15. Jeremiah 49:15, 21

a trace of her former self, after God had laid her land waste, Edom still spoke proudly of her abilities.

"We are impoverished," the Edomites said, "but we will return and build the desolate places."

"They shall build," replied the Lord, "but I will throw down."[16]

In Isaiah 9, God warned the Israelites that their doom was sure. They would be further punished for their dishonesty and idolatry, even though they were struggling to survive and shake off judgment. But Israel stoutly resisted the inevitable.

"The bricks are fallen down, but we will build with hewn stones," they claimed arrogantly. "The sycomores are cut down, but we will change them into cedars."

"For the people turneth not unto him that smiteth them, neither do they seek the Lord of hosts," Isaiah exclaimed. "Therefore the Lord will cut off from Israel head and tail, branch and rush, in one day."[17]

Hosea echoed the same sentiments, charging the Israelites with blatant rebellion against obvious judgment. "The pride of Israel testifieth to his face," he cried, "and they do not return to the Lord their God, nor seek him for all this."[18]

There are many modern examples of proud reactions. While smoke still rose from the rubble of the Twin Towers, American leaders promised that the towers

> **God restrains boastful mankind by sinking the unsinkable and conquering the unconquerable, often by surprisingly simple means.**

---

16. Malachi 1:3, 4
17. Isaiah 9:9-14
18. Hosea 7:10

would rise again. While much of hurricane-ravaged New Orleans still lay under water, people said that America without New Orleans was unimaginable, and that this great city would be rebuilt.

Even in heavy adversity, few sinners turn to God. But this does not mean that God's work with them is of no effect. One of God's main purposes in dealing with nations is to humble men and to keep wickedness from reaching pre-Flood heights. He wants men to know that they are men. He will never let them get to the point where they can honestly think that they have everything under control. Pride grows and bulges; but at the peak of its conceit, God throws it to the earth.

Nations fall because of violence and immorality.

God sent the Flood because almost everyone on earth was violent and corrupt. God told Noah, "The end of all flesh is come before me; for the earth is filled with violence through them; and, behold, I will destroy them with the earth."[19]

Among the commandments that God gave Moses at Sinai are the precepts for moral purity in Leviticus 18. God warned the Israelites,

> Defile not ye yourselves in any of these things: for in all these the nations are defiled which I cast out before you: and the land is defiled: therefore do I visit the iniquity thereof upon it, and the land itself vomiteth out her inhabitants (Leviticus 18:24, 25).

The writer of Ecclesiastes assures us, "If thou seest the oppression of the poor, and violent perverting of judgment and justice

---

19. Genesis 6:13

in a province, marvel not at the matter: for he that is higher than the highest regardeth; and there be higher than they."[20]

An early example of this High One regarding corruption after the Flood was the destruction of Sodom and Gomorrah. There was so little righteousness left in these perverted cities that they were totally destroyed.

For over a thousand years Assyria grew, and God used her to bring judgment on many other nations, though she was desperately wicked herself. Of all the ancient kingdoms, she was one of the most violent in conquest. The stone and clay records of the Assyrians depict a cruel and immoral people.

Around 713 B.C., about 150 years after Jonah preached at Nineveh, the Assyrian capital, God sent another message to the Assyrians through Nahum.

"Woe to the bloody city!" cried Nahum. "It is all full of lies and robbery....There is a multitude of slain, and a great number of carcases; and there is none end of their corpses; they stumble upon their corpses."

The Assyrians were not only violent, but also immoral and idolatrous. Nineveh influenced "nations through her whoredoms, and families through her witchcrafts." God promised to shame her before other nations, "cast abominable filth" upon her, and set her "as a gazingstock."[21]

In 612 B.C., the Babylonians sacked Nineveh, ending Assyrian rule, and became the next world power. The region of Babylon (Babel) was occupied soon after the Flood, and it was the site of one of God's earliest judgments on politics. For several thousand years before Christ, Babylon's strength rose

---

20. Ecclesiastes 5:8
21. Nahum 2, 3

and fell. At times she conquered large areas, at times she was overrun by other nations. Her people were idolatrous, and the idolatry grew worse as the centuries passed. But God raised her up to accomplish His purposes.

"For, lo, I raise up the Chaldeans," declared Habakkuk, "that bitter and hasty nation, which shall march through the breadth of the land, to possess the dwellingplaces that are not their's. They are terrible and dreadful. . . . They shall come all for violence: . . . and they shall gather the captivity as the sand."[22]

The idolatry of Babylon was reaching its climax in Habakkuk's day. The story in Daniel 2 shows how Nebuchadnezzar depended on his magicians and how violently he dealt with them when they could not fulfill his bizarre demands. When Daniel revealed the dream to the king, the king fell down and worshiped Daniel, and in the next breath he declared that Daniel's God was truly a God of gods.

In Daniel 3, possibly 17 years after the events in Chapter 2, Nebuchadnezzar set up an idol of unprecedented proportions and expense. At ninety feet tall and nine feet wide,[23] the shining gold image must have dominated the plain of Dura for miles around. When a few Jewish subjects would not bow to it but could not be destroyed in the fiery furnace, Nebuchadnezzar was again brought face to face with the power of this strange God. Shaken, he quickly decreed severe penalties on anyone who spoke against this God, and he elevated the three Jews in his kingdom.

---

22. Habakkuk 1:6-9
23. Based on an 18-inch cubit

However, these experiences had little effect on Nebuchadnezzar's pride. After God deprived him of his reason and let him live with the beasts for a time, Nebuchadnezzar finally began to honor Him and call Him the high God. Yet there is no evidence that the Babylonians' idolatry declined or that they stopped meddling with the powers of darkness. Their violence and immorality grew until God said that He would break their idols in pieces.

"Stand now with thine enchantments," God challenged them, "and with the multitude of thy sorceries, wherein thou hast laboured from thy youth; if so be thou shalt be able to profit, if so be thou mayest prevail. . . . Let now the astrologers, the stargazers, the monthly prognosticators, stand up, and save thee from these things that shall come upon thee."[24]

Babylon had conquered Israel along with many other nations, and she glorified herself and her gods above the deities of the nations she vanquished. Instead of recognizing God as the source of her power, she was deceived by her ability. Her actions were destroying the concepts of right and wrong in the earth, and God would tolerate it no longer. Babylonia fell to the Persians under Cyrus in 539 B.C., and under the Romans the area was depopulated and left desolate in 275 B.C. The cry of her capture echoed among the nations, reminding men that there is a God much higher than the golden image on the plain of Dura.

Nations fall because God's purpose in using them is eventually fulfilled.

When God smashed Judah's pride and served them their just dues, He did it by using Babylon, a nation that was worse

---

24. See Isaiah 47; Jeremiah 50.

than Judah in moral terms. But God was not showing special favor to Babylon to use her like this. She was simply a tool God used until He destroyed it along with other tools that He had used earlier.

> I have made the earth, the man and the beast that are upon the ground, by my great power and by my outstretched arm, and have given it unto whom it seemed meet unto me. And now have I given all these lands into the hand of Nebuchadnezzar the king of Babylon, my servant; and the beasts of the field have I given him also to serve him. And all nations shall serve him, and his son, and his son's son, until the very time of his land come: and then many nations and great kings shall serve themselves of him (Jeremiah 27:5-7).

The "very time of his land" came during Belshazzar's reign, on the day when Daniel was called to interpret the meaning of the handwriting on the wall. Babylon had been weighed in God's balances and found wanting. God had no further use for her. He decided what would happen to Babylon and to whom the nation would be given; the Babylonians could do nothing about it. "They shall lie down together," Isaiah said. "They shall not rise: they are extinct, they are quenched as tow."[25]

Always when a nation or government has fulfilled its purpose, it is brought low or destroyed.

In Isaiah 10, God called the Assyrians "the rod of mine anger." He said that "the staff in their hand is mine indignation," and that He was sending these proud people "against an

---
25. Isaiah 43:17

hypocritical nation." God had given the Assyrians "a charge, to take the spoil, and to take the prey, and to tread them down like the mire of the streets."

But were the Assyrians conscious of all this? Not at all. They did not recognize God; they counted Him among the idols of the nations they had already conquered.

> Howbeit he meaneth not so, neither doth his heart think so; but it is in his heart to destroy and cut off nations not a few. For he saith, Are not my princes altogether kings? Is not Calno as Carchemish? is not Hamath as Arpad? is not Samaria as Damascus? As my hand hath found the kingdoms of the idols, and whose graven images did excel them of Jerusalem and of Samaria; shall I not, as I have done unto Samaria and her idols, so do to Jerusalem and her idols?
>
> Wherefore it shall come to pass, that when the Lord hath performed his whole work upon mount Zion and on Jerusalem, I will punish the fruit of the stout heart of the king of Assyria, and the glory of his high looks.

"By the strength of my hand have I done it," the Assyrian king boasted, "and by my wisdom; for I am prudent." But he was wrong. Assyria's plans for conquest were thoughts that God had placed in her mind to accomplish His purposes.

Nations today have the same attitudes as ancient Assyria. They see their own wisdom and strategy as the reasons for their power, territory, and economic might. But God tells His people to look beyond those surface reasons to what is actually happening. "I said unto the fools, Deal not foolishly: and to the wicked, Lift not up the horn: lift not up your horn on high: speak not with a stiff neck. For promotion cometh neither from the east, nor from the west, nor from the south. But God is the judge: he putteth down one, and setteth up another."[26]

The fall of nations is not always as final as Sodom and Gomorrah's, and sometimes it seems a long time in coming. But always when a nation or government has fulfilled its purpose, it is brought low or destroyed.

Nations fall because they are destined to fall.

In Ezekiel 31 God compares the nations to trees in "the garden of God." This was written when Assyria was declining. Earlier she had been the greatest tree in the garden, and all the other trees had envied her.

God described Assyria as a cedar in Lebanon with fair branches. All other great nations lived under her shadow of authority. No other tree in the garden could compare to her in size or beauty. When God punished her, He was sending a message to every other tree in the garden. He warned them not to "exalt themselves for their height, neither shoot up their top among the thick boughs." He reminded them that "they are all delivered unto death, to the nether parts of the earth, in the midst of the children of men, with them that go down to the pit."

This message was part of Ezekiel's prophecy against Egypt, who flexed her military muscles as Assyria's power decayed. She wanted to become the next superpower, but in God's plan, Babylon was going to occupy that position. In the struggle to dominate, Egypt would end up in "the nether parts of the earth, . . . with them that go down into the pit."[27]

---

26. Psalm 75:4-7

27. This was fulfilled in 608 B.C., when the Egyptian king Necho II marched toward Assyria, hoping to take advantage of the Assyrian and Babylonian struggle. King Nebuchadnezzar II devastated the Egyptian army and took control of all of Egypt's Asian territory. See also 2 Kings 24:7.

2 • Why Nations Fall

God could not have described the fate of earthly nations in clearer terms. In Ezekiel 32:18-30, He named power after power that had reigned over much of the known world in different periods, and He said that Pharaoh would see them all in the place where he was going. We can extend that list much farther: the cohorts of Babylon and Persia are there; mighty Greece is there; and invincible Rome lies there in shame. Every nation will eventually be there.

God gave Jeremiah a symbolic cup full of His fury, saying that all the nations to whom the prophet was sent would be made to drink from this cup. Judah was first, followed by a long list that included all the peoples in the known world of that time. "Drink ye, . . . and fall, and rise no more...The Lord hath a controversy with the nations," Jeremiah cried. "He will plead with all flesh; he will give them that are wicked to the sword, saith the Lord."[28] God still has a controversy with the nations; it will go on until the end of time.

In Daniel 2, God revealed that all the mighty kingdoms of the earth would eventually be blown away like chaff before the wind. In Revelation, nations are repeatedly mentioned as having the same character and suffering the same fate.[29]

> The beast of political power was and is not (Revelation 17:8). The whole system of political power in the world has this nature. It is, yet it is not. Good kings and bad kings alike come to power only to be removed and replaced by another. Nations and civilizations rise and fall. The great powers of the earth were once in Asia, then in Africa, then they returned to Asia, and then moved to Europe.

---

28. See Jeremiah 25:15-33.
29. Examples include Revelation 11:18; 13:7; 14:8; 18:3, 23; and 19:15.

Now they are in North America, and only God knows what direction they will take next. Pharaoh, Artaxerxes, Alexander, Charlemagne, Napoleon, Churchill, Roosevelt, and many others once controlled large and powerful armies. For a time, they all seemed to hold in their hand the destiny of the world. But now they are all gone as if they never were.[30]

These examples and prophecies confirm that despite surface differences, all historic and modern nations are only temporary; all are destined to fall.

---

30. Virgil Schrock, *The Lamb, the Lion, and the Light in the Book of Revelation* (pre-publication manuscript), p. 92, 93.

The king's heart
   is in the hand of the Lord,
   as the rivers of water:
he turneth it whithersoever he will.

Proverbs 21:1

3

How God Influences Nations: An Old Testament Survey

Who is in control?

When Adam and Eve fell, they came under the partial control of the devil. Yet God was still in control of the situation. He removed mankind from the Garden and limited the devil's power. He promised to bruise the devil's head under Jesus' heel.[1]

In the land of Shinar, mankind united to build a tower dominating the earth. With one stroke God halted that project. In Sodom and Gomorrah, the devil tried to prove that people could defy God and still prosper. But God showed that He was in final control when He poured a fiery judgment from the sky.

---

1. Genesis 3:15

For hundreds of years before the plagues recorded in Exodus, Egypt had sunk deeper into idolatry. The Pharaoh to whom Moses was sent employed sorcerers who communicated with the devil. Satan enabled them to counterfeit God's miracles in changing wooden rods to snakes, turning water into blood, and producing frogs. The devil was controlling Pharaoh, to a great extent. But ultimately, God was. God used Pharaoh's stubbornness to judge Egypt, and finally He drowned the Egyptian army in the Red Sea. About this man, God said, "Even for this same purpose have I raised thee up, that I might shew my power in thee, and that my name might be declared throughout all the earth."[2]

Satan used his children to crucify Jesus, hoping to overthrow God's plan of salvation. The apostles charged the Jews with that murder, saying, "The God of our fathers raised up Jesus, whom ye slew and hanged on a tree." But in the very next sentence comes the evidence that a higher hand was controlling the whole situation. "Him hath God exalted with his right hand to be a Prince and a Saviour, for to give repentance to Israel, and forgiveness of sins."[3]

Men can withstand God's spiritual work in their hearts, but they cannot resist His ultimate control over their physical actions and affairs.

There is no doubt that the devil rules much of the world. But though the devil enslaves man, he has not succeeded in keeping God's hand away from his slaves. God has ultimate control over everyone, and He moves them to fulfill His purposes.

---

2. Romans 9:17
3. Acts 5:30, 31

3 • How God Influences Nations: An Old Testament Survey

When the Bible describes God's control over nations, it typically shows that He controls them without their knowledge. Men can withstand God's spiritual work in their hearts, but they cannot resist His ultimate control over their physical actions and affairs. They are often not even aware of the divine control.[4]

Daniel's vision by the river

Daniel 10 gives one of the clearest pictures of the struggle in the spirit world for the control of nations. In this chapter, Daniel was mourning the captivity of the Jews. He longed for his people to be restored to Jerusalem. He fasted and prayed until God talked with him.

While Daniel prayed for understanding, there was spiritual fighting between God and Satan for the control of Persia. On the one hand, the passage describes the heavenly beauty of God's messenger and identifies his helper as the angel Michael. On the other hand, the enemy that fought God's spiritual messengers is called "the prince of the kingdom of Persia," apparently an agent assigned by Satan to resist God's work with Persia.

Satan hates not only God's spiritual work and His people; he also hates the "remote control" that God exercises over man. He fights God on every spiritual front. If he could have stopped the Jews' deliverance and made them disappear among the heathen nations, he would have. If he could break down the blighted concepts of civil order that man still has after the Fall and make the earth degenerate into a murderous anarchy, he would.

---

4. See Exodus 14:8; Ezra 6:22; and Proverbs 21:1.

But the devil can never completely win in the fight to control kings. He could not make God's agents leave the king of Persia. The time would come when Persia would slip away into history, and then the contest between God and Satan would be waged for the control of Greece. Again, God would win.

> **Nothing political happens without God's knowledge and permission.**

God's control of nations is further explained in Daniel 4. In this chapter, "watchers" and "holy ones" come down from heaven and give commands regarding nations. Perhaps these messengers are the same agents that God used in Daniel 10. Whoever they were, they show us that God is watching earthly kingdoms. Nothing political happens without His knowledge and permission.

God's methods of influence

The Old Testament records that God used spirits, dreams, rumors, prophets, and other methods to influence nations.

Spirits. In 1 Kings 22, God was finished with evil King Ahab and was planning his downfall. God influenced Ahab to fight the king of Syria to reclaim Ramoth-gilead, an Israelite city, from Syrian forces.

> And the Lord said, Who shall persuade Ahab, that he may go up and fall at Ramoth-gilead? And one said on this manner, and another said on that manner. And there came forth a spirit, and stood before the Lord, and said, I will persuade him.
>
> And the Lord said unto him, Wherewith? And he said, I will go forth, and I will be a lying spirit in the mouth of all his prophets. And he said, Thou shalt persuade him, and prevail also: go forth, and do so.

3 • How God Influences Nations: An Old Testament Survey

> Now therefore, behold, the Lord hath put a lying spirit in the mouth of all these thy prophets, and the Lord hath spoken evil concerning thee (1 Kings 22:20-23).

Besides putting a lying spirit in the mouth of Ahab's prophets, God also placed a specific thought in the mind of the Syrian king. He told his servants to disregard the common soldiers of the enemy and fight only with the Israelite king.

God brought Egypt low by giving their counselors a "perverse spirit." The Egyptians were well known for their wisdom, and they could boast about hundreds of years of successful empire building. But when God wanted to bring them low, He simply gave their counselors a foolish spirit. They made so many mistakes in judgment that the Lord described them as staggering like a drunken man.[5]

The same influence is described in the struggle between Absalom and David for Israel's throne in 2 Samuel 15 to 18. David had a counselor named Ahithophel whose political insight was legendary in those days. As David fled from Jerusalem to seek refuge in the wilderness beyond the Jordan, he heard that Ahithophel had joined Absalom. That added to his already perilous situation, and he cried, "O LORD, I pray thee, turn the counsel of Ahithophel into foolishness." He sent another counselor, his friend Hushai, to be a court spy on Absalom and to supplant Ahithophel's counsel.

Ahithophel told Absalom that he should take twelve thousand men and pursue David immediately. No doubt this plan would have succeeded if the Lord had not intervened. He moved Absalom to ask Hushai for his opinion on how to

---

5. Isaiah 19:11-14

take David. Hushai's plan obviously allowed David time to get away and organize a counterattack. But the Lord influenced Absalom to think it was better than Ahithophel's advice, thereby bringing judgment on Absalom.

Dreams. Genesis 41 records how Pharaoh in Egypt dreamed about cattle coming out of the river. When Pharaoh told his dreams to his magicians and wise men the next morning, no one could tell what they meant. Finally the king called Joseph. Joseph explained the dream and told Pharaoh that God was showing him what He was about to do.[6]

By that dream God set in motion a plan involving Israel's time in Egypt and His eventual judgment on Egypt's heathen ways. No doubt Pharaoh dreamed many other dreams and never thought twice about them. But there was something outstanding about these dreams, and God troubled Pharaoh's spirit about them. God knew what it took to get Pharaoh's attention and begin a chain of events in a heathen nation.

God gave one of the Midianites a dream that encouraged Gideon's faith.[7] While Solomon slept, God asked him what He should give him, and Solomon chose wisdom and understanding for his great task.[8]

King Nebuchadnezzar also had dreams that troubled his spirit. He even forgot one of them, but God made him determined to discover the dream and its meaning. Daniel told him, "But there is a God in heaven that revealeth secrets, and

---

6. Genesis 41:25-32
7. Judges 7:13-15
8. 1 Kings 3:5-15

3 • How God Influences Nations: An Old Testament Survey

maketh known to the king Nebuchadnezzar what shall be in the latter days."[9]

Rumors. When the Lord was ready to make the Edomites "small among the heathen, and greatly despised among men," He sent a rumor to other heathen nations to bring them up against her. Perhaps the rumor said that Edom was preparing for new conquests, and struck fear among the surrounding peoples. Or perhaps they heard that Edom's fabled strength was waning and that now was an ideal time to attack her. Whatever it was, Jeremiah wrote that the rumor acted like an ambassador passing from nation to nation, making alliances and gathering an army to perform a task that the Lord had planned.[10]

The Old Testament prophets. The prophets of Israel preached to wicked kings, idolatrous priests, and the common people. Sometimes they gave the word of the Lord on a political situation, such as if and when to go to war and what to do with prisoners of war. Down through Jewish history, one could easily forget God's purpose for shaping and steering that untoward nation were it not for these lonely, faithful men.

Occasionally God also used these prophets to warn other nations. God told Jeremiah to make bonds and yokes of the type used for taking prisoners of war into captivity, and to use them in proclaiming messages to five nations around Judah. He was to tell them to submit to Babylon in order to avoid further punishments from the Lord.[11]

---

9. Daniel 2:28
10. Jeremiah 49:13-15
11. Jeremiah 27:3-6, 8, 9, 11

God called unwilling Jonah to witness against the sins of the Ninevites. His message affected the Assyrian king, the most powerful man in the world at that time.

The prophet Daniel too may have ministered to his people in captivity; but most of the Book of Daniel describes his relationship to several kings, along with the visions God gave him of future events. He had a special assignment from God to influence some of the Babylonian and Persian kings by interpreting their dreams and living a godly life in a heathen court.

Other methods of influence. After giving the Israelites His laws for them as a nation, God described all the terrors He would send if they refused to keep His words. Sickness and disease, drought, death, danger, and enemy attacks were some of these punishments.[12]

God also occasionally used these methods to speak to other nations. For example, when the Philistines took the ark from Israel and placed it in their idol's house, God struck them with disease until they sent the ark back.[13] But God did not always punish ungodly nations in these ways. He only warned Israel of these terrors for a particular period of time in reference to a certain revelation. Many wicked nations lived in general prosperity for many years without suffering the same calamities as apostate Israel.

No person on earth can stop God's sovereign movements within his mind.

However, God can use these punishments on anyone. His entire creation is at His disposal for purposes of judgment.

---

12. Leviticus 26:15-25
13. 1 Samuel 5;6

3 • How God Influences Nations: An Old Testament Survey

On the last day of the Babylonian Empire, God sent a visible hand to write on a wall before Belshazzar and a thousand of his lords. Shaking in fear, Belshazzar sent for Daniel and discovered his doom. Daniel reminded him that he was not living according to his knowledge of "the God in whose hand thy breath is." God was giving the king an opportunity to repent of the sins on his conscience.[14]

Other Scriptures also indicate that God moved political leaders and nations, but they do not say how He did it. The Lord "stirred up an adversary unto Solomon."[15] The Lord "stirred up the spirit of Pul king of Assyria, and the spirit of Tilgath-pilneser king of Assyria," so that they would carry Israel into captivity.[16] The prophet Isaiah wrote that "the LORD of hosts mustereth the host of the battle."[17] Jeremiah recorded that God would "send and take all the families of the north" and bring them against Judah.[18] When it was time for the Jews to return home from the Babylonian captivity, the Lord "stirred up the spirit of Cyrus king of Persia," charging him to see that the temple was rebuilt.[19] How did God do these things? We do not know.

What we do know is that God communicates to and influences nations and their leaders. He may do it with or without their knowledge, and He does it to both the religious and the most godless people.

---

14. Daniel 5
15. 1 Kings 11:14
16. 1 Chronicles 5:26
17. Isaiah 13:4
18. Jeremiah 25:9
19. 2 Chronicles 36:22, 23

The holy angels are at God's command, and the world of nature runs to do His will. The Creator of the human mind is inexplicably able to influence that mind. Fallen men may reject the plan of salvation; that choice is left to them. But no person on earth can stop God's sovereign movements within his mind.

> "And all the inhabitants of the earth are reputed as nothing: and he doeth according to his will in the army of heaven, and among the inhabitants of the earth: and none can stay his hand, or say unto him, What doest thou?" (Daniel 4:35).

And ye shall be brought
   before governors and kings for my sake,
   for a testimony against them
   and the Gentiles.
                        Matthew 10:18

4

How God Influences Nations: A New Testament Survey

The first section in this chapter shows a continuation in the New Testament of the type of influence we have observed in the Old Testament. The remainder discusses the New Testament teachings and examples on how Christians influenced civil government in that time.

New Testament examples of divine influence

The dream of Pilate's wife. In Matthew 27, God used a dream to speak to Pilate. Throughout the account of Jesus' trial, Pilate was uncomfortable with pronouncing the death sentence on "Jesus which is called Christ." He knew that the Jews had brought charges against Jesus because they envied Him.

But even though Pilate seemed afraid to execute Jesus, he was even more afraid to deny the Jews their wish. When he was finally about to pass judgment on the matter, his wife sent him a message. "Have thou nothing to do with that just man," she pleaded, "for I have suffered many things this day in a dream because of him." God was giving Pilate another warning to leave the case alone, but he pushed it off and satisfied the Jews' demands. Hoping to rid himself of his guilty feeling, he washed his hands before the tumultuous crowd and proclaimed that he was innocent of this unjust death.

The death of Herod Agrippa I. This Herod, mentioned only in Acts 12, was a clever man. He extended his administrative power under the Romans and pleased the Jews at the same time. He cunningly saved the Jews from having a statue of a Roman emperor erected in the temple. He saw that persecuting the Christians pleased the Jews, so he killed James the brother of John and captured Peter, intending to do the same with him.

After Peter was miraculously delivered and Herod killed Peter's innocent guards, tradition tells us that Herod went to a festival at Caesarea. Apparently, there Herod gave a speech and his listeners praised him as a god. He did not give God the glory for this, and God allowed him to be eaten by worms.[1]

There is no doubt from the Bible and secular records that Herod Agrippa I was a proud man, but he was not obnoxious. He was sensitive to the tensions among the different Jewish religious groups. He made friends with other kings under Roman rule in the lands surrounding his holdings. He had enough means and power to hold a sumptuous banquet for the Roman emperor, and enough position and diplomacy to sway the Roman senate on important matters. His Jewish countrymen liked him, and the Roman officials respected him.

---
1. Acts 12:20-23

His speech that day in Caesarea moved the multitude and represented years of accumulated diplomacy. But he died in the flower of his reign because, like Nebuchadnezzar, he took glory to himself that belonged to God.

Josephus reported that "the king did neither rebuke them nor reject their impious flattery." That this man died because he took God's glory to himself was not a bit of information that stayed in heaven, off the human record. It was a lesson to the Jews, the Romans, and the civil leaders Herod Agrippa I associated with.

The judgments in Revelation. The judgments recorded in Revelation show that God spoke to man in the past and that He will continue speaking until the end of time. The four horses of chapter 6, for example, can be explained as historical time periods or as describing judgments that have affected the world throughout history. Either way, it is obvious that God allows men to suffer under war, famine, disease, and death so that they consider eternal values. Chapter 18 records the destruction of the "great city Babylon"—a typical scene that has happened repeatedly in world history. The story of Tyre is an example of one of these scenes.

"Ye shall be... a testimony against them."

> And ye shall be brought before governors and kings for my sake, for a testimony against them and the Gentiles (Matthew 10:18).

The Gospels of Mark and Luke give us similar thoughts. Jesus informed His followers that civil and religious leaders would question, beat, and imprison them. He pointed out that such persecution was for His sake, and that every case of it would turn into an opportunity for testimony. "I will give you a mouth and wisdom," Jesus promised, "which all your adversaries shall not be able to gainsay nor resist."[2]

What was this testimony, and what was it against? We find an answer in the apostles' actions the first few times they were apprehended for their faith. In Acts 3, after healing a lame beggar, Peter preached a stirring sermon at the temple. Some five thousand people gathered to hear him, and many of them believed the Gospel message. However, the Jewish authorities noticed the large crowd, arrested Peter and John, and jailed them for the night.

In the morning, the Jews asked the two apostles, "By what power, or by what name, have ye done this?" Peter answered by preaching another evangelical message. After their release, Peter and John prayed with their brethren, asking God to give them boldness to preach the Word in spite of the threats.

Acts 17:2 describes Paul's manner, which was to reason from the Scriptures. His entire testimony throughout the Book of Acts is the same. Even when he suffered illegal treatment, he did not change his testimony. After his arrest in Acts 21 and all through the experiences that finally brought him to Rome, Paul asked for hearings wherever he could get them, and he preached the kingdom of God at all of them. This was the preaching that led King Agrippa to think about repentance.

The apostles always preached to individual souls about their sin and how Christ could save them.

"King Agrippa, believest thou the prophets? I know that thou believest. Then Agrippa said unto Paul, Almost thou persuadest

---
2. Luke 21:15

4 • How God Influences Nations: A New Testament Survey

me to be a Christian. And Paul said, I would to God, that not only thou, but also all that hear me this day, were both almost, and altogether such as I am, except these bonds" (Acts 26:27-29).

Paul had no desire that King Agrippa would simply become a better ruler. His message was Jesus Christ, and his hope was that men would choose Christ, leave the world of politics with all its corruption, and become just like Paul except for his chains.

These examples show what Jesus meant when He said, "Ye shall be . . . a testimony against them." They tell us what God meant when He told Ananias in Acts 9:15 that Saul was a chosen vessel to bear His Name before kings, Gentiles, and Jews. The early Christians preached salvation to every ruler they could. They never tried to help the rulers serve God better in their political office. They never threatened them by saying that God would judge Rome unless the nation turned around. Always they preached to individual souls about their sin and how Christ could save them.

The apostles could have talked to the Jewish and Roman leaders about granting freedom of worship to Christians. They could have pleaded with the Romans to tend to civil order and curb the plague of immoral lifestyles, abortion, corruption, murder, and violent entertainment in their culture. They could have had a stirring message of moral reform, but they were called to something higher.

Moral Decay in the Apostles' Time

Some professing Christians today speak publicly against certain evils of culture, and warn society of God's judgment unless they reform in these particular areas. However, there is no record of Christians doing that in the New Testament. Was this because people of that time were not as immoral as modern societies?

The Roman statesman Cicero (106-43 B.C.) wrote that to expect young men to be morally upright is a good principle, but that no one would be so severe as to require such a thing. Further, he said, such a requirement would be at odds with the loose "customs and concessions of our ancestors. When indeed was [immorality] not done? When did anyone ever find fault with it? When was such permission denied?"

Around 18 B.C. the Roman emperor Augustus[3] tried to curb the Romans' immorality through laws. City populations were growing, and with this came a rising tide of contraception, abortion, and infanticide. Many Romans avoided marriage altogether, preferring the "freedom" of an immoral lifestyle. A significant proportion of marriages were made for financial or political reasons, while the partners agreed to do as they liked with their private lives. Divorce was common.

Augustus' laws had an effect for a while, but the immorality in his own family exceeded that of the general population and became the gossip of the cities. In one city it was said that the sole crime was to bring up children. While that was an exaggeration, many aristocrats and wealthy businessmen were very wicked. Besides the immorality, wealth brought indolent luxury, and violent games became popular. Homosexuality was illegal but tolerated by custom, and it flourished boldly. Caligula (reigned A.D. 37-41) and Nero (reigned A.D. 54-68) were extremely coarse rulers whose lust and licentiousness knew no bounds.

This was the character of the cities and most of the ruling classes, but it would not be fair to say that morality was dead in these times. Some family values, as well as economy and sobriety, lived on among the poorer people, especially those in the countryside. A number of tombstone epitaphs contained records of fidelity. One mentioned that marriages seldom lasted without divorce until death, but in this case the couple was true to each other for forty-one years.

The debased culture of the day was part of the reason why Paul said in Galatians 4:4 that Jesus Christ came "in the fulness of the time." It seems obvious that the Roman roads and shipping lanes, and the widespread use of the Greek and Latin languages, were part of this "fulness of the time." Yet more impressive than these physical preparations was the deepening and spreading moral corruption that defied human remedy.

That the Gospel was written in and for immoral cultures is also clear in the New Testament record. In the Sermon on the Mount, Jesus addressed lust and divorce. In John 4 He ministered to a woman who had married five husbands, and in John 8 He forgave an apparently repentant woman who had been caught in adultery. Nearly every New Testament book after the Gospels discusses purity and what it means for the Christian. The apostles spoke to believers about purity, fidelity, and many other

---

3. Augustus, also called Octavian, was the first emperor of Rome. He ruled from 63 B.C. to A.D. 14.

4 • How God Influences Nations: A New Testament Survey

> issues; to the world they spoke of heart needs, Jesus Christ, and salvation. They realized that before morals could improve, people needed to repent and be born again.

Rome's morals decayed greatly after Rome conquered Greece[4] (completed in 146 B.C.) and reached their worst under Nero, in whose persecutions both Paul and Peter are thought to have died. In those times, Christians lived under a far more brazenly immoral ruling class than has yet been seen in North America. In fact, those Roman rulers appear to have been the worst rulers any Christians have ever lived under. Yet even in those days, the apostles preached godly living to the church and preached Christ to the unsaved crowds.

The apostles sometimes mentioned the wickedness of their times. But their witness did not leave people with the impression that Christ came to change a few of the most glaring sins, or that God's aims in the world could basically be accomplished with some good laws.

There is no better example of this than Paul's sermon in Roman-occupied Athens, on Mars' Hill, recorded in Acts 17. Surrounded by the Epicureans (supporters of rich, immoral Rome) and the Stoics (supporters of Rome's tradi-

The apostles realized that before morals could improve, people needed to repent and be born again.

---

4. In the 300s B.C., the Greek orator Demosthenes said that in Greece the men had "courtesans for the sake of pleasure . . . concubines for the sake of daily cohabitation . . . [and] wives for the purpose of having children legitimately." This immorality permeated Roman society when the Romans annexed Greece. See William Barclay, *Letters to the Seven Churches* (Nashville, TN.: Abingdon Press, 1957), p. 52.

tional values),[5] he refused to be drawn into the culture war. Instead, he taught both groups of people to get ready for Judgment Day. The Epicureans and the Stoics both needed the same message.

If the apostles had wanted to challenge civil rulers with Scriptural principles, they could have used verses such as "Righteousness exalteth a nation: but sin is a reproach to any people."[6] Men like Paul had studied the Old Testament for years as part of their education. They had a far greater understanding than ours of the civil aspects of the Old Testament law, yet there is no record that they ever addressed any leader on that basis. In fact, there is no record that the Holy Spirit ever used any New Testament believer to give political advice or condemnation.

> **There is no record of the Holy Spirit using a New Testament believer to give political advice or condemnation.**

"Ye must needs be subject."

In Romans 13:1-7, Paul teaches that Christians are subject to government because government is part of God's plan for the world. We obey the government as long as its laws do not conflict with God's commands.[7] We obey not just because we fear the consequences of disobedience but because we

---

5. The Greek philosophies of the Epicureans and the Stoics, adopted and adapted by the Romans, were much broader than Rome's moral issues. But historians often use the term *Stoic Rome* to describe the older, more traditional Rome, and *Epicurean Rome* to describe the later, passion-mad Rome. Stoics taught that people should be unaffected by pain or pleasure, and accept their experiences as the gods' will for their lives. Epicureans taught that people should seek pleasure and avoid pain, and they did not believe in gods or an afterlife.

6. Proverbs 14:34

7. Acts 5:29

4 • How God Influences Nations: A New Testament Survey

understand civil government's function in God's plan. This godly obedience is one of the most powerful influences that we have on civil government.

Verse 3 says, "Do that which is good, and thou shalt have praise of the same." When we do well, our civil leaders will sometimes praise us for it. Almost every government in history has praised some good works. However, almost every government has also penalized some good works. Remember that the setting of Romans 13 was an empire under a frivolous, immoral, and maniacal ruler who hated and killed Christians and executed anyone who stood in the way of fulfilling his immoral passions.

So Paul could not have meant that good works will *always* bring the approval of the world and its government. Paul received very little such approval in his life. And since Paul's day, at most times and places in the world, following Christ has brought contempt and derision. It is unlikely that this verse means we can *expect* to be praised by government powers if we do well.

The first sentence in verse 3 says, "For rulers are not a terror to good works, but to the evil." But many governments since Paul's time have tried to terrorize faithful Christians. Throughout much of the Middle Ages, holy Christian living was considered a mark of a "heretic." During the Reformation, anyone who lived a decent moral life was suspected of being an Anabaptist. Sometimes the good works of Christianity were all the evidence needed to jail or execute a person.

So the statement that "rulers are not a terror to good works, but to the evil" is not a promise that God will keep rulers from making life difficult for Christians, or that He will appoint only those rulers who tolerate Christians. Indeed, such an interpretation would go directly against Jesus' warning, "Ye shall be hated of all men for my name's sake."[8] Rather, this is a general statement of rulers' commission by God to maintain law and order.

The statement also means that no matter what rulers do, they cannot strike terror into a Christian's heart. When a Christian senses the approval of God, he obeys the government as far as possible and rests in that, even in prison. But if he disobeys the rulers in areas where God has commanded submission, he will be terrified by their finding out, and he is also guilty before God.

Peter explained this concept further in 1 Peter 2:12-23. Christians should be honest and submit to law, he said, because this is God's will and it will "put to silence the ignorance of foolish men." As we relate to government we will sometimes suffer for doing well, but we need to take this patiently. Christ was patient in suffering, and silent when reviled, and He made no threats. We are called, Peter emphasized, to follow His footsteps.

Patient, undeserved suffering brings conviction on government leaders. It makes them reflect on righteousness. It shows them the ways of God. It reminds them of their personal standing before God.

This has often happened in times of persecution. No matter what governments did, they could not become a terror to true Christians. The Christians imprisoned on charges of civil insurrection sat in jail and went to execution with a clear conscience; they knew the charges were false. The government leaders who jailed them and executed them could not comprehend their peace; it was present in the absence of all earthly security.

---

8. Luke 21:17

Indeed, the civil leaders were the ones often struck by terror as they saw the Christian martyrs' supernatural peace and power. Many of the people who actually performed the persecution of Christians hated the job. Some proclaimed the innocence of those they destroyed, some quit their civil service, and some were so convicted that they joined the remnant and suffered the same penalties they had once inflicted on others.

Many people use Romans 13 to justify opposition of the government's methods or views. On the basis of this chapter, they define the limits of civil government's jurisdiction and resist any authority that goes beyond those lines. For example, on the basis of verse 3 they might say any government that imprisons a person for good works is an illegitimate government.

> **No New Testament writer ever described any civil government as illegitimate.**

But we must face a simple fact: all the New Testament writers lived under governments that persecuted some good works. Christians in that time were often misunderstood, defamed, and resisted. In spite of that, no New Testament writer ever described any civil government as illegitimate. Nor did they intend that anything they wrote, such as Romans 13, would become a basis for Christians to resist or defame a government. They taught obedience to every government, as long as it did not conflict with God's commands, even as they sat in prison for doing well.

Peter said that governments are set up to punish evil, and in the same passage he told believers to expect suffering at their hands for well doing. So while the apostles understood that the basic purpose of government is to maintain order and punish evil, they realized that sinful man's concept of evil is deficient and blurred. As they try to control what they consider evil, they will sometimes punish good instead.

In this problem lies a wonderful opportunity to be like Christ, "who before Pontius Pilate witnessed a good confession."[9] Subjection to rulers, especially in unfair circumstances, is a powerful influence on both authorities and the watching world.

"I exhort therefore, that... supplications... be made."

Prayer is a powerful tool that Christians can wield to influence their government. It is the least visible influence, and probably the most neglected.

> I exhort therefore, that, first of all, supplications, prayers, intercessions, and giving of thanks, be made for all men; for kings, and for all that are in authority; that we may lead a quiet and peaceable life in all godliness and honesty. For this is good and acceptable in the sight of God our Saviour; who will have all men to be saved, and to come unto the knowledge of the truth (1 Timothy 2:1-4).

We hear almost nothing about this influence in nominal Christianity's pressure on the government. Perhaps the humility of prayer, the childlike nature of committing matters to God for Him to work out as He will, seems too simple and naïve to appeal to modern religion.

Note the commands for these prayers. They are unconditional; the Bible does not say, "Give thanks for leaders who rule the way you think is best." We should give thanks for all

---

9. 1 Timothy 6:13

4 • How God Influences Nations: A New Testament Survey

our leaders, from the king or president to the tax collector. Paul gave thanks for rulers who persecuted him as well as those who treated him sensibly, such as Agrippa.

Giving sincere thanks to God for our civil leaders—even if we are sitting in prison for doing well—helps us to respect them. It also gives a powerful testimony for true Christianity when we can explain to our neighbor, after he complains about the rulers, why we give thanks for them every day.

We are to pray "that we may lead a quiet and peaceable life in all godliness and honesty." It is not selfish to do so; it is the will of God.

We are also to pray for our rulers' salvation. They are serving the kingdoms of earth and are constantly reminded of the shallowness of worldly glory. Some of them have reached the height of their careers, perhaps the position to which they had aspired for years, and still have not found satisfaction. From the highest leader to the policeman on the corner, they also face the draining task of constantly trying to check men's evil desires. Much of their time is spent punishing men for bad deeds; they can do little about the fact that men are bad, or that many leaders resort to the same crimes they were put in place to curb. God uses these factors to convict leaders of their own sinfulness.

Prayer for conviction in a ruler's heart may have an effect on his actions, even if he does not respond personally to God's call. Millions of people live with nagging consciences and troubled hearts, unwilling to leave their sins yet trying to be moral in many ways, hoping that these efforts will appease God in the end. Civil rulers are in the same shoes. Stronger conviction and deeper guilt often lead a ruler to strive harder in his own ability to do right. This helps to restrain the downward slide of morality, and it helps to maintain some of the godly character of civil laws.

Salt and light

> Ye are the salt of the earth: but if the salt have lost his savour, wherewith shall it be salted? it is thenceforth good for nothing, but to be cast out, and to be trodden under foot of men.
>
> Ye are the light of the world. A city that is set on an hill cannot be hid. Neither do men light a candle, and put it under a bushel, but on a candlestick; and it giveth light unto all that are in the house. Let your light so shine before men, that they may see your good works, and glorify your Father which is in heaven (Matthew 5:13-16).

Salt is a preservative. Christians are a living example of Bible truth, and by that they preserve for mankind an example of what the Bible means. Christians are also a preservative as they plead with God to be merciful and extend opportunities for sinners to repent.

Without the preserving influence of Christianity, the world would be a far worse place. God does speak through the conscience, and all nature testifies of His existence. But God depends on His people to hold before the world a living example of true discipleship. Many people have been convicted of the existence of God as they observed the order and marvels of creation, but a tree cannot explain how to be saved. The conscience torments sinners, and their heart is lightened when they do right; but the conscience cannot teach things such as justification by faith. These are things that God asks us to do.

Salt is necessary, yet we hardly notice it unless it is missing. We might exclaim over an excellent beefsteak or fresh young peas and potatoes, but for most people these foods are drab without salt. We might ask who raised the steer or the potatoes, and what kind they are, but we never ask where the salt was mined or what brand it is.

So it is with Christians. Being necessary to the world does not make us important in the world's eyes. Sometimes we are persecuted for belonging to another world and not fitting in on earth. Sometimes they exclaim over how quaint our lifestyle is or how we hold the same morals as their grandparents. But most of them will never admit the guilt that a true, salty Christian brings to their heart. However, the effect of salt is there. Some of them will think twice before they divorce their spouse, and some will try harder to teach their children good ethics, because of the salt they tasted.

A simple thing such as a Gospel sign by a mailbox helps to salt the earth. In a repair business I once owned, a small sign like that kept some customers from using foul words or telling evil stories. Two men once entered the shop—a younger man who had been there previously and an older, near-sighted companion who liked to tell dirty stories. While I examined the parts they had brought, the older man started into one of his stories, but the younger one gave him a poke in the side before the first sentence was finished. "Don't tell that one here," he said. "He won't like it. Didn't you see the sign at the end of his lane?"

Salt helps to preserve truth in the world. It keeps alive the consciousness of right and wrong. Society's morals continue to erode, and sin brings a constant downward slide. But the slide is slowed by salt.

Jesus also said that Christians are the light of the world. They help men to see spiritual truth. Their lives shed light on things that are dark and mysterious to the natural man—on life, death, and eternity.

When God makes a light, He does it to show things to people. We are to let our light shine before men so that they may see holiness in action.

When men see the truth in us, they will not necessarily become Christians or openly acknowledge the truth. But even in the hardest of them, it will stir guilt about their sinful ways. It will remind them of facts that they pushed to the back of their mind for many years. When a worldling observes true Christian character, the ideals of right and wrong are reinforced in his mind. He often gives mental assent to what he sees, even though he may have no interest in living that way himself.

Whether we witness to a government official, a taxi driver, or a store clerk, the salt and light are the same and the effect is the same. It is salt because it preserves things that men would rather forget. It is a light because it shows men by word and deed the way of the cross. It is one message for one world with one need.

Again, the devil taketh him up
>   into an exceeding high mountain,
>   and sheweth him all the kingdoms of the world,
>   and the glory of them;

And saith unto him,
>   All these things will I give thee,
>   if thou wilt fall down and worship me.

Then saith Jesus unto him,
>   Get thee hence, Satan: for it is written,
>   Thou shalt worship the Lord thy God,
>   and him only shalt thou serve.

Matthew 4:8-10

5

Are There Godly Nations?

When we understand why nations exist and how God influences them, it is easier to understand why there are no godly nations. The origin of nations, their character, and the methods God uses to control them all stand in stark contrast to true Christianity. This chapter explains why both the concept and the possibility of a godly nation are foreign to God's New Covenant.

What of Israel?

In Babylon, captive among the heathen, a few Jews hung their harps on the willows and refused to sing. "How shall we sing the Lord's song in a strange land?" they cried. "If I forget thee, O Jerusalem, let my right hand forget her cunning. If I do not remember thee, let my tongue cleave to the roof of my mouth; if I prefer not Jerusalem above my chief joy."[1]

Why did they talk that way? Why were they not content simply to make the best of life and dwell in peace among strangers? By far, most of them did settle down in Babylon, and their children were absorbed into that heathen world. But there was a remnant who remembered the Lord, and these people returned to Jerusalem after seventy years to form God's special nation again.

It *was* a special nation. Israel was the nation whose God was the Lord, whom God had chosen for His own inheritance.[2] As the years passed by, multitudes of Jews filtered out into the heathen nations around them and lost their place among the people of God. Multitudes more apostatized and lost their relationship with God even though they lived in His chosen nation. But a few of them never forgot the ringing declaration of Moses before his death.

> For ask now of the days that are past, which were before thee, since the day that God created man upon the earth, and ask from the one side of heaven unto the other, whether there hath been any such thing as this great thing is, or hath been heard like it? Did ever people hear the voice of God speaking out of the midst of the fire, as thou hast heard, and live? Or hath God assayed to go and take him a nation from the midst of another nation, by temptations, by signs, and by wonders, and by war, and by a mighty hand, and by

---

1. Psalm 137:4-6
2. Psalm 33:12

5 • Are There Godly Nations?

a stretched out arm, and by great terrors, according to all that the Lord your God did for you in Egypt before your eyes?

Unto thee it was shewed, that thou mightest know that the Lord he is God; there is none else beside him. Out of heaven he made thee to hear his voice, that he might instruct thee: and upon earth he shewed thee his great fire; and thou heardest his words out of the midst of the fire. And because he loved thy fathers, therefore he chose their seed after them, and brought thee out in his sight with his mighty power out of Egypt; to drive out nations from before thee greater and mightier than thou art, to bring thee in, to give thee their land for an inheritance, as it is this day (Deuteronomy 4:32-38).

Israel received these marvelous privileges for the sake of the whole world. God promised that all the families of the earth would be blessed through Abraham. The apostle Paul explained this promise in Galatians 4:4, saying that the Old Covenant was fulfilled when Christ was born. Hebrews 10 says that Christ's work took away the first covenant and established the second. Paul told the Roman Christians, "Christ is the end of the law for righteousness to every one that believeth."[3]

> **The main purpose of the Jewish nation was to preserve a righteous remnant through which God could send a Saviour into the world.**

The main purpose of the Jewish nation was to preserve a righteous remnant through which God could send a Saviour into the world. After the Saviour lived among men, died, and

---

3. Romans 10:4

rose again, was there yet a purpose for this special nation? Jesus answered:

> Did ye never read in the scriptures, The stone which the builders rejected, the same is become the head of the corner: this is the Lord's doing, and it is marvellous in our eyes? Therefore say I unto you, The kingdom of God shall be taken from you, and given to a nation bringing forth the fruits thereof (Matthew 21:42, 43).

In Jesus' time, many of the Jews hoped to overcome the Romans and reestablish their own government. The reason for Jesus' many strong statements against the hope of a Jewish state is that many of His own followers expected Him to fulfill that hope. But regardless of His explanations, and right up until His crucifixion, most of the disciples continued to believe that Jesus would rule as an earthly king.

Looking at the situation from our perspective today, we wonder how they could have been so blind. Their problem was not simply blindness; it was the deep-settled belief of practically the whole Jewish society that the Messiah would reestablish the nation of Israel. Jesus did not succeed in changing their minds until after He rose again, even though He repeatedly explained the nature of His kingdom.[4]

The apostle Paul explained in Romans 2:28, 29 that the term *Jew*, as referring to a member of God's chosen people, is now applied to all true believers. He carried this concept further in Romans 9:6-8, stating "they which are the children of the flesh, these are not the children of God: but the children of the promise are counted for the seed."

---

4. See Matthew 16:21-26; Luke 9:51-56; John 18:36.

5 • Are There Godly Nations?

In Galatians 4:22–31, Paul said that Christians are the children of the promise. Everyone who rejects Christ is a child of Hagar and the literal Jerusalem, and cannot enter the kingdom of God.

Through the prophets, we detect that God had become increasingly disturbed by the Jewish abuses of His Law and His intentions, and He desired to establish something better. In human terms, we might say that God could hardly wait to show the world the glories of the kingdom He really wanted to build on earth. He wanted to burst the national ties of the Old Covenant and establish a new, spiritual covenant. It seems that one of His greatest delights in the Old Covenant was to prophesy of His coming spiritual nation and to tell how disconnected it would be from any earthly nation.

In the New Testament era, the Jewish nation is reduced to the civil status of all other nations. Christ and the apostles (after Pentecost) never identified with the Jewish dream of a national homeland under Israelite control.

Nations are used, not approved.

In Habakkuk 1, God declared that He would raise up the bitter, fast-moving Chaldeans to punish many nations. He described them as terrible, dreadful, violent, and derisive. As their conquests grew, they praised their idols for their strength. Habakkuk could hardly stand this and began to question God about it, saying,

> Thou art of purer eyes than to behold evil, and canst not look on iniquity: wherefore lookest thou upon them that deal treacherously, and holdest thy tongue when the wicked devoureth the man that is more righteous than he?

It was an ancient question, and it is still being asked today. How can a nation be God's *instrument* when it is not God's *people*, and especially when it is not even *good*?

Habakkuk may be forgiven for his lack of insight. He did not have a copy of the complete Old Testament Scriptures, and he could not experience the provisions of the New Covenant. He lived in God's chosen nation and looked at life through that filter. With the whole Scriptures, we have a much clearer answer to Habakkuk's question.

The Old Testament accounts of how God used sinful nations to fulfill His plans show that God's use of a nation does not imply His approval of that nation. Often, the same text that tells how God used a certain people also describes the wickedness of those people. So the fact that God uses a nation says nothing about the nation's character, nor does it prove anything about its relationship with God.

A nation does not have to be good to be great.

The Lord emphasized this truth even to Israel, His special nation in the Old Testament. In Deuteronomy 9, as Israel was preparing to cross the Jordan and overcome the Canaanites, God emphatically told them that they should not think that He was giving them the land because they were righteous. "Understand therefore, that the Lord thy God giveth thee not this good land to possess it for thy righteousness; for thou art a stiffnecked people. . . . Ye have been rebellious against the Lord from the day that I knew you." Rather, He said, He gave the land to them because the people that were occupying it

5 • Are There Godly Nations?

were so wicked, and because He wanted to show Egypt that He was Almighty God.[5]

The New Testament further emphasizes this by describing righteousness and the function of the state as two differing realms. For example, Christ and the apostles taught that the New Testament church is nonresistant and that Christians love their enemies. In contrast, the state is ordained to be a revenger and to wield the sword. The New Testament does not imply that the state should love its enemies and sheathe its sword. It only calls individuals from the coercive, vengeful service of the state into the voluntary, loving service of Jesus Christ.

In Romans 13, after explaining the role of the state, Paul urged us to love our neighbors as ourselves, put on the armor of light, and put off strife and fleshly lusts.

A nation does not have to be good or righteous to be great. Greatness in a nation is no sign of God's approval. In fact, God has made some wicked nations great for a long time to accomplish certain purposes. The Assyrians and the Romans are examples of great, wicked nations that lasted over five hundred years.[6]

The Babylonians, Persians, and Greeks were also great in their turn, but did that make them good? Was Genghis Khan, the Mongol conqueror, great because he was good? Did the English, French, Chinese, and Russians reach the heights of power because of their goodness?

---

5. Dueteronomy 9:4-6; 24, 27-28.
6. The Assyrians dominated world events from 1100 to 610 B.C. (510 years), and the Romans dominated them from 50 B.C. to A.D. 476 (526 years).

Nations are controlled, not led.

As stated in previous chapters, God uses a variety of influences to affect or control nations. The contrast between this impersonal, mechanical control and God's gentle, fatherly leading of His children is another reason why no nation can be godly.

Christians are sensitive to the voice of the Holy Spirit. They obey the Word of God and the voice of His people. Christians *follow*. On the other hand, governments must be pushed or pulled. They do not keep control of their countries by listening to the still, small voice of God.

This contrast is apparent in how God worked with the rebellious Pharaoh when it was time for the Israelites to leave Egypt. God hardened this sinful man's heart so that He could accomplish His will through him.[7] The same thing happened with Sihon, king of Heshbon, who refused to let Israel pass through his land on their way to Canaan.[8] God sent the Assyrians to judge other nations, but at the same time He prophesied the punishment coming on the stout heart of the king of Assyria.

On the other hand, God is near to "them that are of a broken heart" and saves those who are of a "contrite spirit."[9] He has promised to pay attention to the person that "trembleth at [His] word."[10]

Nations are carnal, not spiritual.

Leaders struggle to gain power and stay in power by using wealth, force, boasting, argument, and compromise, not by

---

7. Exodus 9:12; 10:1, 20, 27; 11:10; 14:8; Romans 9:17, 18
8. Deuteronomy 2:30
9. Psalm 34:18
10. Isaiah 66:2

5 • Are There Godly Nations?

loving others and being humble. Contrast their actions with the godliness described in the Sermon on the Mount. Nations and their leaders are not generally poor in spirit, meek, or pure in heart; nor do they consider themselves blessed when men revile them and persecute them. They turn the other fist, not the other cheek. They do not give their cloak to a thief who stole their coat.

This is not to say that nations and their leaders know nothing of love and kindness. Many of them love their families and friends. Many respect their parents and other elderly people. Most of them appreciate virtues such as honesty, fidelity, respect for law, and fair business practices. But those noble principles are not the chief motivating force of any nation, nor are they required in the life of a statesman. What drives nations as a whole is materialism, greed, pride, lust for power, and nationalism.

> **Though every nation appreciates the effects of some godly values, each one is sinful and is driven by ungodly principles.**

Every nation has a carnal, exalted view of its own culture. The Biblical view that all people are made of one blood has affected some nations, yet no nation has ever succeeded in erasing the selfishness, arrogance, and disdain that exists between different groups, even within the same nation.

Unbelief in any form is ungodly. The Bible establishes no pattern of carnality that may be called Christian. Though every nation appreciates the effects of some godly values, each one is sinful and is basically driven by ungodly principles.

Nations want patriotism, not simple obedience to law.

In America, nonresistant people are often praised for their virtues during peaceful times. But when war comes, this goodwill has often turned into mocking, fines, confiscations, destruction of property, mob threats, imprisonment, physical abuse, and even death in a few cases.[11]

This is because nations want their citizens to be patriotic. The leaders want their people to believe in the superiority of their nation, its ideals, and its people. They want their citizens to glory in the causes of the country and to be willing to die for those causes. To encourage that loyalty, governments use propaganda to make their people think and act in certain ways.

Such loyalty to a nation is actually a form of idolatry. In Matthew 4, Satan showed Jesus the kingdoms of the world and all their glory, offering to give it all to Jesus if He would only worship Satan. But Jesus replied, "Thou shalt worship the Lord thy God, and him only shalt thou serve."

To receive the patriotic glory of the nations requires bowing to Satan, the god of the nations. Being willing to glory in or die for a national cause is worshiping the nation as a god. Even though a national cause is portrayed as a "just war," a struggle against tyranny, or some other noble effort, any cause or interest that makes us disobey God is an idol.

To any nation, a true Christian is always a nonconformist who can be tolerated only to the point that national interests

---

11. It is true that a few American leaders and citizens retained their respect for nonresistant people in periods of war. But the general feeling of the country usually turned against these harmless citizens who refused to fight for what was considered the common good.

may proceed. Even nations that grant religious freedom do not want their citizens to consider God and His Word as their highest authority. No nation understands the Bible doctrine of the two kingdoms, or why the Christian must consider his obligation to his nation as less than his obligation to God.

In every war that America has been involved in, most Americans felt strongly that their goals were God's goals, and it made little sense to them how someone could say that because of his allegiance to God, he could not fight for his country.

No nation can be godly, because every nation asks its citizens to give it their highest loyalty—something that belongs to God alone.

Part Two

Early America—

a Christian Nation?

Introduction

The six chapters in this section discuss American religious history from a Biblical perspective. Christian principles inspired some of the settlers and leaders of this nation. But history also shows that America is not an exception to the Bible teaching that all nations are ungodly.

Although life in America has had special tests and temptations for Christians, God has used this country to provide great blessings for many of His people. True Christians in America should be deeply thankful. As we view history, we have no cause for spite, mockery, or anti-government feelings. Instead, we want to see America through the eyes of the New Testament. This will help us to understand history correctly and to relate to our country in a Biblical way today.

Chapters

6. Religion in Puritan New England
7. Religion in the Middle Colonies and in the South; the Great Awakening
8. A Righteous Revolution?
9. The Religious Views of the Founding Fathers
10. American Protestantism in the 1800s
11. American Social and Moral Issues in the 1800s

> Thus stands the cause
> between God and us.
> We are entered into Covenant
> with him for this worke.
> —*John Winthrop, 1630*
> *Governor of Massachusetts*

6

Religion in Puritan New England

On November 11, 1620, as the *Mayflower* bobbed gently in the Cape Cod Bay, forty-one of the forty-four men on the ship signed the Mayflower Compact. About one-third of the people were called Pilgrims or Separatists. These people had separated from the Church of England and been persecuted for that decision. The rest were members of the Church of England; but most of them agreed to sign the Compact which the Pilgrim leaders had drawn up. Part of it read as follows.

> Haveing undertaken, for the glorie of God, and advancemente of the Christian faith, and honour of our king and countrie, a

voyage to plant the first colonie in the Northerne parts of Virginia, doe by these presents solemnly and mutualy in the presence of God . . . combine ourselves togeather into a civill body politick, for our better ordering and preservation and furtherance of the ends aforesaid; and . . . to enacte . . . just and equall lawes . . . as shall be thought most meet and convenient for the generall good of the Colonie . . .

The Mayflower Compact established no specific laws, but obviously the signers had good intentions. Their settlement was Plymouth Colony, and it was the first permanent colony

Pilgrims signing the Compact in the hold of the Mayflower.

6 • Religion In Puritan New England

in America to allow freedom of religion.[1] To some degree, they also practiced separation of church and state. Early American history may have been written differently had these settlers had an opportunity to spread their style of government to new colonies. But the Puritans, who first arrived in 1628, were much more numerous than the Pilgrims. They soon absorbed the smaller, poorer Plymouth colony, with the result that freedom of religion disappeared.

A colony patterned after Old Testament Israel

In the New World, the Puritans wanted to establish a "New Israel" based on a covenant with God such as Israel had. They also wanted to adopt certain parts of the Old Testament Law. They expected that the God of Israel would make them such a glorious, famous colony that their English friends back home would follow their example on English soil, and that every succeeding colony in North America would want to be like them.

> Thus stands the cause between God and us. We are entered into Covenant with him for this worke. . . . [If God] bring us in peace to the place [Massachusetts] wee desire, then hath hee ratified his Covenant and sealed our Commissions [and] will expect a strict performance of the Articles contained in it. . . . Beloved, there is now sett before us life, and good, deathe and evill in that wee are Commaunded in this day to

The Puritans made a tremendous effort to return to Israel's laws and to claim the privileges of Israel's covenant with God.

---

1. The first permanent settlement was Jamestown, established in 1607, but it allowed only the Anglican religion.

love the Lord our God, and to love one another to walke in his wayes and to keepe his Commaundements . . . and his lawes, and the Articles of our Covenant with him that we may live and be multiplyed . . . or perishe out of the good Land. . . . Wee must consider that wee shall be as a city upon a hill. The eyes of all people are upon us.

—John Winthrop, first governor of Massachusetts, 1630

Capitall Laws

1. If any man after legall conviction shall have or worship any other god, but the Lord God, he shall be put to death.
2. If any man or woeman be a witch, (that is hath or consulteth with a familiar spirit,) they shall be put to death.
3. If any man shall Blaspheme the name of God, the Father, Sonne or Holie Ghost, with direct, expresse, presumptuous or high handed blasphemie, or shall curse God in the like manner, he shall be put to death.
4. If any person committ any wilful murder, which is manslaughter, committed upon premeditated mallice, hatred, or Crueltie, not in a man's necessarie and just defence, nor by meere casualtie against his will, he shall be put to death.
5. If any person slayeth an other suddaienly in his anger or Crueltie of passion, he shall be put to death.
6. If any person shall slay an other through guile, either by poysoning or other such divelish practice, he shall be put to death.
7. If any man or woeman shall lye with any beaste or bruite creature by Carnall Copulation, they shall surely be put to death. And the beast shall be slaine and buried and not eaten.
8. If any man lyeth with mankinde as he lyeth with a woeman, both of them have committed abhomination, they both shall surely be put to death.

9. If any person committeth Adultery with a maried or espoused wife, the Adulterer and Adulteresse shall surely be put to death.
10. If any man stealeth a man or mankinde, he shall surely be put to death.
11. If any man rise up by false witnes, wittingly and of purpose to take away any man's life, he shall be put to death.
12. If any man shall conspire and attempt any invasion, insurrection, or publique rebellion against our commonwealth, or shall indeavor to surprize any Towne or Townes, fort or forts therein, or shall treacherously and perfediouslie attempt the alteration and subversion of our frame of politie or Government fundamentallie, he shall be put to death.

—Some laws adopted in 1641 by the Massachusetts colony [2]

The Puritans made a tremendous effort to return to Israel's laws and to claim the privileges of Israel's covenant with God. When the Puritan author Thomas Prince wrote a history of his people in the early 1700s, he began with the Creation. He was convinced that all history before the "New Israel" experiment was simply a prelude to this most amazing work of God.

A state church system

Because of this effort to model the Old Covenant, the Puritans established a state church. But they were conscious of some of the evils of European state church systems. Though

---

2. Puritan covenant excerpts here and later in this chapter are cited from Thomas Jefferson Wertenbaker, *The Puritan Oligarchy* (New York, Ny.: Charles Scribner's Sons, 1947), 58; Edwin Gaustad and Leigh Schmidt, *The Religious History of America* (New York, Ny.: Harper Collins Publishers, Inc., 2002, revised edition), 53; Edmund S. Morgan, editor, *The Founding of Massachusetts: Historians and Sources* (Indianapolis, In.: The Bobbs-Merrill Company, 1964), 191; and Edmund S. Morgan, editor, *Puritan Political Ideas* (Indianapolis, In.: The Bobbs-Merrill Company, 1965), 197-199. Most of the other quotes in this chapter are also from these sources.

they never intended to give their people freedom of religion,[3] they made an attempt to keep the two institutions separate. They decreed that the church had power to deal with the spiritual faults of any civil officer, but that church discipline, even to the point of excommunication, did not put a man out of any civil office that he was holding at the time. They specified that the civil officers, not the church officers, were to enforce the laws so that this would be done "in a Civill and not in an Ecclesiastical way."

With such an arrangement, the civil and ecclesiastical authorities were soon hopelessly trapped in the state church problems they had hoped to avoid. In most cases, church leaders did not directly rule the colonies, yet they felt responsible to monitor the civil process. This caused friction between the civil leaders and church leaders. And if the church leaders felt that there was no one else who had the education and godliness necessary to fill state offices, they would fill those roles themselves.[4]

A person did not have to be a member of the Puritan church to live in the New England colonies. But only church members could vote and hold public office. As the colonies grew, they included many people whom the leaders did not want in public offices. So they gradually tightened the requirements for

---

3. The Puritans are sometimes blamed for seeking religious freedom in England but denying that freedom to others after they crossed the ocean. However, the Puritans never upheld religious freedom as a civil ideal. Their goal in England was to purify the Anglican Church and the English government, not to grant freedom to all religions existing in England at that time.

4. This practice was opposed by John Winthrop, long-time governor of Massachusetts Bay Colony. He said that ministers who took state offices were doing little good, that they unnecessarily doubted the abilities of others to fill these roles, and that they were meddling in affairs that were not their business. But the church leaders would never completely let go of the reins, because they feared that "worldly" people would gain power in the government, and that their church would be persecuted as it had been in England.

church membership to keep these people out of their church and thus ineligible for government posts.

Some of the people who came to live in the Puritan colonies were worldly-minded. Others held differing religious views, such as the Quakers, Baptists, and Anglicans. The Puritans permitted none of these groups to form churches. All the colonists, regardless of their religious persuasion, were forced to pay for the support of the Puritan Church and her ministers.

Modest successes

In the first generation, the Puritans mostly accomplished their goals for a "New Israel." They were hard-working, disciplined people. They enlarged their colony town by town in an organized fashion, always trying to keep the church at the center of new developments and trying to make it possible for all settlers to attend church at least several times per month. Few Puritans fit the typical pioneer image of an independent family pushing into the lonely backwoods.

The Puritans valued systematic education for their children. In the early years in Massachusetts, every fifty families hired a teacher. These teachers, usually capable housewives, coached children in reading, grammar, and writing. Apparently they circulated among the homes or gathered children from several families for instruction. Puritan law required any settlement with one hundred families or more to build a school. About forty years after the Puritans landed in North America, New

Especially in their first generation in America, the Puritans' morals were better than those of the other colonies.

England had a well-developed elementary public school system and compulsory attendance laws.

Nor did the Puritans' education system stop with the elementary level. In 1638, colonial leaders opened a college to provide higher education in literature, arts, sciences, and the Bible. One aim of this college was to produce men who could provide intelligent leadership after the death of the ministers educated in England. John Harvard, a Puritan minister, left a large sum to the fledgling college when he died in 1638. After that the college was named for Harvard, and today it is the oldest college in the United States.

Especially in their first generation in America, the Puritans' morals were better than those of the other colonies. The reason was not only the Puritan laws—though in comparison with other colonies, Puritan laws were more thorough and sometimes the punishments for lawbreakers more severe. A greater reason was the long arm of the church and the orderly settlement pattern that helped to keep people accountable.

Further, the people who chose to live in such a regulated culture tended to be more upright. Pioneers seeking independent frontier living away from authority tended to settle in other areas of North America.

In the early years, the Puritans encouraged a personal relationship with God. They favored spontaneous prayers and opposed prayer books. They understood that the church leaders had a calling to teach and discipline the flock, yet they realized that the clergy did not stand between the membership and God. The Puritans used no images or statues, and they avoided anything in their building design that would detract from the simplicity of worshiping God in the heart.

They had able ministers, and they observed Sunday carefully. They warned so strongly about the danger of participating unworthily in the Lord's Supper that some of their people were afraid to partake of Communion.

Roger Williams' challenge

The first strong criticism of the "New Israel" came from Roger Williams. A Puritan minister, Williams had moved from England to Boston in 1631. He did not believe that the Puritans in North America were in a special covenant with God.

The Puritans taught that the main duty of the state was to protect the church, but Williams believed that the state was an earthly organization, with no special commission from God such as Israel had in the Old Testament. He believed that God had ordained the civil government, but that He had not established only one right way to exercise civil authority. He told the Puritans that Israel had no successor in the modern world and that there never would be another such nation, because Christ did not rule by force. He also said that the state should not create churches, collect taxes to fund churches, or control the religious beliefs of its citizens.

The Puritans said that there could be no civil peace if the religious beliefs of the population were wrong. But Roger Williams replied that historians and travelers had long noted that there were many kingdoms and governments in the world who enjoyed civil peace, even though their religions were corrupt and Jesus Christ was not mentioned among them.

There was another serious flaw in the Puritan scheme, Williams said. The Puritans took their land from the Indians without paying them anything. They thought this was their right under the "New Israel" covenant. By virtue of their safe passage to America, *God* had given them the land. They were living on it and farming it; it was *theirs*. The Indians were nothing but nomads. Besides, they were heathen like the Canaanite tribes that the Israelites had driven out. As for Roger Williams, the Puritans concluded, he had a windmill in his head, and he too must be driven out.

In the fall of 1635, the court ordered Williams to leave the Puritan colonies. He was told that he could stay until spring if he hushed his foolish talk. But Williams could not keep quiet. When plans were made to arrest him and deport him to England, he and his wife fled to the Narragansett Indians in what is now Rhode Island, south of the Massachusetts Bay Colony. Other outcasts from the Puritan colonies eventually fled to the same area. There they founded settlements on land purchased from the Indians. The English government authorized these settlements to govern themselves, and in the charter they allowed Williams' idea of complete religious freedom to stand.[5]

Great declines

However, the Puritans learned that they could not escape the effects of sin by leaving them behind in England or by banishing them to Rhode Island. By 1645, vain styles in women's clothing were coming into the colonies, and a minister declared that women who followed such styles had nothing but

---

5. One likely reason that the English authorities allowed freedom of religion in Williams' colony was that they were displeased at the Puritans' refusal to share government power with non-Puritans, especially the Anglicans. The Puritans technically were "purified" Anglicans, so they considered this an irrelevant point; but in effect they kept anyone devoted to the established Anglican Church from gaining any power in the colonies. The Anglicans did not consider the Puritans to be Anglicans; in fact, the Anglicans sent missionaries into the Puritan settlements in the 1700s.

squirrels' brains. Yet even the ministers were inconsistent in relation to fashions. They made a difference in what was allowable for servants and other people of the lower class as compared with people of higher standing and more wealth. So in some cases, a maidservant was punished for wearing something that was considered acceptable for her minister's wife. Part of the aim of the laws on clothing was simply to maintain the "proper" relationship of inferior people to superior people.

Married people occasionally fell into immorality, and even more of the servants did so. While some of the second- and third-generation Puritans held nearly as high a standard as their parents and grandparents, there were a number whom the ministers described as debauched wretches, prodigies of wickedness, and children of Belial, even though they had some outward forms of godliness. Church leaders and writers expressed such concerns hundreds of times in their sermons and writings.[6]

In 1674, a minister mourned that New England was becoming exceedingly corrupt.

In 1674, a minister mourned that New England was becoming exceedingly corrupt. Drunkenness, extravagance, profanity, and lewdness were on the rise in nearly every settlement. A court order promoting reformation said,

> Notwithstanding the wholesome lawes already made by this Court for restreyning excesse in apparell, yet through corruption in many, and neglect of due execution of those lawes, the evill of

---

6. The New England colonial records have examples of masters forcing servants into impure relationships, of abortion, and of infanticide.

pride in apparrell, both for costlines in the poorer sort, & vaine, new, strainge fashions, both in poore & rich, with naked breasts and armes, or, as it were, pinioned with the addition of superstitious ribbons both on haire & apparrell.

Many people traveled and engaged in secular activities on Sunday; some even worked. Profanity was very common, and one minister said that his people's oaths and blasphemies had crowded God out of their thoughts. Drinking houses did a brisk business in most of the towns.

Stylish hair was outlawed successfully for about forty years, but in 1675, authorities recorded that great pride was evident in the hair of many men, which was as long as a woman's. That style became almost universal by 1700; even most of the Puritan ministers had long, flowing locks. Wigs came into style before 1700, and soon many of the clergy succumbed to the practice in spite of the fact that they at first preached against it. In 1675, the General Court of Massachusetts reported,

> Whereas there is manifest pride openly appearing amongst us in that long haire, like weomens haire, is worne by some men, either their oune or others haire made into perewiggs, and by some weomen wearing borders of haire, and theire cutting, curling, & immodest laying out theire haire, which practise doeth prevayle & increase, especially amongst the younger sort . . .

Family life suffered from carelessness, indulgence, and lack of discipline.[7] Some families had no Bibles (through lack

---

[7]. This is illustrated by the common practice of couples courting in winter. They were generally allowed to spend time together in a bedroom under quilts because the only warm room in the house was the one with the fireplace, where the rest of the family was gathered. Jonathan Edwards decried this practice as too tempting. Some of his fellow Puritans accused him of having impure thoughts.

of interest, not funds), others had them but did not read them daily, and many others neglected daily family prayers. Churches suffered from bitterness and disputes between members, and the gossip that once would have brought a visit from the minister became standard fare.

For years, tremendous efforts were made to get the "New Israel" back on course. Preachers preached, cried, and prayed. Clergy convened and made reform pleas and plans. Magistrates tried to legislate morality, and theologians wrote books. But it all had little effect on the moral decline of the people.

Cotton Mather (1663-1728) was one of the most prominent Puritan ministers.

The leaders pointed to disasters like the wars and skirmishes with the Indians (especially in 1675) and the Boston fire (1711) as proof that the people had broken their covenant with God. If they would only return to God, He would protect them and their assets and make them flourish spiritually and economically.

The witch trials in Salem in the 1690s were one of the clergy's reactions to spiritual decline. Some of the clergy actually

The Wonders of the Invisible World:

Being an Account of the

TRYALS

OF

Several Witches,

Lately Excuted in

NEW-ENGLAND:

And of several remarkable Curiosities therein Occurring.

Together with,

I. Observations upon the Nature, the Number, and the Operations of the Devils.
II. A short Narrative of a late outrage committed by a knot of Witches in *Swede-Land*, very much resembling, and so far explaining, that under which *New-England* has laboured.
III. Some Councels directing a due Improvement of the Terrible things lately done by the unusual and amazing Range of *Evil-Spirits* in *New-England*.
IV. A brief Discourse upon those *Temptations* which are the more ordinary Devices of Satan.

By COTTON MATHER.

Published by the Special Command of his EXCELLENCY the Governour of the Province of the *Massachusetts-Bay* in *New-England*.

Printed first, at *Boston* in *New-England*; and Reprinted at *London*, for *John Dunton*, at the *Raven* in the *Poultry*. 1693.

Cover page of Cotton Mather's 1693 booklet on the Salem witch trials.

seemed to welcome this problem as an opportunity to show their people the seriousness of sin, and to prove to the "Sadducees" (their name for the less spiritual people) that the colonies urgently needed revival. In 1692, this affair cost nineteen people their lives and countless more their peace of mind.

The problem started when two slaves told a few children some witchcraft stories, and the children took to acting out the stories and pretending that evil spirits and witches were afflicting them. The attention that the community leaders gave the case fanned the flames of imagination; and soon all it took to have an honorable person in the community on trial for witchcraft—even if he was a minister—was for someone to present "evidence" that he had been haunted by a specter of that person.[8] While those prosecuting the cases were convinced that they were driving the devil out of Salem, others were convinced that the devil was working through the prosecutors to destroy good people of the Lord. Several courageous people did their best to prove the fallacy of the accusations. But these voices did not make much difference until the heat of the moment had passed.

The hysteria faded when some of the judges and accusers (or their spouses) were themselves accused of meddling with the powers of darkness. After this happened four or five times, most of the people prosecuting the cases turned against any further investigations. Five years later, one of the judges acknowledged in shame that he was partly to blame for the

---

8. The leaders questioned children and alleged witches for hours, until many times the accused persons simply assented to the assumptions being put to them. One historian commented that if parents had given direction to their children in the early stages of the problem, the matter would likely have been solved.

miscarriage of justice, and he asked the church and the Lord to forgive him for his great sin.

Before the 1700s, the "New Israel" had definitely failed morally and spiritually. The Puritans never realized their goal of forming a righteous society that would start an international revival.

In 1684, the English government revoked the Puritans' original charter. In 1691, King William III gave the colony a new charter that established voting rights and eligibility for office for colonists who were not a part of the Puritan church. This ended the church's political monopoly and the "New Israel" experiment. However, the Congregationalist churches, as the Puritans' churches had come to be called, continued to hold considerable political power until after the Revolution.

The Village as the Center of Puritan Life

The Puritan ideal envisioned a hardy, resilient government and culture based on a covenant with God. But their government was the work of man, and it turned out to be fragile—even more fragile than many other forms of government. It could not deal with the real political conditions faced by any government in any part of the world.

The village church and minister were the center of life in early Puritan communities. Each day, the village folks traveled to their fields around the village, to the river or sea to fish, or to the forest for firewood. Everyone interacted; no one could hide. The clergy was able to maintain a "righteous" order.

But as New England grew into its second and third generations, a village did not have enough room to continue this arrangement. There was not enough land nearby for all the young farmers to reach easily. Eventually they were traveling several miles to reach their land, perhaps walking or driving an ox team with implements. Many of these farmers and their families began living on their land instead of in the village. This was the beginning of farmsteads in New England.

It was also the beginning of the end for strict accountability to the Puritan clergy. Eventually, the village was no longer the center of the settlement. A minister could not supervise his flock as before, nor could he reach them easily for visitation and encouragement.

The spreading out resulted in power struggles in the settlements. Citizens of large settlements disputed over where to place meetinghouses, all of them hoping to avoid many miles of walking. In one case, the western inhabitants of a settlement won the right to build a meetinghouse in their area, and they had begun work on the building. But people from the eastern part came by night and tore down the walls erected earlier in the day. The leaders finally solved the problem by dividing the settlement, and the settlers of both parts built their own meetinghouses.

Along with spreading out, the settlers increased the size of their herds and farms. Many of them became prosperous, yet they were unsatisfied and striving for more. At the same time, other settlers began fishing for a living and spent days out at sea. Some began businesses and stopped farming altogether. The villages in prosperous areas grew into towns and the towns into cities.

The grandfathers of these busy farmers and workmen had viewed themselves as God's chosen people and had tried to please God. They were in a new land where they had to suffer and struggle to make a living. But later generations were more concerned about economics than about their condition before God. Instead of humbly trusting God, they were confident in their own virtues and abilities.

Their political view had also changed. Their grandfathers had focused on keeping the people under the control of the government, but these men focused on keeping the government under the control of the people.

The Puritan ideal was no match for the growing forces of population and economics. As the old establishment tried to govern the church and the community, both grew until they were out of the reach of its arm, and it lost control of both.

Puritan contributions to American culture and politics

Certain things in the early Puritan vision live on. All through American history, right into the 21st century, political leaders have invoked the image of America as a city on a hill and a light to the world. The Puritans were the first to apply these phrases to a state instead of to the church, as the New Testament intends.

The Puritans brought to America new ideas about national law. Even in England, the Puritans had pressed for greater accountability of the leaders to the people. Their views influenced the American focus on limited government, checks and balances in government, and a large degree of state and local autonomy.

The Puritan views of self-government in congregations, towns, and states also became a strong influence in the Revolution, when that concept was extended to rebelling against English rule.

Ironically, a major influence toward religious freedom for all Americans was the lack of such freedom in the Puritan colonies. When the United States was being formed in 1776, support for religious freedom was lower in the Puritan regions of Massachusetts and Connecticut than anywhere else. Even in the 1780s, Massachusetts allowed no one but Protestants to hold government offices.[9] This was looser than their original position, but it still made Baptists, Quakers, Jews, Catholics, and others ineligible. Around 1820, these sidelined groups joined forces and filed lawsuits that brought down the last barriers to their religions in Massachusetts and Connecticut. Freedom of religion for America was won by those who rebelled against Puritan order.

The Puritans' high value of education and their energetic work habits helped to shape American views of family life and labor. In most countries of the world, hard work is associated with low-class people and is avoided by those who can afford hired help. But that has not been the mentality in much of North America. Part of the credit for this goes to the Puritans, who were estimated by some historians in the mid-1800s as being the ancestors of one-third of the entire white population in the United States.

---

9. There were similar rules in Georgia, South Carolina, New Jersey, and New Hampshire at the time. In addition, Massachusetts considered poor men ineligible for some offices.

The early Puritans' emphasis on good works also influenced the new country. An example is the 1675 court order for reformation to regain the blessing of God on the Puritan battles against the Indians. This document laments the great backsliding and decrees greater surveillance of the people and greater punishments for a variety of unrighteous deeds. Anyone who wore stylish clothing was to be fined.

Because some people left church before worship services were over, men were appointed to close the doors and keep the people inside until the proper departure time. Youth who were rowdy in church were to be admonished for their first offense, and fined, whipped, or jailed for later offenses. Anyone who overheard someone swearing was to report the offender to the magistrate or constable. To restrain drunkenness, the county courts were commanded to issue tavern licenses only to sober people of good report. Village residents were forbidden to enter these establishments; they were only for travelers and strangers.

> **While the Puritans failed greatly in teaching true Christianity, they managed to keep an emphasis on good works in their culture for well over two hundred years.**

While the Puritans failed greatly in teaching true Christianity, they managed to keep an emphasis on good works in their culture for well over two hundred years. They tried to impress all America with the fact that New England was religiously superior to all other regions. In 1844, a Congregational writer boasted that likely there was nowhere in the world where fewer infidels or openly irreligious people could be found.

"Christian" but carnal

Puritanism was possibly the most "Christian" influence in the beginning of America. However, the evil forces that plague all nations were present among the Puritans as well.

The Puritans were proud of what they were doing; they believed that the "eyes of all people" were watching them and their experiment. This attitude was especially strong among the early leaders, whose aim was more than simply to establish a "New Israel." They intended to prove to their political opponents in England that they could establish a righteous state if only they had the opportunity to do so. When that pride faced inevitable failure, these leaders became desperate. Their desperation was one of the forces behind the witch trials.

The Puritans did not understand true repentance. Because they believed that they as a people were under a covenant with God, they watched each other closely to make sure no one would sin and bring the whole colony into danger. Especially in the early days, they thought that sin would cause the whole colony to fail. A generation or two later, when the economic success of the colony was obvious, the Puritans taught that sin would be detrimental to the colony's prosperity. So in their settlements, sin was a problem more because it harmed the community than because it was an offense against God. Repentance meant mourning for one's sins because they had endangered the public welfare. It was an outward correction instead of an inward transformation.

6 • Religion In Puritan New England

The Puritans felt that they were God's chosen people. This resulted in class distinction, nationalism, and persecution. Leaders and wealthy people were held in esteem while servants and other lower-class people were denied the privileges of the upper classes. Though the Puritans made a few halfhearted attempts to evangelize the Indians, their true feelings about Indians were exposed in how they fought them to preserve their settlements.

The heroic mission efforts of New Englanders such as Roger Williams, John Eliot, and David Brainerd availed little when the average citizen viewed the Indians with distaste and arrogance at best, and as animals at worst. The settlers were the "New Israel," and Israel did not respect heathen tribes. Cotton Mather (1663-1728), one of the most influential Puritan leaders, wrote in 1702 that "probably the *Devil* decoyed those miserable savages hither, in hopes that the Gospel of the Lord Jesus Christ would never come here to destroy or disturb his absolute empire over them." Such reasoning provided a religious rationale for any action necessary to remove the Indians from land that the Puritans wanted. After all, if they were fighting the devil, no measures could be too harsh.[10]

The Puritans fought the Pequot Indians in 1636-37, killing warriors and also slaughtering some women and children. When the battle was questioned by surviving Pequots as well as some people in England, the Puritan army captain replied

---

10. Such attitudes prevailed for years in New England and elsewhere in America. Elias Boudinot, a Connecticut statesman, worked against these sentiments in the early 1800s by publishing a book alleging a connection from the ten lost tribes of Israel to the American Indians. Boudinot also adopted a Cherokee lad. But when the young man married a white girl, their Connecticut town was outraged and closed the school where the two had met.

109

that God's Word had guided the battle. One minister claimed that God Himself had conquered the Pequots.

The Puritans exiled numerous upright citizens simply because they disagreed with some Puritan doctrines. They hanged four Quakers in the 1600s. In 1675, the General Court suggested that God was using an Indian attack to punish the Puritans for various things, including the toleration of too many Quakers. At that time the court issued strict orders against them, claiming that Quakers taught damnable heresies and abominable idolatry. Anyone who attended a Quaker meeting was to be arrested and jailed. The offenders were to be worked on bread and water for three days or pay a heavy fine.

An Appeal from New England Quakers to the King of England

In the mid-1600s, the Quakers in New England appealed to the king of England to make the Puritans heed the freedom that the crown had granted Quakers. With the appeal, they sent a list of the atrocities that the "New Israel" had inflicted on them.

1. Two honest and innocent women stripped . . . and searched in an inhuman manner.

2. Twelve strangers in that country, but freeborn of this nation, received twenty-three whippings, most of them with a whip of three cords with knots at the ends.

3. Eighteen inhabitants of the country, being freeborn English, received twenty-three whippings.

4. Sixty-four imprisonments of "the Lord's people," amounting to five hundred and nineteen weeks.

5. Two beaten with pitched ropes, the blows amounting to an hundred and thirty-nine.

6. An innocent old man banished from his wife and children, and for returning put in prison for above a year.

7. Twenty-five banished upon penalties of being whipped, or having their ears cut, or a hand branded.
8. Fines, amounting to a thousand pounds, laid upon the inhabitants for meeting together.
9. Five kept fifteen days without food.
10. One laid neck and heels in irons for sixteen hours.
11. One very deeply burnt in the right hand with an H after he had been beaten with thirty stripes.
12. One chained to a log of wood for the most part of twenty days in wintertime.
13. Five appeals to England denied.
14. Three had their right ears cropped off.
15. One inhabitant of Salem, since banished on pain of death, had one-half of his house and land seized.
16. Two ordered sold as bondservants.
17. Eighteen of the people of God banished on pain of death.
18. Three of the servants of God put to death.
19. Since the executions four more banished on pain of death and twenty-four heavily fined for meeting to worship God.

One instance of the injustice mentioned in number 16 occurred in May 1659, when the court of Boston ruled that a son and daughter of Lawrence Southwick, a Quaker, be sold for slavery in Barbados. In addition, another Quaker was hanged after this appeal was written, bringing the total to four.

The Baptists also suffered at Puritan hands. Obadiah Holmes came from England to support the Baptist cause in New England, but in the 1650s he was beaten with thirty lashes in Boston. Holmes testified that he rejoiced to share in the sufferings of Jesus Christ, and that such punishments would not make him ashamed of his Lord.

Safe in Rhode Island, where Baptists enjoyed peace, Roger Williams reproached the Massachusetts leaders for their treatment of Holmes. When they persecuted other religions, Williams asked, how could they be sure that they were not fighting against God? But the Puritans were more concerned about preserving the "New Israel" than about practicing true Christianity, and they outlawed Baptist meetings until 1682.

Although there were probably sincere Bible-believers among the Puritans, especially in their early years, as a whole they fell far short of the principle in the Sermon on the Mount. They were not among the poor in spirit or the meek of the earth. They tried to uphold high morals without emphasizing purity of heart. They taught love and forgiveness among themselves, but they hated their enemies. When the Puritans were cursed or despitefully treated, they did not feel blessed; they believed that God was judging them for not faithfully upholding His commandments.

Had Anabaptists been in the Puritan colonies, they would have refused to fight to protect the villages. They would have insisted on holding separate Anabaptist worship services. They would have rejected some of the civil values as well as the Calvinism that the Puritans taught in their schools. They may have had their own schools and disobeyed the Puritan government schools' compulsory attendance laws. The Puritans would have persecuted, exiled, or killed Anabaptists for these reasons.

The Puritans had the best conditions that any state ever had in order to succeed with "righteous" order. But their commonwealth could not overcome the power of the evil nature within. There is no better example in history of the fact that no earthly government can stop moral and spiritual decline.

That diabolical, hell-conceived principle
   of persecution rages among some. . . .
This vexes me the worst
   of anything whatever.
There are at this time in the adjacent county . . .
   well-meaning men in close jail
   for publishing their religious sentiments,
   which in the main are very orthodox.
—James Madison, 1775

7

Religion in the Middle Colonies and in the South; the Great Awakening

The Puritan "New Israel" experiment offers one perspective on Christianity in colonial America. The religious freedom of New York and Pennsylvania, and the Anglicanism of Virginia and the southern colonies, provide other perspectives. Regardless of their varied religious characteristics, all the colonies had much moral laxness and indifference to religion by the early 1700s. This atmosphere was partly due to the Enlightenment, a European movement that minimized God and magnified man and his abilities.

Between 1725 and 1750, and especially in the 1740s, the Great Awakening challenged the religious indifference in America. But this emotion-filled revival made only a superficial difference in many of the colonists. The majority remained as unconcerned about religion as before. Also, the Great Awakening was followed by a religious slump that largely erased any spiritual gains it had made. By the time of the Revolution, spiritual indifference again prevailed in all the colonies.

New York

The Dutch established New Amsterdam on Manhattan Island in 1626. They were lenient toward religion, so New Amsterdam became a center of religious diversity.

In 1628, two years after New Amsterdam was founded, the first Dutch Reformed minister stepped ashore on Manhattan Island. He observed that the colonists were rough and unrestrained, and that the Indians were savage, wild, and wicked. By 1629 the Dutch Reformed Church was established as the official religion of New Amsterdam, but the colony continued to be a haven for other Protestants such as Lutherans and Presbyterians, English dissenters such as Quakers, and Roman Catholics.

Peter Stuyvesant arrived in 1647 to take charge of New Amsterdam. The colony was facing numerous problems, including disputes with Indians, confusion in the local government, and land disputes with English colonies. Stuyvesant's iron will and stamping wooden leg were more than a match for the political problems, but he could not establish the religious order he wanted. He favored only the Dutch Reformed Church, he half-tolerated the Protestants and Catholics, he tried unsuccessfully to deport the Jews, and he simply hated the Quakers.

Officers of the West India Company, a Dutch commercial enterprise in charge of New Amsterdam, often blocked

7 • Religion in the Middle Colonies and in the South

Stuyvesant's efforts to persecute other faiths. They sided with people imprisoned for matters of conscience. Even the citizens of New Amsterdam were unhappy with their governor's rules against Quakers. Eventually, Stuyvesant's heavy fist worked him out of a job. When English warships sailed into the New Amsterdam harbor in 1664, Stuyvesant's people refused to fight for him; and the colony passed peacefully to the English. Stuyvesant soon sailed for Holland, and New Amsterdam became New York.

In the conditions of surrender, the English agreed to tolerate the Dutch Reformed faith, but they opposed the flourishing sects. Yet the religious scene became ever more varied. By 1678, Anglicans, Dutch Reformed, several kinds of Presbyterians, several kinds of Quakers, Jews, Anabaptists, Catholics, and other denominations were represented among the settlers. At that time the governor reported that every sort of religious opinion was present in New York, but that most of the people had no religion or at least no religious affiliation.

An artist of that time drew a picture representing religious conditions in New York. His drawing shows two ministers preaching to a crowd of people who have their backs turned to the speakers. Only a few are seeking the narrow gate to eternal life; the majority are heading toward hell. Drinking, pride, usury, extortion, chambering, and wantonness are among the sins of the crowd.

In the early 1700s, the English attempted to bring order to what they considered the chaos in New York's religion. For a time, they did not let any Dutch Reformed ministers come into the colony, and they forced Dutch churches that needed ministers to accept Anglican preachers. But though such efforts hampered non-Anglican churches for a time, the English were unable to overcome the precedent set in the colony's first several generations.

Pennsylvania

William Penn started his colony in 1682, decades after the founding of Jamestown, New England, Rhode Island, and New York. From the older colonies, Penn had learned about the struggles of establishing settlements in the New World. He encouraged his settlers to bring supplies that would help them get through the first months in the American wilderness. He did not promise them an easy living; rather, he said that with hard work and a willingness to do without some European comforts, a good living would come in due time.

Penn labored for a good government and a virtuous and industrious society. In many ways, he accomplished his hopes.

Penn also said that everyone who agreed to obey the law and live in peace was welcome to live in his "Holy Experiment." People of different religions were not just tolerated but *invited*. Penn's invitation was similar to that of Roger Williams in Rhode Island, but it came at a time when Quakers and Anabaptists in particular needed a place of refuge. Those people came by the hundreds, along with German Protestants, Schwenkfelders, Dunkers, Seventh-day Baptists, Moravians, Presbyterians, Baptists, Methodists, and even a few Catholics and Anglicans.

Penn labored for a good government and a virtuous and industrious society. In many ways, he accomplished his hopes. He attracted more true Christians to his colony than any other colony had done. Many of his citizens were peace-loving,

7 • Religion in the Middle Colonies and in the South

nonresistant people who were willing to give up comforts if they could practice their deep faith without interference. Such people made solid citizens, especially in a colony that officially rejected warfare and pursued honest, friendly relationships with the Indians.

Yet Penn's "Holy Experiment" contained much that was unholy. Penn faced many disappointments among his own quarreling Quaker group as well as in his family. He seemed to think that offering religious freedom would attract faithful people or convert the unfaithful who came; but in real experience, the freedom in his colony attracted some unruly people

The Quaker plan for civil government did not reckon with the inevitable clash of arms that all states eventually face.

who would not have survived the stern Puritan regime. And even in areas such as Lancaster County, where many citizens had a deep faith, the government found it necessary to establish courts, judges, and prisons to deal with the "Vagabonds & other dissolute People" who lived among the more upright citizens. In later years, Penn sadly acknowledged that liberty without obedience results in confusion, and considered his colony a failure as far as spirituality was concerned.

Some of the greatest struggles in Pennsylvania were between the nonresistant peoples who populated the safer, more expensive regions such as Philadelphia and Lancaster, and the Scotch-Irish Presbyterians, Irish Catholics, and German Calvinists who bought cheaper land on the frontier. This population division was not without exception; some Lutherans lived among the nonresistant groups, and a few nonresistant people lived on

Settlers on the frontier usually bore the brunt of Indian attacks.

the frontier. But in the main, the frontier people were willing to fight and had little concern about observing Penn's policy of respecting the Indians.

The frontier people were usually the first ones attacked by Indians. Those settlers fought back; but because of the large number of nonresistant people in Pennsylvania, they often felt that they were fighting alone. They believed it was unfair for them to bear the burden of protecting the frontier so that the nonresistant people could dwell securely in their homes.

As long as the Quakers had control of the government, they refused to support military action against the Indians. By the 1750s, though only one-fifth of Pennsylvania's population was

Quaker, the Quakers still held two-thirds of the seats in the Assembly of Pennsylvania. Part of their success in holding on to such a disproportionate number of seats was due to the ballots cast by other nonresistant groups who wanted the Quakers to rule. Almost everyone in these groups was more ready to send gifts to the Indians than to fight them.

But finally the hard facts of civil defense drove the Quakers to the sidelines, where their nonresistant beliefs could no longer hinder mustering troops or building forts on the frontier. In 1756, most of the Quakers in the Pennsylvania Assembly were replaced by men who would use force to build the state. The Quaker plan for civil government had not reckoned with the inevitable clash of arms that all states eventually face.

Maryland and Virgina

In 1634, the colony of Maryland was started by Catholic and Protestant settlers under the leadership of a Catholic, Cecil Calvert (Lord Baltimore). He ordered the Catholic settlers to live peaceably with the Protestants, partly because he was under English pressure to tolerate Anglicans but mostly because he believed that religious persecution would hinder the economic success of his colony.

The settlements in Maryland were at peace for several years. But in the early 1640s, the Protestants seized control of the government and forced the Jesuits (Catholic teachers) to leave the colony. The Calvert family regained control in 1646. Hoping to defuse tensions between the Protestants and Catholics, Calvert persuaded the Maryland government to pass a law of religious toleration in 1649. This law granted all Christian groups the freedom to worship as they chose.

But struggles continued—with power held sometimes by Catholics and sometimes by Protestants, and with those in power persecuting their opponents—until the Protestants finally won permanently in 1692. The Catholics suffered some persecution afterward, and they lost their right to vote in 1715; but Maryland remained a center for Catholics. Not until after the American Revolution did the Catholics in Maryland regain equal political footing with the Protestants.

The oldest permanent settlement in America began in 1607 at Jamestown, Virginia, as an officially Anglican community. Religious laws and their enforcement were more relaxed than in Puritan New England, yet other groups (including Protestants) were severely restricted. Virginia law stated that anyone who denied the Trinity should go to prison for three years. Parents who belonged to some sects could have their children taken from them and placed in other homes. Baptists in particular suffered a great deal from beatings and imprisonment, in addition to indignities such as being spit on and openly mocked. Persecution of dissenters was stronger in Virginia than in England.

The English commercial authorities in charge of Virginia advised the colony that persecution would hamper their wealth, and they ordered the rulers to abide by the Declaration of Religious Toleration that England passed in 1689. That ruling made the leaders a bit more careful. But they were far away from England, and they continued persecuting dissenters for almost another century with little interference from English authorities.

Through persecution and legislation, the Anglican Church eventually reached a greater height of power in Virginia than in any other colony. After more than a century of such

7 • Religion in the Middle Colonies and in the South

power, James Madison commented that it produced proud, lazy ministers and an ignorant laity, both of them bigoted and superstitious. During the Revolution and afterwards, Virginia's James Madison and Thomas Jefferson were some of the strongest voices against any involvement of the government with the church. Their objections were based mainly on their experiences in colonial Virginia.

In Maryland and Virginia, morals appear to have been lower than in New England and in Pennsylvania. In 1652, William Mitchell, an officer on Maryland's governing council, had immoral relations with his maid and eventually forced her to take a potion that caused an abortion. When the case was tried, the maid testified that Mitchell had also tried to make her to deny Christianity and had blasphemed Jesus Christ and the Holy Ghost. Other cases of abuse, rape, incest, and abortion also appear in the Maryland colonial records.

Though most Maryland settlers were not involved in such activities, yet the religious condition of the populace was far from ideal. The Anglican church in England sent Thomas Bray to study the condition of the colonial Anglican Church in Maryland, and he observed that many of the English people in Maryland had fallen to atheism and infidelity. Bray was concerned enough to start an organization designed to support missionaries and ministers and to regain Maryland for the church.

Morally, Virginia got off to a bad start. Its first settlers were not sturdy country people expecting to farm the land and raise their families in peace, but English gentlemen hoping to find easy profits in precious metals or by using Indian labor to produce crops. After the colony struggled along for seventeen years, it finally became well established in the 1620s by raising tobacco and exporting it to England. Despite the original settlers' lack of character and the fact that they eventually survived by selling an enslaving drug, the Anglican leaders of Jamestown saw themselves as a special people of God.

As in all state church situations, some Anglican pastors in Virginia contributed to the colony's moral problems. A number of the pastors sent from England were actually trying to run away from problems in their finances, their marriages, or their personal character. In 1632, the Virginia government tried to regulate the ministers' conduct:

> Ministers shall not give themselves to excess in drinking, or riot, spending their time idly by day or night playing at dice, cards, or any other unlawful game; but they shall . . . occupy themselves with some honest study or exercise, always doing the things which shall appertain to honesty, and endeavor to profit the church of God... to excel all others in purity of life and . . . be an example to the people to live well and Christianly.

For their part, the Anglican ministers were more concerned about the Baptists than about their own failures. They were shocked to hear that unordained men preached in Baptist meetings and that even women rose to teach the congregation Yet the Anglicans could not comprehend that the cold deadness and moral failures of their own church were bolstering the numbers in the emotional evangelical sects.

The Carolinas and Georgia

Farther south, in the Carolinas and Georgia, the Anglicans were not able to gain the control that they had in Virginia. Missionaries sent from England to bolster the official church

7 • Religion in the Middle Colonies and in the South

often became discouraged with the settlers' lack of interest in religion or their lively interest in other groups. One of these missionaries said of Savannah that its English citizens seemed to have little more religious knowledge than the Indians. Another missionary reported that the people of Charleston, South Carolina, were the vilest people on earth, not having honor, honesty, or enough religion. Another Anglican reported of North Carolina that its shiftless citizens did not know Sunday from any other day. Still another accused the Baptists of baptizing women in skimpy dresses and of tolerating impurity among their youth and married people.

These reports may have been exaggerated; the Anglicans tended to see any non-Anglican as a wretched person. Nevertheless, some religious people resorted to extremely coarse methods in struggling against the Anglicans. One Anglican preacher reported that dissenter hooligans stole his horse, disturbed his preaching services, and even placed excrement on one of his Communion tables.

How both Anglicans and non-Anglicans treated slaves is another evidence of poor moral conditions in the southern colonies. South Carolina's population in 1750 was about 64,000, of which about 40,000 were black slaves. The English used unmerciful measures to keep this huge slave population under control, fearing what would happen if such a large group should revolt. Many a slave owner would inflict horrible punishments on his slaves, yet piously kneel for prayer at church on Sunday. Some slave owners said that slaves had no souls; others said that Christianity made their slaves proud and lazy. Very few treated their slaves with respect.

The Great Awakening

The Great Awakening was a religious movement in England and America that lasted from about 1725 to 1750, peaking in the 1740s. This movement focused on rescuing people from moral decline and on recovering churches from cold formalism to a spiritual walk with God.

Part of the reason for the spiritual deadness in the colonies was the Enlightenment. Enlightenment philosophy was that reason, or thinking rationally, was the path to success and was responsible for all the positive achievements of mankind. Certainly the ability to reason is a gift from God, but the philosophers of the Enlightenment influenced people to worship reason instead of God, even though many of them still believed in the existence of God.

Enlightenment teachings eroded Christian precepts such as the reliability of God's Word and submission to authority. These philosophers blamed the Catholic Church for teaching blind acceptance of authority, saying that it produced ignorance and superstition. This is true, but the philosophers proceeded to dismiss all unquestioning acceptance of authority, including that of God and the Bible. They rejected many cultural values and traditions. Many of them were motivated by anger toward abusive and selfish governments that pampered a few at the expense of many. Churches affected by the Enlightenment, including the Anglicans and the descendants of the Puritans, became colder, placing a heavier emphasis on reasoning as the path to salvation instead of trusting in the blood of Christ.

Leaders in the Great Awakening sought to reverse this religious decline. One of its main evangelists was Jonathan Edwards (1703-58), who taught that heart affections and a transformed life are the most important marks of true religion. He did not believe that one could become a Christian only by changing his mind or studying a set of Bible propositions. The Great Awakening was characterized by strong emotion, but Edwards taught that the true measure of the Christian life is not how much emotion a person displays but how well he follows God in daily life.

How the Great Awakening Affected Puritan Society

In spite of the charter change that England had forced on the Puritan colonies in 1691, the Congregational churches (the descendant of the Puritan colonial churches) still held tremendous political power at the time of the Great Awakening. The Awakening became a primary force in unraveling that carefully maintained power.

Great Awakening evangelists taught that both a person and a congregation are free in Christ, and this idea divided the people of New England into four groups. The divisions were already present in some ways; but before the Great Awakening, the colony was mostly indifferent spiritually, and the religious differences were not as marked.

The Old Lights considered the revival both foolish and outdated. They were New Englanders whom Enlightenment ideas had influenced the most strongly. Old Lights rejected the Trinity and some Calvinist teachings about human depravity.

The Old Calvinists were diehard Congregationalists. They were committed to maintaining the established social and political order of New England and wanted no revival.

The Moderate New Lights wanted to purify the Congregational Church, much as the original Puritans wanted to purify the Anglican Church. They mostly remained a part of the Congregational Church. Jonathan Edwards identified with this group.

The Radical New Lights did not believe that the established New England churches could be rescued from their evils. They started their own churches, emphasized personal salvation, and practiced church discipline.

The struggles between these four groups created a great upheaval in New England. In the struggle, the Congregational Church fell from its high position, and some of the Puritan concepts about the church, the state, and society were

> disproved. The fact that a Christian revival helped to overthrow some of the Puritans' wrong ideas gives some indication of how far the "New Israel" was from God's will.
>
> The Great Awakening had some unsound emphases, and it disregarded some important Bible principles. Because of these faults, it drew a few Christians away from strong faith into a weaker and more shallow Christian experience. The Great Awakening was not a revival for these people. But in New England, where the social and religious atmosphere for years had actually hardened many people against salvation, the Great Awakening was a revival of some important truths; and it helped many people draw closer to God for a time.

George Whitefield, a British Anglican minister who supported the Great Awakening, was a more bold and fiery preacher than Jonathan Edwards. His preaching contributed to the conversions of John and Charles Wesley, who started the Methodist movement. Whitefield's preaching was so sharp that he was soon barred from many Anglican pulpits in England. He traveled to the North American colonies seven times between 1738 and 1770, preaching widely and gaining the criticism of many colonial Anglican leaders. He often preached outdoors to crowds of thousands, and he moved many listeners to new commitments to the Lord.

These men and many of the less renowned preachers of the Great Awakening had good intentions, and much of their teaching was sound. A minority of people truly found the Lord in this time and remained faithful to Him after the Great Awakening died down. But while the Awakening countered the coldness and formality of the established churches, it failed to set forth clear doctrines for the true church, as the Bible does. The emphasis on conversion and fruit bearing was good; but the great majority of Great Awakening converts had only an emotional experience of repentance, and they failed to go on in genuine Christian living. The Methodist movement in

7 • Religion in the Middle Colonies and in the South

England experienced the same declines. John and Charles Wesley lamented at how rapidly Methodism changed into just another worldly church.

In fact, it was the excitement of the Great Awakening that contributed to the hooligans' thieving and vandalism against an Anglican preacher as described earlier in this chapter. Edwards and Whitefield would have condemned these antics, but such happenings nevertheless were motivated partly by the emotions of the revival campaigns.

The strong assertions of the Great Awakening evangelists easily incited men of lesser character to vandalism and other foolish actions. George Whitefield called the Boston ministers "dumb dogs, half devils and half beasts." Gilbert Tennent, another Awakening preacher, said in 1743 that "the greatest part by far of the Ministers in this land, were carnal unconverted men, and that they held damnable *Arminian* principles."

> **The great majority of Great Awakening converts had only an emotional experience of repentance, and they failed to go on in genuine Christian living.**

Various terms became popular during the Great Awakening, such as "the tyranny of sin," "liberty in Christ," and "virtue." In the next generation, that of the Revolution, these changed from having religious meanings to having political connotations. In America, the tyranny of sin was transferred to the tyranny of England, and liberty in Christ changed into American independence. The Revolution did not directly result from the Great Awakening, but the general spirit, the

George Whitefield (1740-1770) was a fiery, dramatic speaker. Many English and American Anglican leaders did not allow him in their pulpits because he strongly challenged people to a deeper spiritual life.

forceful expressions, and the common ideas promoted in the Awakening became elements of the Revolution.

Did the Anabaptists consider the colonies Christian?

The Anabaptists, while glad for freedom and the chance to spread their wings outside the confining Palatinate and Swiss valleys, still felt like a people apart. They became alarmed when war clouds floated thick on the horizon in 1754 (the French and Indian War). In 1755 they realized that in their naturalization agreement with the Pennsylvania government in 1729, they had promised to fight for King George II if necessary. They had not recognized what they were promising, for they had not understood English (and many still did not, twenty-six years later).

7 • Religion in the Middle Colonies and in the South

Now they appealed to the government to be considerate of their situation. According to Benjamin Franklin, they hoped that if they were quiet, law-abiding people, the French would leave them alone if they took over the British colonies.

The Anabaptist groups in Pennsylvania recognized the Biblical distinction between the church and the world. They did not feel that they lived in a Christian colony; in fact, they often felt like aliens among the English and Irish settlers around them. Colonial documents referred to these German-speaking peoples as "the Dutch," "Swissers," or "long-bearded Switzers."

Pennsylvania Governor Patrick Gordon in 1727 wrote that these strangers, "being ignorant of our Language & Laws, & settling in a Body together, make, as it were, a distinct People." But after observing them for over a year, he said, "They have...behaved themselves well, and have generally so good a character for honesty and industry as deserves the esteem of this government." For their part, the Mennonites in a 1727 letter to the Pennsylvania public explained their relationship to the world like this: "It behoves and becomes a right and true Christian that he should be little and low in the World, and shun the greatness of the same, and keep himself like the lowly ones." Further, the letter

> ... expressed a traditional Mennonite amazement "that so many high gifted, and understanding and excellent men," who had "received Knowledge and clear shining Light of the Gospel," had "so little altered themselves" from the sub-Christian "Customs" of the world. . . .
>
> "We can understand nothing else out of the New Testament, but that the Lord Christ hath so learned, and with his own

131

Example gone before us. . . . ." If we live according to the example of Christ, our conduct will be "a great light, worthy of the Christian Name, lighted and set upon the Candlestick." . . .[1]

This letter, written almost fifty years before the Revolution, shows that the Mennonites did not become estranged from their new country only in the great crisis of the 1770s. In 1727, none of them had been in America for more than sixteen years, and hundreds of them had arrived even more recently. The American Mennonites of the earliest years obviously did not consider themselves part of mainstream colonial American culture.[2] Their beliefs about worldly society were much the same as those of true Christians today.

That Anabaptism was out of step with early American society is also illustrated by the insight of William Duke, an Episcopalian minister in Maryland. In 1795, Duke wrote *Observations on the State of Religion in Maryland*, which observed that the Washington County, Maryland Mennonites had a "scheme of discipline as clashes with the common methods of government and civil society." Yet these people did not intentionally cause

In religion, American society was much like the European societies from which the colonists came— not truly Christian, but influenced by Christianity.

---

1. John L. Ruth, *'Twas Seeding Time* (Scottdale, Pa.: Herald Press, 1976), p. 221, 222. Used by permission.

2. Nor were they the only religious people that considered the colonial world sinful. Henry Muhlenberg, a Lutheran pastor in Lancaster County, believed that the Revolution came because of the sins of American society rather than the so-called outrage of the British against the Americans.

7 • Religion in the Middle Colonies and in the South

"disturbance or innovation and they are remarkably peaceful and passive, and therefore are readily tolerated and excused."

In religion, American society was much like the European societies from which the colonists came—not truly Christian, but influenced by Christianity. The mere fact that society was influenced by some Christian principles did not make dedicated Christians feel at home in the colonial world. They had to separate themselves from colonial society in order to maintain the true faith. They needed to stand against social trends to keep from apostatizing. Colonial society drew people away from truth, just as the Bible says that all worldly societies do. God's call to "come out from among them" and to "touch not the unclean thing" was just as relevant to colonial Christians as it is to us today.

By failing to remember this part of their own story,
    even conservative Mennonites
    allowed a vacuum in their identity,
    into which could gradually creep
    the myth of a God-ordained United States of America,
    born from the matrix of Revolutionary War.

—*John L. Ruth*
The Earth Is the Lord's, *2001*[1]

---

1. John L. Ruth, *The Earth Is the Lord's* (Scottdale, Pa.: Herald Press, 2001), p. 320. Used by permission. It is true that the government of the United States is ordained by God according to the principle of Romans 13:1. But it is a myth that the United States is special to God in a way that other nations are not.

8

A Righteous Revolution?

I n this chapter, we will look at the American Revolution in the light of the New Testament. How did godly people in Revolution times view the drama into which they were innocently thrown? Did the Revolution happen because colonial Americans were following God's leading, and did it result in a Christian nation more precious to God than other nations?

Revolutionary rhetoric and Anabaptist responses

The patriots stirred anti-British feelings with rhetoric like Patrick Henry's famous declaration: "Give me liberty, or give me death!" Many Protestant preachers in the colonies also helped to rouse support for the patriots' cause. In Maryland, Presbyterian John Craighead "declaimed in such burning and powerful terms against the wrongs we were then suffering, that after one glowing description of the duty of men, the whole congregation arose from their seats, and declared their willingness to march to the conflict."

In Lancaster County, a Presbyterian named John Carmichael preached that nonresistance was foolish. Had not God created all the animals with means of defense? Man, "the noblest creature in the lower world," could not "be destitute of this necessary principle!" Of course, Carmichael added, a Christian must be sure that he conducts his warfare in a righteous way and that his cause is just. If it is, Christ has no problem with His people going to war. In fact, he emphasized, all the angels of heaven were supporting the patriots because truth and justice were on their side!

Samuel Sherwood was a Congregational minister in Connecticut during the Revolution. His words give a taste of what Puritan preaching sounded like in those days.

> God almighty, with all the powers of heaven, is on our side. Great numbers of angels, no doubt, are encamping round our coast for our defense and protection. Michael stands ready, with all the artillery of heaven, to encounter the dragon, and to vanquish this black host. . . . It will soon be said and acknowledged that the kingdoms of this world are become the kingdoms of our Lord, and of his Christ.

The British laws were described as intolerable slavery and clanking chains that would soon drag the colonists down in disgrace. When the British said the colonies were in rebellion, the patriots flashed back that the British soldiers were butchers and murderers of innocent people. The patriots said they would not submit to Britain's yoke; instead—understanding their great duty to God and the country—they would learn the art of war! And learn they did, while accusing, threatening, and persecuting people who refused to be whipped into the frenzy of the moment.

The Anabaptists and other nonresistant groups watched all this in bewildered amazement. They could not understand why a few taxes should cause a rebellion, much less why they—citizens who refused to rebel—were now considered traitors. Who were these patriots, who considered people enemies for simply keeping their promises to the king? What kind of God would agree that it was a sacred duty to break agreements and fight the powers that be? What kind of honor would cause people to burn or bury English lords and tax collectors in effigy? What kind of country would charge a citizen with treason because he questioned these things?

Based on how the patriots were acting, the Anabaptists and others wondered whether this new government would provide the same peace and liberty they had had under the English.

Christian Newcomer, a Mennonite in the Cumberland Valley, said that the Revolutionary fervor "caused considerable distress with me being conscientiously opposed to war and bearing arms. I was thereby placed in many instances in disagreeable situations, respecting both my temporal and spiritual concerns; I desired to have nothing to do with the war, and be at peace, bearing goodwill toward all mankind."[2]

In 1775, the Mennonites, Amish, and Dunkers of Lancaster County addressed the Pennsylvania government as follows:

---

2. Edsel Burdge, Jr., and Samuel L. Horst, *Building on the Gospel Foundation* (Scottdale, Pa.: Herald Press, 2004), p. 106. Used by permission.

> We have dedicated ourselves to serve all Men in every Thing that can be helpful to the Preservation of Men's Lives, but we find no freedom in giving, or doing, or assisting in any Thing by which Men's Lives are destroyed or hurt. We beg the Patience of all those who believe we err in this Point.

Individual Mennonites did sometimes lose their tempers—and control of their tongues—during the Revolution (see chapter 13). Almost to a man, if they expressed their private thoughts, they supported the English government because they had so promised and because it was the legitimate power over them. Gradually, however, the Mennonite emphasis on loyalty to England shifted to a wait-and-see approach. As early as 1776, acceptance toward the upstart government began to show up, especially in the family of bishop Christian Funk. What if the Americans won? The new Pennsylvania Constitution promised to support freedom of worship and to honor every citizen's rights regardless of his religious beliefs. Might it be as good as the old English charter?

Godly people during the Revolution understood that human nature, not injustices, were at the root of the drive for independence.

Christian Funk began to urge that the Mennonites consider shifting their loyalties to the newly formed American government. But in 1776 his church was still far from ready to do that; the members firmly considered the new government rebellious. Because Christian Funk moved too far and too fast to suit his brethren, he was excommunicated in 1778, mostly over political issues.

For the Mennonites as a whole, it was not until the 1780s that they could accept the new government as legitimate. Up until 1783, the new authorities still oppressed the nonresistant people with fines, taxes, and harassment. For over fifteen years, the nonresistant groups had watched the patriotic fervor, endured community hostility, paid huge fines, suffered the destruction of property, been jailed numerous times, and experienced some executions as well as other deaths caused directly or indirectly by the Revolution. A minority even moved to Canada to find a peaceful home under English rule.

Today we might think the issues were fairly simple. When the colonists set up their own government, it should have been clear to the Mennonites what power was over them. But the transition was not simple; it took years for things to become clear. Nor was the matter of government legitimacy the only question they faced. Should they sell grain and cattle to soldiers? If their crops were going to be confiscated for the war effort, should they plant at all? Should they allow their horses to be used for government hauling? If they used the money that the patriots minted, would they be breaking their promise to the king?[3] It was a difficult time for many normal citizens and especially the Anabaptists, who above all were a people of tender conscience and strict Bible obedience.[4]

Godly people during the Revolution understood that human nature, not injustices, were at the root of the drive

---

3. Another question was at an ordinary level: would the colonial money have any value in the future.

4. Excellent accounts of Revolution experiences can be found in *'Twas Seeding Time* and *The Earth Is the Lord's,* by John L. Ruth.

A club-wielding mob of "liberty men" in Virginia force a Loyalist to sign a document supporting the Revolution. On the left, another Loyalist is led toward a gallows standing in the background on the right, from which hangs a sack of feathers and a barrel of tar.

Colonists prepare to tar and feather a Loyalist seated on the ground as another Loyalist hangs from the gallows with a rope around his waist. The artist titled this drawing "The Tory's day of judgment."

for independence. They were not convinced that the patriots knew God's will. They believed that they needed to wait until circumstances showed them where their loyalties should lie. They understood the Revolution to be a carnal cause that brought great distress to the church and that represented a loss, not a gain, for the principles of Christianity. The Revolution strengthened the Anabaptist understanding that the world is no friend to grace.

It would be presumptuous for believers today to contradict the opinion of godly people who suffered through those times. The following sections describe further why Anabaptists in those times viewed the Revolution as they did.

A theology of rebellion

The Anabaptists believed that in Romans 13:1, "the powers that be" are any political powers under which Christians find themselves. They appreciated benevolent governments, but for most of their history they had not experienced this blessing. Nevertheless, they believed that they should respect and obey any government, regardless of how it treated them, unless doing so violated a New Testament command.

Contrast this to the beliefs of the early American Protestants. They generally held that in Romans 13:1, "the powers that be" could refer only to powers that were just and fair. How *could* any power claim to be ordained of God if it did not act right? That was simple, straightforward reasoning, so simple that it entirely overlooked the nature of all the governments under which the New Testament Scriptures were penned.

During the Revolution, Protestant ministers preached that a government could be legitimate only if it secured the property, rights, and happiness of its subjects. Any king or government who did not do so was obviously not ordained of God, and resistance to such a government was righteous. This doctrine, called the *right of rebellion*, was widely taught in the churches and political arenas (often synonymous) of Revolution times.

We are thankful that God overruled in those rebellious times to make a nation where Christians can live in peace. But that does not make the rebellion honorable or righteous. The Anabaptists of those times saw no way to reconcile the right of rebellion with New Testament teaching. If England chose to command and tax the colonies without colonial representation, they would obey her. If civil laws resulted in hardship or persecution, they could respectfully petition the government or emigrate elsewhere; but under no circumstances would they resist or reject their government. Instead of the right of rebellion, the Anabaptists taught the duty of submission.

A confusion of political and Biblical themes

To church leaders who taught the right of rebellion, the cause of America was the cause of God's kingdom itself. A Lutheran minister in Lancaster reported that many preachers viewed "those who have been killed on the American side . . . as martyrs. . . . [If only] the human race were for once as zealous and unanimous in asserting their spiritual freedom as they now are here in America in respect to bodily freedom!"

Before the Revolution, some Great Awakening teachers had taught that the fervent spiritual activity of that campaign was part of the end times, and that right after it God would usher in the millennial kingdom of Christ on earth. As one Virginia preacher watched the European struggle between English

Protestants and French Catholics in the 1700s, he thought he was viewing the great end-time conflict between the Lamb and the beast. He prophesied that if the French were defeated, the Lamb would bring in a new heaven and a new earth.

Such visions mostly faded as years rolled on after the Awakening, but the fervor of the Revolution revived this thinking. Many colonists believed that they had been mistaken in considering France as the beast; was not Great Britain herself now acting much more like a beast? Samuel Sherwood called the British laws the work of the Antichrist. The seven-headed beast that the apostle John saw rising from the sea, Sherwood believed, was the British system of tyranny and oppression.[5] On this basis, the Revolution was a holy war, a Protestant "jihad" against God's enemies. Some colonial Protestants believed that America had to win the war in order to ensure the survival of Christianity.

Especially in New England, many viewed the Revolution as a godly defense of religion just as much as a war for liberty. In this religion, sin was oppression and righteousness was liberty. The British not only represented the wrong side; they were actually called sin with a capital *S*. Thomas Paine, the most-read writer of the Revolution era, mixed sacred and profane themes all through his writings.[6]

---

5. Revelation 13:1

6. In 1776, Thomas Paine published a booklet called *Common Sense* in support of the Revolution. Later that year, he wrote several booklets titled *The American Crisis* to encourage the colonies to continue the fight against Britain. In 1787 he went to Europe to support the French Revolution, and there he wrote *Age of Reason*. In this book, Paine attacked churches and described the Bible as a wicked book of lies. Because of this mockery, Paine was considered an atheist and died a lonely outcast.

8 • A Righteous Revolution?

> Tyranny, like hell, is not easily conquered; yet we have this consolation with us, that the harder the conflict, the more glorious the triumph. . . . Heaven knows how to put a proper price upon its goods; and it would be strange indeed, if so celestial an article as FREEDOM should not be highly rated. . . . [The patriots] have suffered in well-doing. . . . Throw not the burden of the day upon Providence, but "shew your faith by your works," that God may bless you. . . . I should suffer the misery of devils, were I to make a whore of my soul by swearing allegiance to one whose character is that of a sottish, stupid, stubborn, worthless, brutish man. I conceive likewise a horrid idea in receiving mercy from a being, who at that last day shall be shrieking to the rocks and the mountains to cover him, and fleeing with terror from the orphan, the widow, and the slain of America.

In one of the most famous speeches of that time, Patrick Henry referred to the Revolution as a holy cause. He spoke of a just God who would support the Americans, and of the battle as not being only for the strong (the British) but also for the brave and vigilant.

Ministers interpreted the call to Christian liberty in Galatians 5:13 to mean that God was calling the Americans to resist British domination. Exodus 1:8, "Now there arose up a new king over Egypt, which knew not Joseph," was used to describe the English government and how they would destroy the colonists' rights and property. In support of the American campaign against drinking British tea, one preacher used Colossians 2:21: "Touch not; taste not; handle not." Old

The patriots gave the Revolution an honor that belonged to God alone.

Testament prophecies about the greatness of Israel were applied to the rising, hopefully free, America. And the "curse of Meroz" was a handy epithet for people who did not support the Revolution as the patriots thought they should. "Curse ye Meroz, said the angel of the Lord, curse ye bitterly the inhabitants thereof; because they came not to the help of the Lord, to the help of the Lord against the mighty" (Judges 5:23).

The patriots were so convinced about their cause that the Revolution became an idol. They gave it an honor that belonged to God alone. Soon after the Revolution, Ezra Stiles, president of Yale University, preached that the "glorious act of Independence" was "heaven inspired. . . . the ardor and spirit of military discipline was by Heaven . . . [Independence] was sealed and confirmed by God Almighty in the victory of General Washington. . . . time would fail me to recount the wonder-working providence of God in the events of this war."

An inconsistent cry for liberty

For many Americans, the cry "Give me liberty, or give me death!" had the emphasis on the first *me*. Liberty for the thousands of African slaves or for the American Indians was not worth considering. A few of courageous voices did ask how the demand for liberty could be consistent with slavery in America, and some pronounced it absolutely inconsistent. But those voices were so few that the roar for *my* liberty drowned them out.

Samuel Hopkins, a minister in Rhode Island, asked how the colonists could possibly call Great Britain's laws slavery when they themselves held people in a far worse slavery. He wrote,

> The slavery the Americans dread as worse than death, is lighter than a feather, compared to their heavy doom; [our condition] can be called liberty and happiness, when contrasted with the most abject slavery and unutterable wretchedness to which they are subjected. . . . Behold the sons of liberty, oppressing and tyrannizing over many thousands of poor blacks, who have as good a claim to liberty as themselves.

Quaker Anthony Benezet wrote in 1772 that black slavery was unnatural and barbarous, and that it caused the blacks tremendous suffering. In the same year, Baptist John Allen of Massachusetts said that for people who called themselves Christians, slavery was unthinkable, bloody, and inhuman. Everything about true Christianity, he said, demanded emancipation of the slaves and putting an end to the trade of man stealing.

As George Washington prepared to lead the patriots to battle against Great Britain, he was troubled that the English were forcing America to "be drenched with Blood, or inhabited by Slaves" (referring to white citizens). But Washington himself owned over 150 slaves when he penned this, and he owned over 270 slaves when he died in 1799.

Thomas Jefferson, who could write in glowing terms about the unalienable rights of life, liberty, and the pursuit

The drive for liberty included ideas that eventually brought freedom to the slaves, but the patriots of the Revolution considered black slavery not at all comparable with the so-called American slavery to the British.

of happiness for all men, owned about 200 slaves. But he acknowledged that slavery was morally wrong and said it would end someday. Reflecting on slavery, he wrote,

> I tremble for my country when I reflect that God is just: That his justice cannot sleep forever: that considering numbers, nature, and natural means only, a revolution of the wheel of fortune, an exchange of situation, is among possible events; that it may become probably by supernatural interference! The Almighty has no attribute which can take sides with us in such a contest.

However, Jefferson felt that his home state was not ready for abolition, nor was he ready for it himself. He spoke of family planning among his slaves in terms of economic profit, and he divided black families as he bought and sold slaves.

So while the drive for liberty included ideas that eventually brought freedom to the slaves, the patriots of the Revolution considered black slavery not at all comparable with the so-called American slavery to the British. The concept of freedom for all men had to develop many more years before it could supersede slavery—and even then it prevailed only by war.

Nor was slavery the only inconsistency about the patriots' cry for freedom. Baptists in New England wondered why the patriots did not grant their own residents the freedom they demanded from Great Britain. If liberty was important enough to die for, why did Baptists suffer persecution and loss of property in Congregational colonies? Most Baptists and other persecuted groups fought in the Revolution despite these inconsistencies. But their questions illustrate how unbalanced the patriots were in their concept of liberty. There was much wisdom in the ideas that produced the Declaration of Independence and the Constitution, but the patriots' thinking had not yet expanded to include everything that those ideas involved.

The patriots complained that the British tried to keep them from publishing materials in support of independence, even while the patriots themselves often tried to keep Loyalist literature from being published. The patriots destroyed the Saur family's print shop in Philadelphia for this very reason, even though the Saurs were well known for printing the Bible and other religious literature.

The patriots accused the British of giving special status to the Catholics in Quebec, yet they asked those same Catholics to help them fight the British. To heighten the irony, Catholic France and Spain entered the war on the side of the Americans, mostly because they wanted to weaken Great Britain. So the people that American theology had once classed as belonging to the "beast" were suddenly on the side of "Christ," without altering their religion. Moreover, the French government actually came to the aid of the colonies that around 1700 had received hundreds of Huguenots (French Protestants) when they fled from persecution by the same French government.

A carnal conflict

It is very common for worldly conflicts to be marked by immorality, abusing the Bible, making alliances with avowed enemies, and denying others the very rights that men are fighting to gain. It is not surprising that the Revolution involved and even gloried in these inconsistencies. What is surprising is that in spite of all these things, some religious people viewed this carnal conflict as serving the kingdom of Christ, and that some religious people today still do the same.

We are thankful that the patriots went on to support a liberty that has resulted in an unparalleled time of peace for godly people. Even though Jefferson's sentiments did not move him to free his slaves, those ideas eventually did contribute to setting the blacks free. The same freedoms may have been granted under English rule, but we do not know that, nor is it important to know. God permitted Americans to become independent for His own reasons, and we should thank Him for the blessing it has been.

Saying this is not the same as saying that the Revolution was a godly cause or that God's blessing was on the American side. No godly person can glory in Revolutionary reasoning and hypocrisy. The Revolution contained some thoughts that sounded spiritual, but it was not spiritual. It used words from the Bible, but it was not Biblical. The Bible was important to some of the colonists, but they disobeyed many Bible teachings.

When people trust the Lord instead of putting confidence in man, they do not view worldly conflict as the world does.

When some colonists thought they had to win the Revolution to save Christianity, they were showing how little they knew of Christianity.

In Pennsylvania, where a higher percentage of the population truly understood Christianity, support for the Revolution was lower than anywhere else in the colonies. This fact often raised the patriots' ire. Thomas Paine said irritably that the Patriots could not afford to lose their fight just because of the "baseness" and "folly" of the Loyalists and of

Pennsylvania's many nonresistant folks. To the leader responsible for Pennsylvania's contributions of soldiers and money for the war, George Washington complained that the battalions of "Pennsylvania, the most opulent and populous of all the states… have never been one third full, and now many of them are far below even that."

It was the great number of Quakers, Mennonites, and Dunkers, authorities complained, that were to blame for this problem. So many of these people lived in Pennsylvania that their convictions kept the war and its supply process from moving smoothly along. Nonresistant people were a problem for the Revolutionary War, just as they have been for all wars.[7]

When people trust the Lord instead of putting confidence in man, they do not view worldly conflict as the world does. It is just as crucial for godly people to understand this today as it was in Revolutionary times.

---

7. Thomas Paine viewed the nonresistant people and the supporters of Great Britain, also called Loyalists or Tories, as basically the same. But this was a mistake. Loyalists aided the British in many ways, including military service; while the majority of the nonresistant people did all they could to remain neutral.

When I was young I was fond of the speculations
    which seemed to promise some insight into that . . .
    but . . . they left me in the same ignorance
    in which they found me. . . .
I have for very many years
    ceased to read or to think concerning them,
    and have reposed my head
    on that pillow of ignorance which a benevolent Creator
    has made so soft for us. . . .
I have thought it better,
    by nourishing the good passions & controlling the bad,
    to merit an inheritance in a state of being
    of which I can know so little,
    and to trust for the future to him
    who has been so good in the past.
        —*Thomas Jefferson, 1801, on the destiny of the soul*

9

The Religious Views of the Founding Fathers

The Founding Fathers of America include the influential men during the Revolution, the main delegates to the Constitutional Convention, and the first few presidents. Who were the Founding Fathers? What were the sources of their ideas about religion, government, and freedom? The six men discussed in this chapter provide an overview of the group that developed the government ideals of the emerging United States.

Patrick Henry

Patrick Henry (1736-1799) made his mark during the Revolutionary period as one of the greatest American orators. He energized his fellow citizens to the fray by speeches such as the following, delivered to Virginia's government leaders on March 23, 1775.

> Three millions of people, armed in the holy cause of liberty, and in such a country as that which we possess, are invincible by any force which our enemy can send against us. Besides, sir, we shall not fight our battles alone. There is a just God who presides over the destinies of nations, and who will raise up friends to fight our battles for us. The battle, sir, is not to the strong alone; it is to the vigilant, the active, the brave. . . .
>
> If we were base enough to desire it, it is now too late to retire from the contest. There is no retreat, but in submission and slavery. Our chains are forged. Their clanking may be heard on the plains of Boston! The war is inevitable—and let it come! I repeat, sir, let it come! . . .
>
> Gentlemen may cry, peace, peace—but there is no peace. The war is actually begun! The next gale that sweeps from the north will bring to our ears the clash of resounding arms! Our brethren are already in the field! Why stand we here idle? What is it that gentlemen wish? What would they have? Is life so dear, or peace so sweet, as to be purchased at the price of chains and slavery? Forbid it, Almighty God! I know not what course others may take; but as for me, give me liberty, or give me death!

Patrick Henry was one of the few Founding Fathers who accepted orthodox teachings of Christianity such as the divinity of Christ, the Trinity, and Christ's miracles.

In an earlier speech against the Stamp Act, Henry said, "Caesar had his Brutus—Charles the First, his Cromwell—

Patrick Henry was a powerful speaker whose choice of words commanded attention. Here, on May 30, 1765, before Virginia's leaders, Henry speaks out against the Stamp Act.

and George the Third—*may profit by their example*. If *this* be treason, make the most of it."

Patrick Henry was one of the few Founding Fathers who accepted orthodox teachings of Christianity such as the divinity of Christ, the Trinity, and Christ's miracles. He had been influenced by the Great Awakening, and he tried to apply many Bible principles in his life. In many ways, Henry could be described as evangelical. He lived in a society that valued reason over revelation, matter over mystery or miracle, and experience over doctrine; but Henry did not accept these "enlightened" ideals. Among the Founding Fathers, his beliefs were considered old-fashioned. In 1785, during one of his terms as governor of Virginia, Henry tried to establish Christianity as Virginia's state religion.

Before the Revolution, Anglicanism enjoyed the protection of the Virginia government and used its power to persecute dissenters. After the Revolution there was a period of uncertainty as to how the new United States government would relate to religion. Pennsylvania and some other colonies supported full freedom of religion, but the Virginia leaders were not sure that they should so radically change the historical pattern of their colony. Had not the Anglican Church provided a moral anchor for 150 years?

Dissenters, of course, did not agree that established churches had been a benefit to the colonies. To the Baptists and numerous other sects, legal Anglicanism had been a disgrace and a hindrance to Virginia.

Patrick Henry had a solution for these conflicting views. In 1785 he proposed to the Virginia legislature that no single church or sect should enjoy a privileged status with the

9 • The Religious Views of the Founding Fathers

government, but that Christianity itself should be established as Virginia's official religion. Under the "Bill Establishing a Provision for Teachers of the Christian Religion," all Christian churches would have equal rights and security. This would help to promote, said Henry, the morality and justice that every state needs. Henry's bill would not totally disconnect the government and religion, but neither would it allow any persecution. It would support every sect that was peaceable and faithful, but it would allow the state to combat the unbelief and moral laxity that plagued the colonies.

The Virginia sects rose as one man against the bill. They had suffered too long to tolerate another civil-religious experiment. What would keep them from being persecuted again if the primarily Anglican government decided that their teachings were not in accord with the ambiguous meaning of *faithful*? But the sects alone were too weak to withstand Henry's political power.

Thomas Jefferson was in France at the time, but his close ally James Madison took up the challenge of defeating Henry's bill. These men promoted full religious freedom not because they favored the sects but because they opposed any kind of tyranny. They considered any law establishing a particular religion as tyranny.

Madison constructed his case carefully, gathering signatures of many supporters and collecting numerous historical facts showing that persecution always accompanied an established religion. In true Enlightenment fashion, Madison argued that reason alone should dictate what sort of religion was right for an individual to follow. After all, had not the Revolution been fought to rid the colonies of tyranny? Why establish it again?

Let the government concern itself with civil matters, and let religion be a matter between people and God.

The Virginia leaders followed Madison's advice and passed the "Statute for Religious Freedom," a law based on a statement by Jefferson. The bill said that God had made men with free minds and that they should be kept free. If God had seen fit to allow religious freedom, how arrogant it would be for a government to legislate religious faith. Some would say that error and lies will spread everywhere if the government does not control them. But truth is great, reasoned Jefferson; and if left to herself, she will prevail. No one should be compelled to attend worship services or support any faith, and no one should be punished for his opinions or beliefs. The Virginia decision was important because it influenced the course of the whole United States in relation to religion.[1]

John Witherspoon

John Witherspoon (1723-1794) was the only minister to sign the Declaration of Independence. He was also a delegate to the Continental Congress.

Like his fellow Presbyterians, Witherspoon enthusiastically promoted colonial independence. The Scottish Presbyterians had a long history of war with the English, and they poured their fervor into the Revolution. In fact, one English leader described the American Revolution as a Presbyterian rebellion.

---

1. Patrick Henry was not the only one who tried to establish Christianity as the religion of a state. This also happened a number of times in New England. For example, Congregational politicians in Connecticut made a final attempt in 1816 to secure government funding in support of Christianity. This legislation, called the "Bill for Support of Literature and Religion," would have authorized $68,000 to Yale University, $20,000 to the Episcopalians, $12,000 to the Methodists, and $19,000 to the Baptists. But even this pluralistic bill did not pass. It was defeated in 1818 with 105 votes against it and 95 votes for it.

9 • The Religious Views of the Founding Fathers

John Witherspoon, a Presbyterian minister from Scotland, came to America in 1768 to serve as president of the College of New Jersey, now Princeton University.

Witherspoon was an orthodox Christian in many ways, especially in his preaching. He believed that Christ's death atoned for repentant sinners, which most of the Founding Fathers rejected. But at the college he was not only a minister; he was also the professor of moral philosophy and political subjects. He leaned heavily on theories of the Enlightenment as he taught these courses. Witherspoon's sermons and his college lectures appear to have come from two different people.

When he preached, Witherspoon taught that Jesus' blood and God's grace are necessary for salvation, and that God will provide an eternal home for the saved. He believed that a society should discourage evil and promote virtue. He said that the emerging American government should be fair, honest, and kind. He taught that God overruled man and could make good things happen out of man's mistakes. He recognized many of the New Testament truths that guide the child of God. He also recognized that the Bible did not contain the political answers that civil leaders needed in the Revolutionary period.

But when he lectured on political themes, Witherspoon adopted the deistic view of God held by most of the Founding Fathers. Deism was the belief that even though God created the world, He takes no active part in controlling or governing the present world. He thought God did not take a direct role in raising and putting down governments. He said that the basis of government is only "natural laws" that man learns by reason and experience.

Witherspoon taught that the basis of government is only "natural laws" that man learns by reason and experience.

Witherspoon accepted Old Testament theology with its themes of a righteous nation and holy wars. To him, fighting the British was righteous, and supporting or refusing to resist them was a gross sin. He taught that fighting for colonial independence was putting first the kingdom of God.

Perhaps Witherspoon, in his two-stance approach, was simply trying to reconcile the two kingdoms to which he felt responsible. He is a good example of what usually happens when a Bible-believing person becomes involved in politics. He was the most Biblically orthodox of all the Founding Fathers, yet his political involvements drove him to compromise his Biblical beliefs; and his theories were inevitably warped as a result.

Benjamin Franklin

From a civil viewpoint, no country could have a more useful citizen than Benjamin Franklin (1706-1790). Some historians believe that his contributions to the Revolution and the new nation were so crucial that without him, America could not have been established.

Franklin's broad range of accomplishments would be hard for anyone to duplicate. He made important discoveries in science, such as in electricity, gardening, and seafaring. He invented the lightning rod, bifocal glasses, the Franklin stove, and many other useful things.

As a public servant, Franklin organized the best postal service up to his time. He improved the streets and the cleanliness of Philadelphia and upgraded the city hospital. He helped military efforts in the period from the French and Indian War through the Revolutionary War. He tried valiantly to keep the American colonies in the British Empire. His success in getting French aid for the American Revolution was crucial in winning that war. Franklin signed all the important documents in the early history of the United States. He was a major force in the drafting and approval of the Constitution. He also called for the new nation to end slavery quickly.

Franklin's father took his son out of school when he was ten years old, but he continued to study all his life. He was an avid reader and writer. He studied logic, arithmetic, science, and five languages besides English. He became an apprentice in the printing trade and owned a print shop by the age of twenty-four. He was diligent in his work habits and careful with his money, and he enjoyed gathering wise sayings, which he published in *Poor Richard's Almanac*.

Franklin's philosophy was that hard work, simple living, and good stewardship will produce health and wealth. Franklin also believed that people and their governments should pursue happiness, be kind and generous with each other, and be respectful and dignified. In his own life, he demonstrated his beliefs by letting others use his inventions freely and by generously sharing his financial resources.

Franklin did not speak bitterly against Great Britain as many other Americans did. In fact, he was the only American in his time to win the respect of the English, the French, and the Americans.

Religious beliefs mattered little to Franklin, but he did not hate, fear, or reject churches or religion.

With all the good that Franklin believed and accomplished, one might expect that he was a man of deep faith and extensive Bible learning. But Franklin was primarily a philosopher of the Enlightenment principles; he was a convinced humanist. While many of his witty sayings reflect Biblical wisdom, Franklin saw the Bible as one source of wisdom among many. Though he loved proverbs, he did not follow God's Proverbs, and had a son out of wedlock.

Franklin seldom attended church, but he sampled the ideas of many different religions in Philadelphia. He considered religion as a science to be analyzed, and tried to avoid making enemies over matters of such minor importance. Religious beliefs mattered little to him, but he did not hate, fear, or reject churches or religion.

Franklin often referred to God with terms such as "the Supreme." In one of his remarks on the nature of America, he called God a mechanic. When a stranger comes to America, Franklin said, people do not ask,

> What is he? But, what can he do? If he has any useful Art, he is welcome; and if he exercises it, and behaves well, he will be respected by all that know him; but a mere Man of Quality, who, on that Account, wants to live upon the Public, by some Office or Salary, will be despis'd and disregarded. The Husbandman is in honor there, and even the Mechanic, because their employments are useful. The People have a saying, that God Almighty is himself a Mechanic, the greatest in the Universe; and he is respected and admired more for the Variety, Ingenuity, and Utility of his Handyworks, than for the Antiquity of his Family.

Here we catch a thread that winds through nearly all of Franklin's religious ideas. His philosophy in summary was, What can God and religion do? What are they useful for? Use them for that, but do not get tangled up in the abstract doctrines that churches wrangle over.

For the same reason, though Franklin was a confirmed deist in his younger years, he became less sure of deism as he grew older. He began to suspect, he said, that although deism may be true, it did not seem very useful.

Franklin believed that God existed and that there was a life beyond the grave in which there would be rewards and punishments. But he was often cavalier about these matters. He thought that a proportionate punishment in the afterlife for sins committed in this life was sensible, but he would hear nothing of eternal punishment. His nonchalance is also evident in his reply to the question of whether Christ is divine,

> It is a question I do not dogmatize upon, having never studied it, and think it needless to busy myself with it now, when I expect soon an opportunity of knowing the Truth with less Trouble, I see no harm, however, in its being believed, if that Belief has the good Consequence, as it probably has, of making his Doctrines more respected and better observed; especially as I do not perceive, that the Supreme takes it amiss, by distinguishing the Unbelievers in his Government of the World with any peculiar Marks of his Displeasure.

Like his deist friends, Franklin was convinced that many people needed religion to make them behave.

> You yourself may find it easy to live a virtuous Life without the Assistance afforded by Religion; you having a clear Perception of the Advantages of Virtue and the Disadvantages of Vice, and possessing a Strength of Resolution sufficient for you to resist common Temptations. But think how great a Proportion of Mankind consists of weak and ignorant Men and Women, and of inexperienc'd and inconsiderate Youth of both Sexes, who have need of the motives of Religion to restrain them from Vice, to support their Virtue, and to retain them in the Practice of it till it became habitual, which is the great Point for its Security. . . . If men are so wicked as we now see them with Religion what would they be without it?

That is classical Enlightenment thinking. In this view, religion is beneficial despite its obvious problems, because it does more good than harm for the masses who do not have the strength to control themselves. Virtue and self-control ranked high in Franklin's priorities; communicating with God and finding forgiveness of sins did not. How people talked and acted was very important; what they thought and believed was unimportant. Franklin once wrote,

> My Mother grieves that one of her sons is an Arian, another an Arminian. What an Arminian or an Arian is, I cannot say that I very well know; the Truth is, I make such Distinctions very little in my study; I think vital Religion has always suffer'd, when Orthodoxy is more regarded than Virtue. And the Scripture assures me, that at the last Day, we shall not be examin'd what we thought, but what we did; and our Recommendation will not be that we said Lord, Lord, but that we did GOOD to our Fellow Creatures.

There is some truth to what Franklin said here. Yet this is also a good example of what was wrong with much of his reasoning: he promoted the truth that he favored and dismissed the rest. All his life he sought a foundation for virtue outside the Gospel of Jesus Christ.

George Washington

Acclaimed as "first in war, first in peace, and first in the hearts of his countrymen," George Washington (1732-1799) is probably the most honored American. Against tremendous odds, he led the often ragged, dispirited, and outnumbered American troops to victory over the British. Just as Franklin's diplomatic skills were indispensable to the Revolution, so

Washington's skills and tenacity as a general were indispensable to that cause. The patriots needed the oratory of Patrick Henry, but they also needed the calm, confident leadership of George Washington.

For all his skill as a general, Washington was a courteous man of high character. Thomas Jefferson described him as follows:

> His mind was great and powerful. . . . It was slow in operation, being little aided by invention and imagination, but sure in conclusion. . . .
>
> Perhaps the strongest feature in his character was prudence, never acting until every circumstance, every consideration, was maturely weighed; refraining if he saw a doubt, but, when once decided, going through with his purpose, whatever obstacles opposed.
>
> His integrity was most pure, his justice the most inflexible I have ever known. . .
>
> He was, indeed, in every sense of the words, a wise, a good and great man. . . . On the whole, his character was . . . perfect . . . it may truly be said, that never did nature and fortune combine more perfectly to make a man great.

Washington's Anglican parents believed in diligence and character. But in his youth on the frontier of Virginia, Washington apparently had little church experience. His father died when the boy was eleven, which left George, his mother, and his siblings in charge of their plantations. Slaves worked the fields, and George was able to get seven or eight years of country schooling. Even as a boy he was prudent, quiet, and careful with his funds. But his life was not all work and study.

9 • The Religious Views of the Founding Fathers

He enjoyed fishing, boating, hunting, dancing, and writing poems about his romances.

Washington gained military experience in fighting the French, who were trying to hold the Ohio River valley against the British. In 1759, after pressures on the frontier eased, he came back to Virginia and turned to farming and business. He also served in government posts. Through inheritances, his marriage to a wealthy widow, and his business sense, he accumulated forty thousand acres by the time he was about forty years old. Renters farmed much of this land. Washington led the life of a Virginia planter, with time for socializing, fox hunting, and playing cards, along with occasionally traveling to nearby cities to purchase supplies and to attend dances, plays, and horse races.

During this time, Washington attended the Anglican Church about ten times a year. While he left an ample record of his experiences and finances, he wrote so little about his religious ideas that it is hard to know where he stood. It appears that he had a strong moral character, but his church attendance seems to have been a social performance, not an evidence of spiritual interest. One author summarized Washington's spiritual life as follows: "He was a Christian as a Virginia planter understood the term. He seems never to have taken Communion; he stood to pray, instead of kneeling."[2]

Washington's way of referring to God may provide the clearest indication of his spiritual understanding. To him, God was the "higher Cause," the "Great Ruler of Events," the "Governor of the Universe," the "Grand Architect," and the

---

2. Marcus Conliffe, *Washington: Man and Monument* (New York, Ny.: New American Library, 1958), p. 60.

167

"superintending Power." He used the same impersonal terms in his speeches as president, such as when he asked the nation to thank "that great and glorious Being who is the beneficent Author of all the good that was, that is, or that will be." In his first inaugural address, he said,

> No people can be bound to acknowledge and adore the invisible hand which conducts the affairs of men more than the people of the United States. Every step by which they have been advanced to the character of an independent nation seems to have been distinguished by some token of providential agency.

Washington rarely mentioned the Bible or Jesus Christ. When Presbyterian leaders complained to him in 1789 that the Constitution did not mention "the only true God and Jesus Christ, whom he hath sent," Washington calmly replied, "The path of true piety is so plain as to require but little political direction."

Washington was not a Christian in the sense that he believed in Christ and tried to follow His teachings. He did little about the immorality that plagued his Revolutionary soldiers. In one case, Chaplain Alexander MacWhorter of New Jersey preached a thundering sermon to Washington's troops against the evils of the British. The chaplain never mentioned the evils of more than two hundred prostitutes who were also listening to the sermon.

A treaty that Washington negotiated with the Muslim country of Tripoli in 1797 reveals his opinion about the relationship of religion to the United States government. The Senate accepted this treaty near the end of Washington's term, and President John Adams signed it into law. Part of it says,

9 • The Religious Views of the Founding Fathers

> As the government of the United States of America is not in any sense founded on the Christian Religion,—as it has in itself no character of enmity against the laws, religion or tranquility of Musselmen . . ., it is declared by the parties that no pretext arising from religious opinions shall ever produce an interruption of the harmony existing between the two countries.

John Adams

John Adams (1735-1826), the second president, was raised in Massachusetts by parents from old Puritan families. He was raised at a time when some New Englanders were accepting the Enlightenment, and he is an example of this shift.

Adams taught school in his early adulthood. He became a lawyer at the age of twenty-three, and by his early thirties he was a leading attorney in Boston. His position enabled him to become a leader in resisting British taxes on the colonies. He believed that it was illegal for Great Britain to tax the colonies at all, and he called the Boston Tea Party a "magnificent movement."

Adams was one of the delegates from Massachusetts at the First Continental Congress. He valiantly defended the Declaration of Independence, wrote most of the Massachusetts Constitution of 1780, and served on a number of important foreign missions to France, the Netherlands, and Great Britain. After spending years abroad, he returned home in 1788 to serve as Washington's vice-president for two terms.

Like Washington, Adams had the casual attitude toward religion that pervaded the educated society of his time. He confessed that in this he was breaking a tradition in his family; his ancestors had been staunch Calvinistic Puritans ever since their arrival in Massachusetts in 1620.

169

During the Great Awakening, Adams became deeply suspicious of revivals and prophets. He considered himself a Christian, which to him apparently meant believing that God exists and following some Bible principles of conduct. But he hated Catholics and was hostile toward some of the central themes of the New Testament.

Unlike Washington, Adams often studied and talked about the Bible. He enjoyed debating religious subjects, but his arguments present a strange mixture of agnosticism, skepticism, and moralism. The following words describe his brand of Christianity.

> The Love of God and his Creation; delight, Joy, Tryumph, Exultation in my own existence, tho but an Atom, a Molecule Organique, in the Universe; are my religion. Howl, Snarl, bite, Ye Calvinistick! Ye Athanasian Divines, if You will. Ye will say, I am no Christian: I say Ye are no Christians: and there the account is ballanced. Yet I believe all the honest men among you, are Christians in my Sense of the Word.

Adams thought that religion should not trouble itself with theological disputes but should promote virtue in everyday life. Why does every religion today, he asked, think that they alone have the Holy Ghost in a vial? "Be good fathers, sons, brothers, neighbors, friends, patriots, and philanthropists, good subjects and citizens of the universe," he said, "and trust the Ruler with his skies."

There will be a future state of rewards and punishments, Adams believed. Without that, he could "make nothing of this Universe but a Chaos. . . . If I did not believe in a future state, I should believe in no God."

9 • The Religious Views of the Founding Fathers

Adams did not appreciate the authors of the Enlightenment who doubted God's existence or charged Him with mistakes. Yet the concept of a close relationship with God was beyond him. He wrote that God is "an Essence that we know nothing of, in which Originally and necessarily reside all energy, all Power, all Capacity, all Activity, all Wisdom, all Goodness."

However, Adams could not accept that Jesus Christ is the Son of God who came to earth in the form of a man.

> The Europeans . . . all believe that great principle, which has produced this boundless Universe . . . came down to this little Ball, to be spit-upon by Jews; and untill this awful blasphemy is got rid of, there never will be any liberal science in the world.

In his older years, Adams said, "The Bible is the best book in the World. It contains more of my little Phylosophy than all the Libraries I have seen: and such Parts of it as I cannot reconcile to my little Phylosophy I postpone for future investigation." But for some reason, he did not like what the Bible societies of the early 1800s were doing. He wrote to Thomas Jefferson,

> We have now, it seems, a National Bible Society, to propagate King James' Bible, through all nations. Would it not be better, to apply these pious Subscriptions, to purify Christendom from the Corruptions of Christianity; than to propagate their Corruptions in Europe, Asia, Africa and America!

In his answer, Jefferson agreed and made his own comments about the societies that were sending Bibles and missionaries to China.

> These Incendiaries, finding that the days of fire and faggot are over in the Atlantic hemisphere, are now preparing to put the torch to the Asiatic regions. What would they say were the Pope to send annually to this country colonies of Jesuit priests with cargoes of their Missal and translations of their Vulgate, to be put gratis into the hands of every one who would accept them?

Certainly Adams was affected by some Christian influences; but his view of God's Word was that it contained some of *his* philosophy, instead of having the truth that he needed to cleanse his heart, save his soul, and amend his life.

Thomas Jefferson

The greatest contribution of Thomas Jefferson (1743-1826) to America was his ability to draft well-written statements. He first proved this gift when he filled several positions in the Virginia government, and then he went on to help the Revolutionary cause in the same way.

The Declaration of Independence stands supreme among Jefferson's works. In writing it, he captured the spirit of the patriots in clear, forceful language. The Declaration has expressed and molded the American spirit more than any other document.

Jefferson served in many public offices during and after the Revolution, though he strongly preferred a private life with his family, books, and estates. He served as Virginia's governor for two years, as a Congressman, as a representative of the United States in France, as a member of George Washington's cabinet, as John Adams' vice-president, and finally as president of the United States from 1801 to 1809.

Jefferson was a nominal Anglican, though his education influenced him with ideas of the Enlightenment. He believed in God as Creator and Judge; he praised good character and appreciated the virtuous teachings of the Bible; but he was a deist. He detested the organized religion of his day and considered himself above the need for strong church ties or a personal walk with God.

Many of Jefferson's ideas, like Franklin's, are appealing for their promotion of character or honor, yet shallow in their spiritual perception. Jefferson believed all his life in the freedom of the common man, and he made statements such as, "Those who labor in the earth are the chosen people of God."

Jefferson believed that traditions, mysteries, miracles, and other "irrational" religious teachings needed to be discarded so that religion could appeal to the enlightened world.

> Cultivators of the earth are the most valuable citizens. They are vigorous, independent, virtuous—and they are tied to their country and its liberty and interests by the most lasting bonds.
>
> Determine never to be idle. No person will have occasion to complain of the want of time who never loses any. It is wonderful how much may be done if we are always doing.

Jefferson believed that traditions, mysteries, miracles, and other "irrational" religious teachings needed to be discarded so that religion could appeal to the enlightened world. This thinking was not entirely wrong; there were many useless traditions and wrong beliefs in the churches that Jefferson knew. But in typical Enlightenment fashion, he rejected many supernatural things about God and retained only what made sense to him.

Jefferson said that he believed the "genuine precepts of Jesus himself" and was a "real Christian . . . sincerely attached to his doctrines, in preference of all others." He believed that Jesus' teachings "tend to the happiness of man . . . that there is only one God . . . that there is a future state of rewards and punishments, that to love God with all thy heart and thy neighbor as thyself, is the sum of all religion."

Yet he rejected the Trinity as "mere abracadabra" (foolish and unintelligible reasoning), and said it was a very sad example of what happens when people believe mysteries. He called the Three-in-One the "incomprehensible jargon of Trinitarian Arithmetic." "I am a sect by myself, as far as I know," he said in 1819. He believed that Jesus Himself denied that He is the Son of God.

Jefferson did not think a person needed the church to help him understand God's will. God had placed a sense of right and wrong within every man, he reasoned, as surely as He had given him legs and arms. This was the main guide for making moral decisions.

Jefferson's words at the beginning of this chapter show how he related to problems that could not be solved by reason. Questions such as why people were evil and whether there was a spiritual world were troubling to him, and he once said that such questions kept him awake at night. Perhaps the soft pillow of ignorance was not always so soft. His life had an aura of sadness after his wife died at a young age. Later his youngest daughter died; and though he concealed his grief behind a stoical exterior, he could not dispel his questions about the nature of life.

9 • The Religious Views of the Founding Fathers

Perhaps these deep questions explain why Jefferson spent so many hours working on his version of the Bible. He read the Bible every day, but he discarded much of the Epistles as the work of men, and from the Gospels he selected only what he considered the pure teachings and morals of Jesus. The result was forty-six pages of pasted-together "pure and unsophisticated doctrine." Jefferson discarded Jesus' miracles and His resurrection as "deliria of crazy imaginations," along with all references to His divinity and to the authority of God's Word.

Although he was a disciplined man who once said, "Never spend your money before you have it," Jefferson was unable to follow this rule in his search for personal happiness. After his return from France, he spent lavishly on imported wines, exotic foods, and French furniture and books. He constantly worked at changing and rebuilding his palace at Monticello, with the result that he ran up large debts and often had to mortgage his slaves.

Jefferson felt guilty about slavery, as noted in chapter 8, but he could not bring himself to disrupt his lifestyle by heeding his conscience. He said, "The man must be a prodigy who can retain his manners and morals undepraved by such circumstances." He knew firsthand what he was talking about; one of the female slaves on the Monticello plantation had six children with a white father—who was either Jefferson himself or a member of his family, perhaps a nephew.

Jefferson's disdain for churches brought him severe criticism when he ran for the presidency in 1800. Ministers and others called him an arch demon, atheist, and infidel. George Washington's beliefs were not much different from Jefferson's, but Washington had been so quiet about religion that many people considered him a godly savior. In contrast, Jefferson had talked about religion so freely and so long that he was a marked man. Anti-Jefferson forces printed advertisements labeling him as the source of all the sins that spring from unbelief. One picture of that era shows angels flying away as the wrath of God descends on a barren landscape. The devil waters the tree of unbelief as a ghoulish volcano erupts in the background and the flames of hell lick the foreground.

In 1801, a Congregational minister in Massachusetts compared Jefferson to Jeroboam. He was naturally gifted, the preacher pointed out, yet he was filled with a wicked and ambitious spirit. He had lived too long in Egypt (France), and he still loved its moral darkness and false religion. When he returned to Israel (America), he plied his evil hand to get the unprincipled majority on his side, thus managing to secure the throne for himself and ending the reigns of the wise and good kings. He destroyed religion, corrupted the people, and set bad examples on every important matter. Jefferson's ascent to the presidential office was seen as a sure sign of the last days.

"The reign of the Goths & Vandals," an Episcopal pastor in Maryland wrote in 1806, "was not more destructive, than the ascendancy of these men has been." These feelings were especially strong among ministers in New England. They were convinced that events were ripe for the punishment of America, the favored but sinful land. True religion was declining, and evil men were leading the nation. Somehow, the nation had changed from being the kingdom of God to being under His judgment like all other kingdoms, simply through an election.

9 • The Religious Views of the Founding Fathers

Religious but not genuinely Christian

The Founding Fathers were disciples of reason, not of Christ. They valued Christianity for its morals just as they valued the Enlightenment for its reason. They liked the Bible because it contained some of their philosophies, not because they sensed a personal need for its teachings. As historian Daniel Boorstin once wrote, they saw in God what they most admired in men.

For many of the Founding Fathers, religion was moralism, not spiritual discipleship. Whatever served morality was useful to them, because it helped to keep people doing the right thing. This has obvious benefits, yet it is a man-centered teaching, not a godly concept. The Founding Fathers emphasized virtue and the place of religion in supporting it, yet they were not genuinely Christian.

Most of the Founding Fathers were fully convinced that human ability would make the United States an ideal country. They believed that God had created man with almost unlimited potential, but they did not understand that man's potential is severely limited by the Fall or that his potential can be restored only by the blood of Jesus Christ.

The New Testament was not the sole base or even the primary base of the men and movements that founded the United States. This does not mean that Christianity had no effect on the founding of America. It had a strong effect, and to deny this influence is wrong. But it is just as wrong to say that the nation was wholly founded on Biblical principles. If we will be an effective witness in a secular age, we need to base our testimony on truth and reality, not on error.

To call the early United States Christian or Bible-based promotes several errors. It puts the approval of God and His

Word on something that at best was a compromising mixture of Biblical, non-Biblical, and anti-Biblical forces. It also keeps Christians and those to whom they witness from properly understanding which values in their present culture are truly Biblical and which ones are merely cultural.

For citizens of the United States, this conclusion does not destroy our respect for our earthly nation. We appreciate the virtues of the early period in its history. We are happy that the colonies insisted on justice and the rule of law. We are thankful that the largely irreligious Founding Fathers promoted freedom of religion for all. Knowing how fragile freedom for nonresistant Christians has been in the world, including the United States, we rejoice that in North America it has long been our lot.

Seeds of secularity

In an increasingly wicked society, we may wish that we could live in a society of people like Benjamin Franklin or George Washington. What would it be like to have neighbors of that character? Even though they would study our Gospel tracts merely as science, would refuse invitations to revival meetings, and would consider us extremely unenlightened, at least they would promote decency and order.

Years ago, a young man used to drive past our Wisconsin home in his old Cadillac, music thumping. We could hear him coming nearly a mile away; when he passed our house, the windows vibrated. His hair was long, he had rings in his ears, and he appeared to be under the influence of drugs. Eventually his oversized music system ruined his alternator, and he came to me to get it repaired. As we talked, it became obvious that he believed in God but had no room for God in his life.

9 • The Religious Views of the Founding Fathers

He spent extra money on his alternator to make sure it would last a long time. Several days later his check came back from the bank marked "Not sufficient funds."

Benjamin Franklin and George Washington did not live as this young man did. But there are some connections that span the centuries between them. They all followed natural reasoning processes that dethroned God from being the Lord of their lives. They all elevated humanistic concepts to a place that only God can fill. To all of them, religion was not a guide for the whole life but only a sector of life equal or subservient to other sectors.

While we certainly live in a more secular age than the Founding Fathers did, the popular ideas in our society are not distinctly different from those of the Founding Fathers. Though there was more virtue in early America than in modern America, early America contained the seeds of secularity that have bloomed into what we see today. "In short," says one historian, "the faith that the Founding Fathers were defending was not a religious concept but the belief in the ability of the American people to decide for themselves how they wanted to shape their own society."[3]

To illustrate the connection between the god of reason in Revolutionary America and in modern America, we need only to hear the late Edward Kennedy's speech at the funeral of his brother Robert Kennedy in June 1968.

> Our future may lie beyond our vision, but it is not completely beyond our control. It is the shaping impulse of America that neither faith nor nature nor the irresistible tides of history, but

---

3. Wilbur Edel, *Defenders of the Faith* (New York, Ny.: Praeger, 1987) p. 72.

the work of our own hands, matched to reason and principle, will determine our destiny. There is pride in that, even arrogance, but there is also experience and truth. In any event, it is the only way we can live.

The American Revolution was not a new beginning for the work of God. Instead, it was the organization of a civil government based on Enlightenment ideals and some traces of Christian beliefs. In the lives of the Founding Fathers, the key of true Christianity was missing—a vital relationship with the Lord Jesus Christ.

Throughout the entire colonial period,
  at least until the colonial awakenings,
  the great mass of the lower classes
  were little influenced by organized religion;
  and only a very small proportion
  of the total population of the thirteen colonies
  were members of the colonial churches.
At the end of the colonial period
  there were undoubtedly
  more unchurched people in North America,
  in proportion to the population,
  than were to be found in any other land in Christendom.
That every frontier was in pressing need
  of moral restraint and guidance
  there can be no reasonable doubt,
  and in most instances the only guardians of the morale
  of these communities were the little frontier churches.
On every frontier from the Alleghenies to the Pacific these
    were the people who fought the battle for decency and order,
    and to a large degree saved the west from semi-barbarism.
            —*Historian William Warren Sweet, 1933*[1]

---

1. "The Churches as Moral Courts of the Frontier," II *Church History*, 1933, 1:3-22.

10

American Protestantism in the 1800s

What kind of nation did the colonists and their Revolutionary leaders become? This chapter discusses the religious conditions in American society of the 1800s.

Differences between the Revolution leaders and the common people

To understand religion in America after the Revolutionary period, keep in mind that many colonists during the Revolution were more interested in peaceful living than in fighting for independence. This changed as the Revolution neared its victorious climax, mostly because the colonists were eager to get the turmoil behind them. They were willing to submit to the new government if it prevailed. They were ready to accept Revolutionary concepts if the Revolution proved successful, though few of them were willing to die for the cause of independence.

On the other hand, the Founding Fathers were fervent believers in the Revolution. They were more highly educated than common Americans and more strongly convinced of Enlightenment ideals. It is important to understand this, because some religious people today glorify the character of early America and implore society to return to the supposed Bible base of that culture. Yet secular historians can argue just as well from the historical record of the Revolution and the Founding Fathers that the Bible was not the base in those times. A key to these opposing views is that the religious views of Americans as a whole appear different from those of the Founding Fathers as an elite group.

Most Americans acknowledged that Jesus is God's Son. They believed in miracles and they accepted the divine authority of the Bible. Few of the Founding Fathers believed these things. While the average American believed that God took an active role in people's day-to-day lives, many of the Founding Fathers denied this.

There are several reasons that the Founding Fathers did not specifically put religion into the early documents of the United States. First, they did not want to; they were not men of Biblical convictions. Second, they correctly saw that virtue cannot be imposed on a population by government effort. Third, they were dealing with a population that generally valued virtue. Despite the failures in the colonies noted in chapters 6 and 7, a higher level of virtue existed in those days than in America today.

The decline of the Enlightenment

The Enlightenment had focused on the power of knowledge and learning. People's decisions should be guided only by knowledge, its philosophers said. Ignorance, superstition, and emotions should be discarded; life should be based on cool reason.

But the Enlightenment could not explain why people who knew better still made decisions that led to their ruin. It was not able to erase ignorance or superstition, and even enlightened people were affected by strong emotions.

In America, the Enlightenment faded in the early 1800s. One influence that replaced the Enlightenment was Romanticism. Among the emphases of Romanticism was the ideal of the noble savage, a free and happy person who has not been spoiled by society. These ideals were present even in the Revolution to some extent, especially with Thomas Jefferson. He idealized the life of the country farmer and supposed that children who grew up unspoiled by culture were virtuous and capable. Jefferson's idea is partly right, but it does not consider that humans themselves are sinful and will do wrong regardless of their environment.

After the Revolution, self-reliance and the pursuit of wealth and happiness became America's religion.

After the Revolution, Americans had a heady sense of freedom, power, and economic opportunity. Most Americans believed that human limitations had nearly vanished. There was no telling to what great heights their vast new land would rise.

The feeling that America was a special nation with special favor from God became very strong at this time. Had not God

"The Floating Church of Our Savior for Seamen" was an example of the efforts to curb wickedness among men with few religious moorings.

vindicated all the arguments that America was righteous and that fighting for her freedom was a holy cause? Some ministers preached that the greatness of Old Covenant Israel was a prophecy of the future splendor and prosperity of the United States. This country, they said, was planted by God himself for the express purpose of exalting Americans among other peoples in praise, name, and honor.

Self-reliance and the pursuit of wealth and happiness became the nation's religion. Ambition, individuality, and spontaneity became more important than the colonial and Enlightenment themes of order, control, and discipline.

Church growth in the early 1800s

When Alexis de Tocqueville described the American society of the early 1830s as the most thoroughly Christian in the world, he was commenting on a situation that developed primarily in the years between the Revolution and his visit to America. Protestantism dominated American culture from 1800 to 1850. The vast majority of Americans were Protestants even though many of them were not active promoters of Protestantism.

In this period, the old churches that tried to control politics and populations had become weaker while the flexible, locally organized denominations such as Methodists and Baptists grew rapidly. By 1850, these two denominations accounted for 70 percent of all American Protestants. Churches in this era were very vigorous, and this period came to be called the Second Great Awakening.

In this period, religious people formed many voluntary associations. These associations commissioned and supported ministers and missionaries, promoted lay teachers and lay Bible studies, and reached out to new immigrants. The associations also supported people struggling with vices, and they helped people who suffered financial or medical needs.

Many missionaries supported by voluntary associations worked to meet the spiritual needs of the growing West and of the sinful cities. Volunteers built churches on rafts to minister to sailors in the ports, hoping to stem the vices that flourished among seamen. Camp meetings brought revivals to many places. Ministers such as Charles Finney promoted the camp meeting as a way to bring lost souls to God and to bolster local church memberships.

The voluntary associations also worked to overcome the influences of radical Enlightenment ideas such as those of Thomas Paine and various French authors. America did not slide into general unbelief and immorality nearly as fast as France did, largely because of these vigorous church efforts.

Many of these voluntary associations were the world's first ecumenical efforts. While they did not cross all denominational lines (Catholics and Protestants still opposed each other), many Protestants of different churches cooperated for common causes. For example, Congregationalists and Presbyterians worked together to found colleges. Schools were also founded by individual denominations, especially the Methodists, Baptists, and Catholics. Smaller groups like the German Lutherans, German Reformed, and Quakers also contributed with their institutions.

In addition, circuit-riding preachers and missionaries preached and distributed tracts in the western settlements. While it is true that the wave of western expansion pushed on ahead of religion, and in some cases frontier life was very irreligious, yet the churches and voluntary societies did a remarkable job considering the size of the country.

In the first half of the 1800s, the voluntary societies did what the government and law could not have done. Bible societies, mission societies, Sabbath societies, and societies against drunkenness held tremendous influence, especially from 1825 to 1850.

However, nearly all the churches promoted a worldly Christianity. Their religion went hand in hand with many carnal practices. They followed vain and immodest fashions of the world with no apparent pang of conscience. Catholics in California complained that covetous Protestant Yankees "came, straining every nerve and energy in the pursuit of wealth." The camp meetings did some good, but politicians seeking supporters, salesmen, and young people looking for social fun also attended them. Because of these features, one historian described the meetings as part serious revival, part county fair, and part carnival.

In the first half of the 1800s, the voluntary societies did what the government and law could not have done.

The Methodists of this time tried valiantly to stem the tide of worldliness. They disciplined their members for sinful words, dishonest and immoral actions, neglect of home and church duties, and disobedience to church order. Matthew 18:15-17 was practically written into their church rules. In some localities they were able to maintain standards clearly different from the world's until the mid-1800s.[2]

---

2. The Methodist Church in America was founded in 1784, and by 1844 it had become America's largest Protestant denomination, with one million members. This incredible growth paralleled an almost universal relaxing of membership requirements. The Wesleyan Methodist Church, which separated from the main Methodists in 1843, maintained the discipleship of the parent group.

Circuit-riding preachers presided in church services, baptized, and officiated in marriages and funerals. Francis Asbury, the first bishop of the Methodist Episcopal Church in America, recruited many young men to serve as circuit riders on the frontier, resulting in rapid growth for the Methodist faith.

Aging Mennonite minister Melchior Brenneman of Donegal, Pennsylvania, was distressed as he compared society to pre-Revolution days. Strange clothing (innovative new styles) on both old and young was an abomination to God, he said, and was an evidence of pride. Other Mennonites of that era, including Christian Burkholder in his *Addresses to Youth*, also spoke of the times as dangerous, decayed, and corrupted.

America was now a huge Rhode Island where man had complete religious freedom on a grand scale for the first time. He could choose whatever religion he wanted, create his own religion if he pleased, or ignore all religions.

Unintended Effects of Great Awakening Revivalism

How Biblical was American religion during the Second Great Awakening? One way to measure this is to evaluate the fruit of its revivals in New York, especially the western part of the state.

During that period, evangelists crisscrossed New York and held earnest and emotional camp meetings year after year. People would dedicate their lives to God and then fall back into sinful living, only to repeat their emotional experiences at the next revivals. Apparently the evangelists supposed that these converts would find their way into the established churches in the region, but only about 10 percent of them actually did so. The evangelists themselves gave little direction on how the new believers should conduct their lives in Christ.

As a result of this hit-and-run evangelism, many people accepted corrupted forms of Bible teaching. Almost anyone who was eloquent and "spiritual" could gather a following in New York in the 1800s, as the following illustrations show.

Joseph Smith organized the Mormon Church near Palmyra in 1830. As a young man, Smith was strongly influenced by the doctrines of New England Puritans and by the various revival groups that flourished in his area. He considered his followers, the Mormons, to be the kingdom of God and literal descendants of the Israelites. This idea was much like the Puritans' "New Israel" concept. Smith implemented many strict, Puritan-like rules, stressing temperance, diligence, and wealth. His church attracted one thousand followers within nine months of its founding, and the rapid growth continued for some time.

John Noyes organized the Oneida Community at Oneida in 1848. Noyes planned that this community would be a utopia of perfection where people could be totally free from sin. But he adopted his own philosophies, not the Bible, as the foundation of his community. Members of the Oneida Community lived communally and replaced the family unit with an immoral system.

The Oneida community was heavily persecuted because of their immorality. In 1880, they stopped such practices. They reorganized themselves as a business and became wealthy by manufacturing steel animal traps, steel chains, thread, and silverware.

William Miller gained a large following in upstate New York when he taught that Christ would return in 1843 or 1844. He believed that Christ would establish a "New Jerusalem" on earth at that time. His followers disbanded after his prophecies failed. Some of them returned to the denominations from which they came, some formed new groups, and others gave up religion entirely.

Ellen White organized the Seventh-Day Adventists in the mid-1800s, mostly from William Miller's disappointed followers. The Adventists moved to Michigan in 1855, and by 1863 the group had over three thousand members in one hundred churches.

Spiritism began near Rochester in 1848. The growth and beliefs of this movement are described in Chapter 11.

The shift from church to nation

In chapter 8 we noted that many ministers equated the Revolution with the cause of Christ. This idea grew stronger after the Revolution succeeded. Some Protestants thought that the Revolution and its effects made it the most important world event since the birth of Christ. Others were sure that the Revolution had prepared America for the millennial reign of Christ, which they thought would begin soon. The way of the Lord had been prepared by "the march of revolution and civil liberty," preached Congregational minister Lyman Beecher. America had become a living epistle to the whole world of how to secure God's special favor; the new nation would now be a fountain of life to all other countries. One minister said that July 4 should be celebrated like the Jewish Passover, and that from the victory celebrated on this day, men would become free indeed.

This was quite natural for the generation that had not experienced the paradoxes of the Revolution first hand. As they exulted in the rapid improvement of economic conditions and general freedom, it was easy to believe that the Revolution had been a sacred cause to attain these great fruits of God's kingdom.

In the early 1800s, the first leaders of the nation became legends. Many citizens came to see the Founding Fathers as great men of God. Washington was especially honored; one European traveler in 1815 said, "Every American considers it his sacred duty to have a likeness of Washington in his house, just as we have the image of God's saints." Churches forgot their former attacks on the wrong doctrines of these "enlightened" men. Instead, preachers referred to George Washington as an "American Joshua" whom God appointed for the great work of leading armies.

While many Protestant denominations were growing at this time, they were also splintering. In colonial times, Protestant denominations considered unity an important mark of the true church, and they usually thought people outside their denomination were lost. But this idea faded in the maze of Protestant groups that sprang from the soil of liberty.

In time, the many religious groups came to stand on equal social and political footing, a situation described as pluralism. As this grew in America, Protestants gradually shifted from focusing on their particular denominations as the center of God's kingdom, to seeing the mainly Protestant American republic as the center of God's work. Most people no longer called everyone outside their denomination lost. To many Americans, God's chosen people came to include everyone in God's "chosen nation" of Protestants, instead of any particular denomination of Protestants.

Protestant bigotry

After the Revolution, certain barriers between social classes and ethnic groups were slowly torn down. But many still remained, and some were even bolstered by Protestant denominations. The most glaring of these was slavery, which is discussed in chapter 11.

The Protestants' lack of Christian love for people of other religions has caused deep and ugly scars in American history. At best, many Protestants deeply disliked groups such as Catholics, Jews, and Mormons; at worst, they hated these other people and used Bible teaching to justify persecuting them. It was a short step from the Protestant "chosen nation" spirit to bigotry against other religions. If Christ had raised up the Protestant "chosen nation," other religions were the devil's work and should be treated accordingly.

Catholic forces in Europe had persecuted almost every Protestant group, but in America the tables were turned. Even though the law prevented official persecution, Protestants found ways to harass Catholics. Authorities often looked the other way because they sympathized with the Protestant cause.

When Catholics in America were few in number, this discrimination was not very pronounced. But from 1815 to 1860 about two million Irish Catholics immigrated to America. By 1850, Catholicism had become the largest united religious group in America, a status that it retains to this day.[3]

Many Protestants were frightened by this change. Some of them formed secret societies that tried to control immigration policies, sought to keep Catholics out of government positions, and opposed the Catholic Church in other ways. Protestant writers and cartoonists rose to fame by promoting the idea that a vast Catholic conspiracy was trying to gain control of America. Incited by such influences, angry Protestants burned several Catholic buildings to the ground. The American public eagerly read the sensational tales of books that pictured the Catholic Church in America as an enclave of immorality and violence.

> **It was a short step from the Protestant "chosen nation" spirit to bigotry against other religions.**

Similar sentiments caused Protestants to drive the Mormons from state to state, and in 1844 such influences caused the murder of Joseph Smith in Illinois. The violence of the Ku Klux Klan, predominately a "Christian" movement, was another expression of this spirit. Many American Protestants were benevolent and open to white Protestants, but tended to despise or hate anyone who did not contribute to that image. This attitude was rooted in old European tensions between Protestants and Catholics. Americans might easily say that they supported liberty and religious freedom for all, but applying those generous policies to everyone was much more difficult.

---

3. About 52 percent of Americans are Protestant, and about 38 percent are Roman Catholics. But because the Protestants are divided into numerous groups, Roman Catholicism is the largest united religious body.

A Methodist camp meeting about 1819.

These Protestant sentiments also gave rise to manifest destiny, the idea that white Americans were destined by God to rule North America from sea to sea. Catholics may have been detested, but Indians were abhorred. Americans despised the Spaniards of Mexico and the West (partly because of their Catholicism); such thoughts helped to swing American public opinion in favor of the Mexican War in the 1840s. Early settlers in Oregon Territory (predominantly Northerners who, ironically, favored the abolition of slavery) barred even free blacks from setting foot on this territory. "Christian" expansionist ideas drove others off the land, at least the productive land, to make room for whites.

Gradually, such persecution diminished and the principles of the Declaration of Independence and the Constitution won out. We should be very grateful for God's hand in moving the civil authorities to eventually reaffirm and expand religious freedom, because this provides a haven for nonresistant Christians. If the Protestant violence had continued, it is very likely that true Christians would have been persecuted just as they were in the Protestant nations of Reformation times.

A misplaced focus

From 1800 to 1900, Protestant churches grew dramatically but had very little emphasis on discipleship.[4] Membership and institutional growth was the measure of success; emphasis on repentance, instruction of new members, and church standards faded or disappeared.

In 1851, a Methodist in Georgia listed the causes of this decline as a weak "discharge of ministerial duty, a misguided defective church policy, [and] a worldly element of pride and self-sufficiency in the membership." Although church history clearly showed the necessity of membership requirements, this professor lamented, people were no longer willing to submit to this. Protestant preaching in this time was in general agreement with what "everybody" believed; seldom did it disturb the sensibilities of the rising rich and middle class.

After one hundred years of such a misplaced focus, the churches were ill prepared for the overwhelming problems of the 1900s. Protestants entered that century without a disciplined army and without clear battle lines. They had few answers to the problems of war, mushrooming divorce rates, and the erosion of morals, or to such movements as modernism and fundamentalism.

---

4. Teachings in many churches had been far from the Biblical ideal already in colonial days, especially during the 1700s. But in the 1800s, discipleship teachings practically disappeared in all the major denominations.

There has not been any war
> between the religion and the slavery of the south.

The church and the slave-prison
> stand next to each other. . . .

The church-going bell and the auctioneer's bell
> chime in with each other;
> the pulpit and the auctioneer's block
> stand in the same neighborhood. . . .

We have men sold to build churches,
> women sold to support missionaries,
> and babies sold to buy Bibles and communion services. . . .

Between the Christianity of this land
> and the Christianity of Christ,
> I recognize the widest possible difference.

> > *--Frederick Douglass (ca. 1817-1895),*
> > *abolitionist and former slave* [1]

---

1. Douglass spoke the first sentences of this quotation at a speech in 1846. The last sentence is taken from his autobiography.

11

American Social and Moral Issues in the 1800s

A house divided

In the early 1800s, slavery reared its head just enough so that no one could forget the issue. Though many antislavery people tried to ignore it, they knew it was certain to cause trouble. Pro-slavery people guarded it, knowing that the Southern plantation hung in the balance. Slavery was the faint but certain wailing of an emergency siren far away, but it became harder and harder to ignore.

As churches became increasingly worldly in the first half of the 1800s, legitimate church discipline issues faded and slavery became the supreme question in most denominations. Slavery took precedence over every other moral or spiritual question, and it divided every major Protestant denomination except the

Episcopalians. Most of the denominations split long before the Civil War actually started, and there was extreme bitterness between the factions.

Early in the 1800s, some people believed that enlightened principles of liberty for all would eventually extinguish slavery peacefully. The government outlawed imports of Africans in 1808, but this did not cause slavery to die out; the slave population continued growing from within. The next step for the abolitionists was to make sure that every new state that entered the Union was a free state. This would restrict slavery to the older Southern states and reduce the influence of the slave states in Congress; and perhaps in the future, slavery could be phased out by a majority of freedom supporters.

But the national leaders could not agree on such a position. Southerners were determined to keep the Northern states from gaining control of Congress, and one way they did this was by maintaining an equal number of slave states and free states.

For twenty-four years, the eight presidents from Martin Van Buren to James Buchanan tried to lead the United States without settling the crucial slavery question. The flames of debate rose hotter and higher, while Scripture fueled both sides and books such as *Uncle Tom's Cabin* blew oxygen on the flames.

On the pro-slavery side, Dutch Reformed minister Samuel How preached in 1855 that the Bible upholds slavery, using such Scriptures as Exodus 20:17: "Thou shalt not covet thy neighbor's house, thou shalt not covet thy neighbor's wife, nor his manservant, nor his maidservant, nor his ox, nor his ass, nor any thing that is thy neighbor's."

Such Scriptures, Mr. How pointed out, establish the fact that slaves are legitimate property of their owners, and that God recognizes this property. God teaches us, he said, to respect the rights of the master. "The desire and the attempt to deprive others of property which the law of God and the law of the land have made it lawful for them to hold," he said, "is to strike a blow at the very existence of civilization and Christianity."

In 1835, Presbyterians in South Carolina stated that slavery was in accord with the examples set by the patriarchs, prophets, and apostles, and it could be conducted with "the most fraternal regard to the best good of those servants whom God may have committed to our charge." The people trying to abolish slavery, said one Presbyterian minister, were atheists, socialists, and communists, and were trying to destroy the principles of security and social order.

Some slavery supporters explained that the slaves are better off under masters than they would be otherwise. They only had to give up their freedom in order to receive care from kindly masters. All that the masters asked in return was reasonable labor and loyalty.

Slavery supporters also charged the abolitionists with not interpreting the Bible correctly. How could they say that the Golden Rule applied to slaves when in fact those very Northerners did not apply the Golden Rule in the same way to their children? If the Golden Rule meant that a master could not have a slave unless the master himself was willing to be a slave, it would also have to mean that a father could not rule his son unless he was willing to be ruled by his son. There are such things as common sense and social order, they insisted, that must be used to apply the Bible correctly.

Slavery supporters said that abolitionists were embracing radical philosophies instead of Bible truth. A Presbyterian minister said that abolitionists become disgusted with the Bible because they could not find enough support for their cause there. Then they sought for "an abolition Bible, an abolition Constitution for the United States, and an abolition God." The fact that terms for lifelong servitude are set forth in the Old Testament (where Protestant people often sought support) was hard for abolitionists to explain. But aside from that, they found many Scriptures to defend their position.

In both the Revolution and the Civil War era, God's Word was an important piece of literature, and its texts were carefully selected and aligned by mortally opposed people on both sides.

Slavery involved much unjust treatment, abolitionists said, while the Scriptures teach kindness and love for others. If all people are of one blood and are made in God's image, how can we treat others as being lower than ourselves? Is not God the only rightful Master of men and women? The fact that the Bible says, "Servants, obey in all things your masters according to the flesh" does not necessarily indicate support for slavery, any more than "Blessed are they which are persecuted for righteousness' sake" indicates support for persecution.

Further, the abolitionists asked, how could anyone possibly defend the physical, emotional, and sexual abuse that went along with slavery? What could justify buying and selling people, dividing families, and even controlling religion so that slaves did not get too taken up with Christianity? Southerners might be able to defend their position with *legal* arguments, Scriptural or otherwise, but they could never do so with *moral* arguments.

11 • American Social and Moral Issues in the 1800s

So the two factions in the Protestant empire drew their lines in the sand and arrayed cannons on either side. Even as they did so, in disobedience to the Lord Jesus who told Peter to sheathe his sword, they invoked the Name and blessing of God.

No person could have better portrayed the northern Protestant view than did Julia Ward Howe (1819-1910). Mrs. Howe had been involved in social reform and the abolition cause for nearly twenty years before visiting the Union army camps at Washington, D.C., in December 1861. During this visit, she was inspired to write the "Battle Hymn of the Republic."

> Mine eyes have seen the glory of the coming of the Lord;
> He is trampling out the vintage where the grapes of wrath are stored;
> He hath loosed the fateful lightning of His terrible swift sword:
> His truth is marching on.

Often the Northerners blasted the South in less dignified terms. One propagandist lashed out, "The most unmitigated set of villains they have in the south are the Methodist, Baptist, Presbyterian, and Episcopal preachers . . . all talking secession . . . drinking mean liquor and advocating the cause of Jefferson Davis and the Devil." Those Northerners who would not rise to this holy cause were criticized as committing treason against God.

On the other hand, William J. Jones, in his 1887 book *Christ in the Camp, or Religion in Lee's Army*, described how the Southern soldiers felt about their cause.

> It was always assumed that the cause for which they contended was righteous; on it was invoked the divine blessing, and the troops were exhorted to faithful service.

> The people were never more religious, and faith in God was never at a higher point. The southern people felt that their cause was just, and prayed with fervor and confidence for success.

In both the Revolution and the Civil War era, God's Word was an important piece of literature, and its texts were carefully selected and aligned by mortally opposed people on both sides. People of the Protestant empire saw God's Word not as their master but as their servant. To the extent that it could serve their present purpose, they used it. But few let its message penetrate their souls and deliver them from sin.

Abraham Lincoln (who did not identify with any church) was one of the few religious people to maintain a more balanced view in this dark time. Though he fought for the North, he refused to claim the approval of God for either side. "It is quite possible that God's purpose," he wrote, "is something different from the purpose of either party." He thought that Americans were too proud and successful to pray to the God who made them. Lincoln knew about all the praying that was being done on both sides, of course, but apparently he was unsure if any of it qualified as real prayer. "Both read the same Bible and pray to the same God," he said in his second inauguration address, "and each invokes His aid against the other. . . The prayers of both could not be answered—that of neither has been answered fully."

How did true Christians view the Civil War? One answer comes from Mennonite Michael Shank, inducted into the army (though he would not fight) at Fort Colliers near Winchester, Virginia. Sad, lonely, and far away from home, he wrote a poem to his wife that ended like this:

11 • American Social and Moral Issues in the 1800s

Oh! May the rulers of our land
Obey Jehovah's great command.
And love their foes as well as friends.
Then wars will cease and strife will end.

And men then seek the Lord to know
Who peace and pardon will bestow.
Then I'll return and with you dwell
And no more bid thee sad farewell.

Michael Shank was hoping for too much in this world of sin. But his thoughts illustrate that although the Mennonites saw many evils in slavery, they did not see the cause of the North as Christ's cause; and neither should we.

Jacob Schwarzendruber, an Amish bishop of Johnson County, Iowa, believed that God had sent the Civil War to punish America for her sinfulness. But he did not name slavery as sin impersonated. Rather, he humbly said, "And who is there that has not deserved it?"

In Lancaster County, Pennsylvania, Amish bishop David Beiler echoed these sentiments. He believed that the prosperity, freedom, and abundance of the early 1800s had led many of his brethren away from God. Perhaps God had allowed this difficulty, he mused, to turn them back to Himself.

The "Battle Hymn of the Republic" is an example of how people overcome by the military spirit are often deceived into thinking that they are working for the kingdom of God. Certainly, God's truth does go marching on. But true Christians do not find His presence and truth "in the watchfires of a hundred circling" military camps. Instead, they find God's truth marching on in His children, who trust and obey the Prince of Peace.

Though war eventually settled the slavery question, Americans faced other religious and social issues that could not be settled by force.

Spiritism

Spiritism (also called spiritualism) began near Rochester, New York, in 1848. Two sisters, Margaret and Katherine Fox, said they had heard mysterious knockings in their home, and they could discover no reason for the noises. They decided that the sounds were coded messages from ghosts or spirits, and they invented a code by which they could decipher the supposed messages. From this beginning in the 1850s and 1860s, spiritism developed into a huge movement. Modern historians sometimes call these spiritists the "New Agers of the 1800s."

George Templeton Strong of New York believed that spiritism was foolishness, but he was amazed at its popularity, as he recorded in his diary on November 26, 1855.

> What would I have said six years ago to anybody who predicted that before the enlightened nineteenth century was ended, hundreds of thousands of people in this country would believe themselves able to communicate daily with the ghost of their grandfathers? That ex-judges of the Supreme Court, Senators, clergymen, professors of physical sciences, should be lecturing and writing books on [spiritism] . . . is surely one of the most startling events that has occurred for centuries and one of the most significant. A new Revelation, hostile to that of the Church and the Bible, [is shaping] intellectual character and morals.

Newspapers often commented on the rapid growth of spiritism. The *Cincinnati Daily Times* reported in 1854 that spiritists were found on every street and corner in the city. The *Cleveland Plain Dealer* said that within about a month, the believers in spiritism had jumped from around fifty to hundreds. And the *New York Times* speculated in September 1855 that spiritism "seems to be the new Mahomet, or the social Antichrist, overrunning the world."

Spiritists said that every person must decide for himself what is right and wrong. They believed that intelligent communication between the living and the dead was possible. Some of them taught and practiced fornication, adultery, and abortion. In 1854, one religious author wrote that such beliefs were breaking up churches, making havoc of religion, and seeming to know no limits on whom they would capture next.

> There are some three hundred circles or clubs in the city of Philadelphia alone. . . . The infection seizes all classes, ministers of religion, lawyers, physicians, judges, comedians, rich and poor, learned and unlearned. The movement has its quarterly, monthly, and weekly journals, some of them conducted with great ability.

In the late 1870s, Dr. Henry Gibbons of California reported that spiritism left a terrible effect on morals; it crazed some of its devotees and intoxicated multitudes more. "Our age and our country," he said, "alive with free and busy thought, have given birth to a number of anomalies, if not monstrosities, religious, intellectual, and moral." He said that a continuous stream of feticide literature had corrupted the country since the 1840s, and that it was largely the result of the idea that between men and women, "spirit-affinity" was more important than marriage.

Dwight L. Moody (center, back) poses with a fellow superintendent and a Sunday School class in Chicago at the North Market Hall Mission, circa 1877. The photographer described the scene as "small boys, whose street names are 'Red Eye, Butcher Kilroy,' etc. . . . As a whole, it represents the mission work in the streets and alleys of our city . . ." Mr. Moody moved to Chicago from Massachusetts at the age of 19 in 1856. He was a shoe salesman until the age of 23, when he devoted the rest of his life to Sunday school, evangelism, and other religious activities.

11 • American Social and Moral Issues in the 1800s

Such terms were common among Americans who had turned to spiritism and its accompanying adultery.

There was a great deal of variation among the spiritists; not all were immoral. Some Americans dabbled in spiritism out of curiosity and not as a matter of personal faith. Many who had lost loved ones in the Civil War grasped eagerly at the hope of communicating with the dead.

Abraham Lincoln and his wife lost a three-year-old son in 1850 and an eleven-year-old son in 1862. Deeply grieved, Mrs. Lincoln sought the help of mediums to communicate with her children. These mediums held at least eight séances in the White House during Lincoln's presidency. The president himself doubted spiritist ideas but attended several of the sessions. People such as the Lincolns did not adopt spiritism as a faith, nor did they approve the immorality of radical spiritism; but neither did they see any conflict between their belief in God and their involvement in occult practices.

According to the best estimates, around 7 percent of the United States population (two million out of thirty million) were spiritists in the middle to late 1800s. But many Americans who were not spiritists accepted some of the concepts of this movement. After it passed, American culture was more selfish and valued children less. By 1900, the average white middle-class family had less than half the number of births that such families had in the early 1800s.

Partly due to the spiritist movement, American culture began to emphasize personal rights more, especially in moral issues. Permissiveness became common; a 1938 study of 777 couples showed that 74 percent of the women born between 1890 and 1900 were pure before marriage; but after 1910, only about 33 percent were. As with many other moral issues, these figures varied widely from one area of the country to another, and it appears that they were far worse in cities than in rural areas.

During the era of spiritist influences, Americans made a major move toward the idea that if a marriage does not "work out," it is better to end it than to continue it. Until the 1930s, marital separation was so disgraceful in some places that spouses who divorced often moved out of their community. But in less socially conservative areas, especially in cities, divorce was losing such stigma already in the late 1800s. Almost every state allowed divorce by the 1850s. In 1867, the first year that the United States Bureau of Census published divorce figures, the annual divorce rate was a little more than one couple per thousand. More recently, the rate was 16.4 divorces per thousand couples in 1998, having fallen from the record high of over 22 divorces per thousand couples in 1979 and 1980.

Urbanization and its evils

After 1850, two things especially changed the face of America. Huge industries developed, and cities boomed. The picture of America as a land of vine-covered cottages, small tranquil farms, and sturdy tillers of the soil was far more accurate before the Industrial Revolution than it was afterward.

Immigration swelled the population of the eastern seaboard cities by two or three times in the fifty years between 1850 and 1900. Some midwestern cities had phenomenal growth; Chicago went from about 30,000 to 1.7 million people in those fifty years (its 1900 population was over fifty times the 1850 population). Cities such as Cleveland, Columbus, Toledo,

11 • American Social and Moral Issues in the 1800s

Indianapolis, St. Louis, Detroit, Milwaukee, Minneapolis, St. Paul, Omaha, and Denver also had major growth.

Cities offered an exciting social life, and factories offered jobs that many people considered easier and steadier than country employment. Also, factory jobs were the obvious choice of many poor immigrants who could not afford land. Cities offered the latest innovations of the Industrial Revolution, much of which took place in the same period of 1850 to 1900.

But this tremendous growth and industrialization came at a terrible price for many Americans. Thousands of immigrants, even children, worked in factories with brutally long hours, poor conditions, and low pay. In 1890, a reporter named Jacob Riis published a book called *How the Other Half Lives*, in which he described the appalling home conditions of many city workers. Riis wrote that parents were so busy trying to feed their families that they had no time for religious and moral teaching. In some neighborhoods, bars outnumbered churches ten to one, and the devil seemed to have far more sway than any religious influence. Catholic bishop John Spalding of Peoria, Illinois, agreed with this assessment.

Urbanization and industrialization came at a terrible price for many Americans.

> The conditions of life are not favorable to purity, and the grossest sensuality prevails. . . . [In the city] people have no settled home and no local traditions, the loss of a good name is often looked upon as a mere trifle. . . . [Morality and manners] cease to be handed down as sacred heirlooms. . . . Lodging-houses

where people sleep and eat are not homes. Hired rooms which are changed from year to year, and often from month to month, are not homes. . . . [A city] is the grave of a family, not its home.

Congregationalist Josiah Strong published *Our Country* in 1891, which pointed out that America had one Protestant church for every 438 persons in 1890. However, per population, the concentration of churches was far greater in the country than in the city. Boston had only one Protestant church per 1,778 citizens, Cincinnati had one to 2,195, St. Louis had one to 2,662, and Chicago had one to 3,601. Strong emphasized that Protestantism was not reaching the majority of the population. This, he felt, was causing great decay in America.

Rapid population growth exceeded the capability of many cities to keep up with utilities, but another factor was that incompetent or exceedingly corrupt officials controlled many cities of this period. Municipal authorities often took bribes and formed partnerships with big business and crime. Alcoholism and prostitution flourished. Watchmen carrying clubs tried to keep order in rough sections, but in some cities they would help a citizen only if bribed to do so.

In many cities, it was dangerous for a young woman to venture out alone on the street in the evening. Many a Protestant boss cared only for his own financial gain, and many a Protestant politician was corrupt. There were some solid family folks who held to morality and virtue, but most of those people lived in the country.

Social Problems in the Late 1800s

The late 1800s were marked by the forming of several labor groups (later called unions) that demanded better pay and improved working conditions. Many employers of that time did not care about their employees. Most of the employee requests were reasonable, but radical men with anarchist ideas sometimes used labor groups to fight the government.

The Knights of Labor, an early union, grew to 700,000 members by 1886. Early in that year, members of this union went on strike at the McCormick-Harvester plant in Chicago. Strikers and strikebreakers fought at this plant on May 3, and several workers were killed or wounded. Enraged labor leaders organized a labor rally for the next day and called for armed resistance to strikebreakers.

On May 4, three thousand workers from McCormick-Harvester and some other factories gathered for the rally at Haymarket Square. The rally was in charge of the city's most radical labor leaders; and when police tried to break up the crowd, someone threw a bomb at them, killing seven officers and one other person. In the shooting riot that followed, many more workers and policemen were injured. Eventually, four of the leaders were hanged, one committed suicide, and three were pardoned.

In 1894, several factors led to a large railroad strike. A federal court condemned the strike because it disrupted the country's postal service. Rioting broke out near Chicago, and President Grover Cleveland sent in federal troops to restore order.

Typical of the corruption in many cities was Tammany Hall, a political machine that controlled New York City for decades. William M. Tweed was the main boss of Tammany Hall from 1860 to 1871. He and his accomplices organized city improvement projects and designated money for them; but instead of being used for the stated purposes, millions of dollars were diverted to the pockets of the "Tweed Ring." Tweed's power was broken in 1871, but Tammany Hall and its scandals continued to rule the city until 1933.

The social gospel

The problems of the late 1800s were not unique to America. The social gospel movement began in England in response to similar problems. Proponents of the social gospel applied the teachings of Jesus Christ to social life—saints and sinners alike. Even though this movement accomplished some good, it further distorted people's views of the true Gospel and of church purity.

The social gospel taught that all people had high potential and that they could attain it if they were given the right environment and proper guidance. This resulted in many helpful programs, such as children's homes in slum areas. Some social gospel leaders maintained that their primary emphasis was conversion, and some of them were men of deep, spiritual convictions who did hard and dangerous work. However, like all movements that emphasize service above discipleship, the social gospel movement went far astray. It became a social and political force to create a society that upheld some Biblical emphases with no significant focus on salvation, holiness, and discipleship. The evangelist Dwight L. Moody decried the social gospel as a substitute for the real Gospel.

Some social gospel leaders thought the kingdom of God was an age that would soon be fulfilled on earth, in which all social injustices would end, and peace and equality would rule the world. Several offshoot organizations of the social gospel built on its principles to support socialism.

The social gospel became an ecumenical force. Almost every Protestant denomination developed social theories, taught them in their seminaries, and linked arms in social para-church organizations. The social gospel inspired many women's movements, which worked to end alcoholism and war and to gain more rights for oppressed classes and for women in general.

> **The social gospel taught that all people had high potential and that they could attain it if they were given the right environment and proper guidance.**

Another important result of the social gospel was the idea that if poverty, dirt, failure, and misery were the devil's empire, then wealth, cleanliness, success, and happiness must be Christ's priorities. A strong connection developed between

11 • American Social and Moral Issues in the 1800s

wealth and virtue. Such theories had been taught already in colonial times, especially among the Puritans, but now they reached new heights.

By the late 1800s and early 1900s, some of the terrible working conditions had been corrected, and there rose an urban consumer society that emphasized wealth and convenience. Shopping culture began, characterized by consumer advertising and tempting displays. Amusement and self-gratification became more and more important, corresponding to the availability of money to spend on personal wants. Protestant and Catholic religion blessed it all as the great American abundance that came from righteous living.

Prayers or sayings like the following became common in these times, often presented to God as the "Spirit of Infinite Plenty."

> God, my opulent Father, has poured out to me all resources, and I am a mighty river of affluence and abundance. I think of myself as a child of God, heir to all the riches of the Kingdom. This is the truth about me. I know that I am worthy of abundance. My prosperity is assured.

The social gospel declined in the World War I era, when the realities of war shattered the optimism of the movement. People began to understand that some of the social gospel emphases were naïve. Yet this movement left a permanent mark on many Protestant churches in the form of social change programs and political involvements.

Abortion in the late 1800s and early 1900s

In 1860, when the United States population was 27 million, there were about 160,000 abortions—an annual rate that is very close to modern figures.[2] Nonwhites were not included in the 1860 figures; there are no records on the frequency of abortion in the slave population.

The official record shows that abortion rates declined slowly after the mid-1800s; then they rose again in the mid-1900s. The reasons for that decline are given in chapter 18. In this chapter, the circumstances of abortion are discussed only because of what they show about morality in that era.

Like spiritism, abortion in the 1800s was not a part of mainstream, middle-class American culture.

In the late 1700s, many American children were conceived outside of marriage—as many as one child out of three in some areas. But very few children were born into single-parent settings. According to the court records of trials in such cases, the father was usually given two options. He could marry the woman, or he could stay single and pay child support for twelve years. The second option was highly disgraceful. With or without a court order, most men decided to marry.

In colonial times, the courts depended heavily on a woman's testimony to determine the father of her child. If several men may have been the father, the woman's word was taken as the strongest evidence, and the result was a "shotgun marriage." Men attacked this in the early 1800s, refusing to submit to

---

2. Further details may be found in *Abortion Rites* by Marvin Olasky (Wheaton, Il.: Crossway Books, 1992). This book gives well-researched documentation of abortion in the 1800s, from the perspective of a conservative evangelical pro-lifer. He sets the record straight after James Mohr, in *Abortion in America* (New York, Ny.: Oxford University Press, 1978) used the same records to prove that Americans always accepted abortion. Mr. Mohr's thesis is false, but so is the idea that abortion was not common in America until after *Roe v. Wade* in 1973.

marriage and child support mainly on the basis of a woman's testimony. Laws were changed accordingly, which resulted in more desperation among single mothers-to-be and a corresponding increase of abortions.

A related factor was the increasing numbers of prostitutes as cities grew in the 1800s. City men often fell into this vice, but history also records a common theme of rural men traveling to the city on business trips and yielding to anonymous immorality that they never would have committed in their home areas.

The spiritism of the 1800s was yet another factor. Even though its radical immorality involved only a small segment of the American population, the loose morals of spiritism affected the way many people felt about families. One result was an increase of abortions, especially among the wealthy.

Like spiritism, abortion in the 1800s was not a part of mainstream, middle-class American culture. Yet it was real, especially in large eastern cities. Many newspapers decried the tragedy, calling abortion the evil of the age. At the same time, the papers also carried thinly veiled advertisements for abortion providers.

Laws to prevent abortion and to prosecute abortion providers were on the books, but conclusive evidence was difficult to obtain.[3] The women who sought the illegal procedure kept quiet about it. Many abortionists were rich, and they often bribed city officials to look the other way. Most of the information available to the public was what leaked out when a woman died because of an abortion, or what was obtained by newspaper reporters posing as a couple seeking abortion services.

---

3. As morality declined in the 1800s, states passed increasingly strict abortion laws. This began in the 1820s, and by the 1870s all the states had such laws.

TO MARRIED WOMEN —MADAME RESTELL, Female Physician, is happy to have it in her power to say that since the introduction into this country, about a year ago of her celebrated Preventive Powders for married ladies, whose health forbids a too rapid increase of family; hundreds have availed themselves of their use, with a success and satisfaction that has at once dispelled the fears and doubts of the most timid and skeptical; for, notwithstanding that for twenty years they have been used in Europe with invariable success, (first introduced by the celebrated Midwife and Female Physician, Madame Restell, the grandmother of the advertiser, who made this subject her particular and especial study,) still some were inclined to entertain some degree of distrust, until become convinced by their successful adoption in this country. The results of their adoption to the happiness, the health, nay, often the life of many an affectionate wife and a fond mother, are too vast to touch upon within the limits of an advertisement—results which affect not only the present well-being of parents, but the future happiness of their offspring. Is it not but too well known that the families of the married often increase beyond the happiness of those who give them birth would dictate? In how many instances does the hardworking father, and more especially the mother, of a poor family, remain slaves throughout their lives, tugging at the oar of incessant labor, toiling to live, and living but to toil; when they might have enjoyed comfort and comparative affluence; and if care and toil have weighed down the spirit, and at last broken the health of the father, how often is the widow left, unable, with the most virtuous intentions, to save her fatherless offspring from becoming degraded objects of charity or profligate votaries of vice? And even though competence and plenty smile upon us, how often, alas, are the days of the kind husband and father embittered in beholding the emaciated form and declining health of the companion of his bosom, ere she had scarce reached the age of thirty—fast sinking into a premature grave—with the certain prospect of himself being early bereft of the partner of his joys and sorrows, and his young and helpless children of the endearing attentions and watchful solicitude which a mother alone can bestow, not unfrequently at a time when least able to support the heart-rending affliction! Is it desirable then —is it moral for parents to increase their families, regardless of consequences to themselves or the well being of their offspring when a simple, easy, healthy and CERTAIN remedy is within our control? The advertiser feeling the importance of this subject and estimating the vast benefits resulting to thousands by the adoption of means prescribed by her, would respectfully arouse the attention of the married, by all that they hold near and dear to its consideration. Is it not wise and virtuous to prevent evils to which we are subject by simple and healthy means within our control? Every dispassionate, virtuous, and enlightened mind will unhesitatingly answer in the affirmative. This is all that Madame Restell recommends or ever recommended. Price Five Dollars a package, accompanied with full and particular directions. For the convenience of those unable to call personally, "Circulars" more fully explanatory will be sent free of expense (postage excepted) to any part of the United States. All letters must be post-paid, and addressed to MADAME RESTELL, Female Physician. Principal office, 148 Greenwich street, New York. Office hours from 9 A. M. to 7 P. M. Philadelphia office, 39½ South Eighth street.
ap10 1m*

An advertisement in the New York Herald on April 13, 1840, advising couples to seek abortion to control family size. Over half of the medical advertisements in the New York Herald in 1867 listed abortion services or medicines.

11 • American Social and Moral Issues in the 1800s

Many Protestant churches were basically silent on abortion in these times. Of the major denominations, only the Presbyterians officially condemned the practice. However, a number of individual Protestant ministers preached and wrote against abortion. Catholics verbally condemned abortion but did not put Catholic abortionists under church censure.

The pro-life movement that grew in the late 1800s was not motivated primarily by churches. Rather, it developed because several doctors' associations and some large newspaper firms worked to expose and report the extent of abortion. These associations often complained that the clergy was so silent on the issue. As with many evils in the 1800s, the fight against abortion was led by volunteers.

In some cases, churches were unwilling to take part in fighting abortion because it was a delicate subject for the pulpit, and because many upper-class church members were involved with it. In the records of this time, it is common to find that abortion was done to hide the immoral affairs of wealthy businessmen and politicians, including congressmen. Many of these people were respected churchgoers. Clergymen of that time were accustomed to ignoring many evils of society, even when such evils were within their congregations, and abortion was generally treated no differently.

The good old days?

Farmer Boy tells the story of Almanzo Wilder, a young boy of northern New York who attended a country school in the 1860s.[4] Almanzo feared for the life of his teacher, a slim young

---

4. Laura Ingalls Wilder (New York, Ny.: HarperCollins Publishers, 1971, Harper Trophy edition).

man named Mr. Corse. In the upper grades were several husky logging boys who intended to thrash the teacher and bring an end to the school term. But Mr. Corse borrowed the Wilder family's blacksnake ox whip. When the boys began their attack, Mr. Corse whipped two of them, threw them out of the schoolhouse, and slammed the door. The other boys escaped through a window.

It makes sense, doesn't it? Right is maintained by the use of a whip, if need be, and the whole school learns what happens to bullies. Surely Almanzo would have missed a valuable lesson if he had been sitting, instead, in a modern school where the students run the teachers and physical punishment is disallowed.

Yet to be fair, we need to consider a few other facts about that upstate New York settlement in the 1860s. Father Wilder was a disciplined man, but he was noted more for his fine barns and for bankrolling his savings than for his family worship and his contribution to the church. It would be difficult for anyone to exceed Mother Wilder's stewardship, yet she dressed her daughters in the latest fashions and sent them to a secular college.

The bullies in that school had driven out two teachers before Mr. Corse, and both times these tough boys had succeeded in closing the school. Mr. Lane, who had taught the year before Mr. Corse, was beaten so badly that he died later. Yet there is no mention that the bullies or their fathers were prosecuted for that death. In fact, Mr. Ritchie (one of the fathers) was proud that his son could beat teachers and force the school to close.

In rural settings, certain virtues were promoted in the 1860s that seem hard to find today. No rock music floated over the fields, no television flashed its pictures, and no sinful magazines

11 • American Social and Moral Issues in the 1800s

defiled the roadside. But the fact remains that godly people in those times were still concerned and at times distressed over conditions in the surrounding culture. The world was no friend to the true church, even in that era.

Had you lived in a rural New York community in the 1860s, one of your neighbors might have been like Mr. Wilder—steady and virtuous but not necessarily godly. Another neighbor could have been like Mr. Ritchie. Your children might have gone to a school so violent that the teacher died of injuries, while your neighbor joked about it and encouraged his son to further violence.

Others of your neighbors might have been devoted to spiritism or to the new teachings of the Mormons, the Oneida Community, or numerous smaller groups in that period of religious ferment. Or when a horse dealer bought horses from you, he might have broken into your house at night to retrieve the money, as happened to a farmer near the Wilders.

True Christians of this period understood that the world of their time was sinful. They did not see their era as a time when Americans were open to the Gospel, when righteousness prevailed, or when the values of society were based on the Scriptures.

Had we lived in those times, we would have agreed with Peter Nissley, an Old Mennonite minister who wrote the following in 1863.

> True religion has always been counted a shame full thing, so that it has always required a holy boldness to make an open profession of it. . . . We are engaged in a Severe warfare, but under the

captain of our Salvation we are assured of victory if we endure faithfull to the End.

It is true that rural living in the latter half of the 1800s had some advantages that are lost today. But we enjoy some blessings now that true Christians in that time did not have. What everyone today needs most is not a return to a contradictory past, but a turning to the Lord Jesus Christ, who is the one solid Rock in the shifting sands of time.

Part Three

A Christian View of

Modern Politics

Introduction

It is important for Christians today to understand the New Testament view of politics and government. During wars and other periods where government values clashed head-on with nonresistance, Christians always experienced a sharp increase in their awareness of the vast difference between the political kingdom and the heavenly kingdom. In periods of rest, however, these principles have nearly always clouded. To be prepared for the inevitable future clash, we need to be convinced today that the simple New Testament rules for church and state relationships apply at all times.

Chapters

12. Understanding Civil Religion
13. A Christian View of Civil Government
14. A Christian View of Officials
15. A Christian View of Laws
16. A Christian View of Culture
17. A Christian View of Foreign Cultures
18. A Christian View of Political Action: Part 1
19. A Christian View of Political Action: Part 2
20. A Christian View of War

Are they willing to turn the world
   over to the Huns and the rulers of the Huns?
Are they willing
   when the Huns are seeking to conquer the world,
   that they be permitted to murder little children,
   cut their throats, cut off their arms and legs? . . .
Are they willing
   that murder and rapine and arson
   and all God's ten commandments shall be broken
   in order that the Kaiser may rule the world?
Are they willing to turn their backs
   upon the religion of Jesus Christ
   which they had practiced so simply
   and has been the inspiration of their church?
   —*Robert Cain, Maryland director of War Savings Stamps Campaign,*
   challenging the Anabaptist position against purchasing war bonds, June 14, 1918

12

Understanding Civil Religion

I t's hard to relate to," a conservative Mennonite told me. "People in politics are usually not very honorable, and our last president certainly wasn't. But this one reads the Bible every day and speaks of how faith changes lives. In some ways, he acts like a Christian. What should we make of it?"

A few weeks later, Dick Benner, pastor of a large mainstream Mennonite congregation, voiced a similar frustration.

> As citizens of the most powerful empire in the world, we are taken with the rhetoric of our "born again" Caesar as he infuses public policy with so-called "Christian" values, even justifying preemptive strikes around the world to preserve the world for democracy and "Christianity." . . . A theocratic government that seems to

share some of our values—but doesn't share our peaceful ways of bringing in the kingdom—is distracting us.[1]

When a political leader is obviously wicked, the Bible description of the worldly kingdoms fits well. But when someone in power seems to echo Christian values such as Bible reading, pro-life sentiments, and good work ethics, it is easy to become confused.

Recognizing the differences between true religion and civil religion will help us to understand the nature of politics, regardless of the surface qualities of any particular leader or government.

Civil religion is the values that hold a worldly culture together.

Civil religion is the values that hold a worldly culture together. It is usually based partly on the major faith(s) of a culture. Civil religion follows principles that seem like common sense to fallen man. It focuses on physical life. It is willing to suffer or fight for earthly ideals. Civil religion lifts up self, not God and the Bible, even though it may speak freely of God and the Bible. Civil religion promotes certain rights or ideals as part of a people's divine heritage, and it asserts that people should fight to the death for those ideals. Civil religion is a drifting base in a changing world.

In contrast, true religion is holiness, obedience to the Bible, a focus on eternal life, and a willingness to die for truth. True religion focuses on Christ, His church, and Biblical discipleship; its adherents give up many personal "rights" in order to seek God's will with fellow Christians. True religion includes

---

1. Dick Benner, "Let all the talking continue," *Mennonite Weekly Review*, August 8, 2005, p. 5.

repenting from sin and bearing fruit for God. True religion is a solid base in a changing world.

Civil religion in all times and places is marked by pride, covetousness, love of violence, desire for power, and hatred or disdain of other nationalities. In nations whose civil religion is based in Christianity, some cultural values will be similar to Christian values. Yet in every such culture, Christian values are mixed with many dark aspects of human nature.

The following sections of this chapter describe some of the characteristics of civil religion, especially in the New World.

Shifts with the times

Since the founding of the nation, Americans have not been governed by absolutes such as the Biblical view of sin, the two eternal destinies of the soul, or the personal accountability of all men to God. Civil religion shifts with the times to reflect prevailing political and moral moods. It replaces God's absolutes with man's thinking. In Revolution times, one absolute was that the colonies must go free or die. Another absolute was that the common man must be independent and have representation in government.

Civil religion changes the Biblical view of sin and righteousness into something easier for people to accept. President Reagan demonstrated this well in the spring of 1983 when he spoke to the National Association of Evangelicals about his expanding defense plans. The president said,

> We know that living in this world means dealing with . . . the doctrine of sin. . . . There is sin and evil in the world. And we are enjoined by Scripture and the Lord Jesus to oppose it with all our might.

229

Then Reagan described exactly what he meant. He said that Communists are "the focus of evil in the modern world" and that the United States must employ every means to contain the "aggressive impulses of an evil empire." The 1,500 evangelical church leaders responded with thunderous applause.

Civil religion loves this kind of rhetoric, in which sin and evil means someone else on some other continent. In this view, serving Jesus Christ is not discipleship but opposing an enemy such as the Communists.

Civil religion displaces the authority of God's Word with the ideals of independence and equality. Since every American is free to think for himself, and all churches and beliefs are considered equal, there is tremendous pressure to disregard the absolutes of the Bible. But there is also a blessing in this freedom. Because Americans are free and independent, true Christians—strange as they seem to mainstream culture—have been mostly left alone.

Civil religion creates its own "absolutes" by means of majority opinion. For example, most Americans (about 7 out of 10, according to some surveys) personally believe that abortion is wrong. But most of them also think that if a woman wants to have an abortion, that is her right.

For the most part, Americans do not feel responsible for what others do, and they prefer not to discuss a subject like abortion as long as it does not affect them personally. They see this as the spirit of democracy; what other people do with their own bodies is a private matter. As one man explained on the subject of abortion, "I know how I feel, and my feelings are valid. These feelings are based on experiences that are mine alone, and you can't tell me they are wrong."

That is one reason why the majority of Americans will never be attracted to true Christianity and Biblical church life. To obey the Scriptures and to teach Bible absolutes as requirements for church membership seems like infringing on people's rights. But God is no democrat, nor can His Word be swayed by public opinion. The Bible does not offer everyone equal say; it requires everyone to fall in silence at the cross.

In America, a church that follows the Bible is regarded as exclusive and perhaps even proud. The belief that unrepentant people are lost is considered religious bigotry. Whatever opposes mutual tolerance is considered sin. These ideas have dominated much of American culture since the Revolution, and especially since the Civil War.

Civil religion displaces the authority of God's Word with the ideals of independence and equality.

Plural and secular

Pluralism is a condition in which varied religious and cultural groups coexist within a society. Law established pluralism in the United States at the birth of the nation, and it has constantly expanded since then, especially in the 1900s. Today in some cases, atheism is accorded the same legal privileges that traditional religions have.

Independence and pluralism themselves have become the personal religion of many Americans. Anything goes, everyone is welcome, and religion is a marketplace of ideas in which the greatest crime is to say that someone else's idea is wrong.

Walt Whitman's theology in 1855 was radical for the time, but it described a growing trend.

> Reexamine all you have been told at school or church or in any book . . . dismiss whatever insults your own soul. . . . I, now, for one, promulge a sublime and serious Religious Democracy... The ripeness of Religion is doubtless to be looked for in this field of individuality, and is a result that no organization or church can ever achieve.

A true Christian's religion is also deeply personal and voluntary, but it is lived within a church where together the believers sense God's leading and interpret the Scriptures. Apostle Paul describes it as "Submitting yourselves one to another in the fear of God."[2]

On the other hand, legal plurality demands that nobody be required to yield to another in his ideas of religion. In American religious and cultural life, the individual is the most important entity, and personal rights are the most important tenets. Most people believe they will be happiest when they are free to think and do as they please. Pluralism, rights, tolerance, and compromise have the last word.

In this atmosphere, religion and politics seem to play on a level field. Religious ideas can be harnessed for secular purposes, and secular ideas for religious purposes, as illustrated by J. Edgar Hoover's comment: "Since Communists are anti-God, encourage your child to be active in the church."

The great American experiment in pluralism is one of the paradoxes of civil religion. While pluralism has helped to provide unparalleled freedom for generations of believers, the free market of religious pluralism has also cheapened religion. True Christians are very thankful for the freedoms resulting

---
2. Ephesians 5:21

from this experiment, but they must guard against personally giving religion the low regard that it has acquired in American culture.

Moral but not Biblical

Civil religion is a key tool in supporting national morality and virtue. This has been true for centuries; in most ancient kingdoms, success or failure in economy and war were directly associated with the people's devotion to their gods. About 150 B.C., the Greek historian Polybius reported on Roman society as follows:

> The quality in which the Roman commonwealth is most distinctly superior is, in my judgment, the nature of its religion. The very thing that among other nations is an object of reproach—i.e., superstition—is that which maintains the cohesion of the Roman state. These matters are clothed in such pomp, and introduced to such an extent in private and public life, as no other religion can parallel.... I believe the government has adopted this course for the sake of the common people. This might not have been necessary had it been possible to form a state composed of wise men; but as every multitude is fickle, full of lawless desires, unreasoned passion, and violent anger, it must be held in by invisible terrors and religious pageantry.

But Roman society fell from that "quality" and suffered severe disorder in the years before Christ's birth. According to the poet Virgil (70-19 B.C.), "right and wrong are confounded; so many wars the world over, so many forms of wrong; no worthy honor is left to the plough; the husbandmen are marched away and the field grows dirty." Augustus Caesar (63 B.C.–A.D. 14) thought the reason for this was that Romans had become careless in worshiping their ancient gods. He tried with some success to reinstate the old religions and the moral laws that accompanied them.

A few hundred years later, Constantine based his acceptance of Christianity on the same thinking. His goal was to establish a religion that would promote unity and virtue among the Romans, and help to secure his throne.

Those themes are recorded many times in history. The comments of Polybius are much like Benjamin Franklin's remarks in chapter 9 on why people need religion. American religion was different from that of the pagan Romans, but the political goals of both governments were basically the same. Both appreciated some of the effects of God's principles while rejecting much truth.

In the Founding Fathers' view, the Bible certainly was a *help* to virtue, and one of the greatest helps at that, but so were the ambiguous "laws of nature and nations"—an Enlightenment expression that simply meant "laws that everybody knows and that nobody needs any particular religion to teach him." Christians recognize that through the conscience and the Scriptures, God is the source of anything good in the "laws of nature"; but most of the Founding Fathers did not make that connection.

What Are the "Laws of Nature"?

Politicians and philosophers have debated the "laws of nature" for hundreds of years. Atheists have argued that these laws exist without God. Some religious people say such laws existed before the Bible, some say the laws are separate from the Bible but in agreement with it, and others give a different explanation. In short, the "laws of nature" have been marshaled to serve a multitude of people and purposes, religious and irreligious.

12 • Understanding Civil Religion

> In Greek and Roman times, both Stoics and Epicureans used the "laws of nature" to support their philosophies—even though the two were directly opposite. The same laws have been used to support evolution, Creation, and mixtures of these. They were used to support many political rebellions and many "purgings," such as Hitler's rampage against the Jews. They have also been used to support the violence of Aryan supremacists in America and other nations.
>
> Any reference to the "laws of nature" that contradicts the Bible or that motivates people to do wrong is deception. When the Bible says that certain behavior is "natural" and that contrary behavior is "against nature" (as in Romans 2), it is simply comparing God-approved and sinful behavior.
>
> The "laws of nature" can never be used rightly to do anything but honor the God who made the world, who gave people a conscience based on truth, and who speaks today through His Word, His Spirit, and His people.
>
> Christians always improve their witness when they use biblical terms, such as the "law of God," rather than philosophical terms, such as the "law of nature." To base our testimony on the "laws of nature" is to retreat from the sovereign, unassailable position of God's Word to the contested terrain of nature and philosophy.

The Founding Fathers elevated reason over truth, common sense over the Bible, and experience over anything eternal. Many of them believed that Christianity was best viewed as a sturdy ally of morality and not as truth to be accepted by faith. What Christianity did at its best, John Adams said, was to teach "the great Principle of the Law of Nature and Nations: Love your Neighbour as yourself, and do to others as you would that others should do to you."

The Founding Fathers failed to realize that their rejection of Bible truth destroyed the foundation of the morality they considered so important.

Jesus' command to fear God and love one's neighbor, Thomas Jefferson said, was the sum of Christianity. No mysteries, miracles, Incarnation, or other unintelligible doctrines were necessary; all those things were theological imaginations. Benjamin Franklin was of the same mind. He had no use for a certain

235

evangelical minister because "he wanted to make persons good Presbyterians rather than good citizens."

What these men failed to realize was that their rejection of Bible truth destroyed the foundation of the morality they considered so important. In the American civil religion that developed from their thinking, morality is based on the flimsy idea that being virtuous is the most sensible thing to do. Certainly it is sensible, but what seems sensible will change with times and people. If Bible absolutes are not to be considered, who finally decides what is sensible and virtuous?

A religion of wealth

Civil religion teaches that wealth is a result of righteousness or virtue. In some ways, this is true. Wealth is most likely to come to those who work hard and practice careful stewardship and disciplined living.

But the idea that righteousness brings wealth is false in many ways. In fact, the New Testament teaches that wealth is more often a curse than a blessing. A man's wealth is *not* a measure of his spiritual life, for his life "consisteth not in the abundance of the things which he possesseth."[3] Jesus also said that man shall not live by bread alone, that a certain rich man was a fool for his investment planning, and that the poor widow who gave all her money to the Lord had given more than the rich philanthropists. Jesus introduced the New Testament concept that wealth no longer means what it did to Old Testament Israel.

Throughout history, all cultures have taught that wealth is an indication of righteousness. This is not a Christian idea, though it is just as present in nominal Christianity as in any

---
3. Luke 12:15

other false worship system. Nor is it an American or a European idea, though it flourishes in those societies. From the first colonial days, when the Puritans taught that God would bless them as He had blessed old Israel, most Americans have believed that their blessings and economy are solid proof that God is pleased with their lives.

Civil religion is always materialistic. In America, the reign of materialism is so complete that when someone asks what a man is worth, it is assumed that they mean financial worth. In the 1800s and 1900s Americans became accustomed to prosperity, and they came to resent anything that interfered with material success. A recession or depression is regarded as the worst evil that can befall the country. The greatest problem that can happen to a political party is to be blamed for an economic downturn. Any law or policy that promises to build wealth is automatically regarded as good, and anything that would reduce wealth or be bad for business is inevitably regarded as an outrage against the unalienable rights of the people.

Throughout history, all cultures have taught that wealth is an indication of righteousness.

In the early 1800s, Alexis de Tocqueville described the relationship between American religion and wealth like this:

> The American ministers of the Gospel do not attempt to draw or fix all the thoughts of man upon the life to come; they are willing to surrender a portion of his heart to the cares of the present. . . . [They] never cease to point to the other world as the great object

of the hopes and fears of the believer, [but] they do not forbid him honestly to court prosperity in this [life].

The "health and wealth" emphasis was part of the of the social gospel movement (see chapter 10). The equations were simple: goodness equals abundance; abundance is certain evidence of goodness. This philosophy fosters a bold faith in material progress. It contrasts sharply with the Bible concept that the wicked may prosper in time, but they will not prosper in eternity.

Was Early American Religion Similar to Anabaptism?

In 2006, after the horrific shooting in an Amish school at Nickel Mines, thousands of website and newspaper commentators praised the Amish for their forgiveness of the criminal and their love and support for his family. Many people held up the Amish as the guardians of virtue in a secular world, and commented that the world would be better if everyone lived like this.

One writer compared "the faith of the Amish" with "the faith of our forefathers." He thought the Amish were showing the goodness or the best of America that still resides in the nation's heartland. In his mind, they were part of a long tradition of Christian living that had also been evident in early America and in the lives of the Founding Fathers.

This mistaken comparison reflects the same sentiment that Chief Justice Warren Burger showed in writing the majority opinion for *Wisconsin v. Yoder* in 1972. Burger extolled the simple life of the Amish as "a life in harmony with nature and the soil, as exemplified by the simple life of the early Christian era that continued in America during much of our early national life." Furthermore, in Burger's opinion, the Amish fit Thomas Jefferson's image of the ideal American as a sturdy farmer who raises his family away from the corrupting influences of society.

Mennonite historian C. Henry Smith confessed after World War I that he had earlier considered Anabaptism and American democracy as twin, overlapping movements of the common people. But after the persecution that Anabaptist descendants suffered in World War I, he realized that the two were at sharp odds.

What is wrong with these statements equating the Anabaptist faith to the faith of the Founding Fathers or the early Americans?

It is clearly an error in understanding history. One of the few colonial places where Anabaptist groups could live in freedom was early Pennsylvania. A number of the other colonies would have driven them out because they did not fit into the prevailing religious patterns. Even in Pennsylvania they were considered odd. An ideal citizen would have fought to protect his land and family against Indian attacks, and he would have supported the American cause in the French and Indian and the Revolutionary wars. The Anabaptists did none of those things.

After the Revolution, religion became very personal. Ecumenism rose as people of many faiths worked together, and church standards declined until they were practically meaningless by the Civil War. Church membership rose steadily through the 1800s (up from a very low point in Revolution times), but the rise in church activity closely paralleled the drift away from Biblical truth. Numbers, not quality, impressed the American church.

Compare that with Anabaptist beliefs in those times. To the Anabaptists, religion was voluntary but not private. The brotherhood together decided how faith was to be practiced; together they understood the meaning of the Bible. Only those who conformed to the congregation's understanding of the Word were able to join the church.

For the most part, the Anabaptist churches would not join the common Protestant causes. They were more concerned about personal discipleship than about religious campaigns such as the social gospel and the temperance movement. In fact, as a whole they were hardly involved in such programs, because they saw Christ's purpose in the world as redeeming souls and forming a faithful church, not as redeeming society from some of its obvious evils.

Nor did they trust in the institutions of the United States. In *The Amish and the State,* Garrett Epps wrote, "The Amish do not regard the Constitution as their bulwark or the courts as their protectors."[4] This reflects the traditional view of Anabaptists. They appreciate the blessings they enjoy under the United States government, but they do not see those blessings as guaranteed by the government. Rather, they see them as privileges that God has graciously allowed and which are fragile at best in this world of sin.

The early American government and colonial people did not hold the values of the early church or Anabaptism. The Anabaptist settlers were not the quintessential, original citizens of the United States. Genuine Christians do not represent "the best of America"; they represent a heavenly kingdom to which many of

---

4. Donald B. Kraybill, ed. (Baltimore and London: The Johns Hopkins University Press, 2003), p. 268.

> America's values stand in opposition. The idea that true Christians made America great has no basis in the Scripture or in church history.

A religion of rebellion and violence

Thomas Jefferson expressed the rebellious nature of American civil religion this way: "Resistance to tyrants is obedience to God." Jefferson was not referring only to the British monarch. Americans in the 1700s came to see tyranny—both political and religious—as the great sin of the times. This was one reason why churches such as the Baptists and Methodists became the largest denominations in America in the 1800s. They had a congregational organization, without an ultimate authority at the top as in the Anglican and Catholic churches, and this appealed to the anti-tyranny Americans.

In this aspect, civil religion is much different from true Christianity. The early believers had nothing but tyrants as their rulers, yet the apostles taught honor and submission to their governments.

Civil religion in almost every nation supports violence. In the quotation at the beginning of this chapter, a Maryland official made one of the simple deductions that violent civil religion tends to make. If the Mennonites would not fight the Germans, then they were aiding and abetting child murderers. They were to blame if plundering and arson flourished and if all the Ten Commandments were broken. Furthermore, they were rejecting the very faith that had inspired them ever since the beginning of their church.

Nonresistant people faced similar accusations in every American war. Before World War I, many Protestant denominations supported efforts to eliminate war; yet when the United States actually went to war, these discussions almost invariably ceased. The difference between Protestant and Anabaptist viewpoints is illustrated by a discussion on September 28, 1917, between Mennonite Isaac Baer and his commander, Colonel Sweeney.

"Do you realize," Colonel Sweeney asked, "that this war is being fought in defense of Christianity as well as democracy?" In the minds of many religious people, Christianity and democracy are practically the same thing—a common error of civil religion.

"Christianity does not call for physical weapons to defend it," Baer replied. "'For the weapons of our warfare are not carnal.'"

We are grateful that most countries will go to considerable lengths to make peace and avoid war. But if war seems necessary, most religious people (regretfully or otherwise) will go to war. To civil religion, the end always justifies the means. "Thank God," a Maryland newspaper article proclaimed in March 1918, "the American people have at last begun to hate the [Germans]." *Answer to War*, by Millard Lind, reports a typical statement made in World War I, from a religious magazine of that era.

Civil religion in almost every nation supports violence.

> As Christians, of course, we say Christ approves [of the war]. But would he fight and kill? . . . There is not an opportunity to deal death to the enemy that he would shirk from or delay in seizing! He would take bayonet and grenade and bomb and rifle and do the work of deadliness against that which is the most deadly enemy

of his Father's kingdom in a thousand years. . . . That is the inexorable truth about Jesus Christ and this war; and we rejoice to say it.

On the other side of the conflict, the German soldiers marched to the conflict with "Gott mit uns" (God with us) engraved on their belt buckles.

"God almighty in his infinite wisdom," proclaimed Colorado Senator Edwin Johnson after World War II, ". . . dropped the atomic bomb in our lap. . . . [W]ith vision and guts and plenty of atomic bombs, . . . [we] can compel mankind to adopt a policy of lasting peace . . . or be burned to a crisp."[5]

The violence of civil religion—even in the culture that considers itself the most Christian on earth—will stop at nothing to accomplish its ends. Blasphemy and lies are justified in the cause of self-preservation; the most blatant disobedience to Jesus Christ is tolerated and even exalted if it serves the carnal purposes of man. One of the most telling illustrations of this is the tombstone in Mississippi that reads, "Here lies J. H. S. In his lifetime, he killed 99 Indians, and lived in the blessed hope of making it 100, until he fell asleep in the arms of Jesus."[6]

It is obvious that there is no significant difference between major religions such as Islam and Christendom on this point. Whoever is not liked, or is not the same as us, or gets in our way, may be treated in whatever fashion society deems good.

In contrast, the true Christian will obey God's Word no matter what the cost. It will make him unpopular with civil

---

5. William H. Chafe, *The Unfinished Journey: America Since World War II*, 4th ed. (New York, Ny.: Oxford University Press, 1999), p. 59.

6. Dallas Lee, ed., *The Substance of Faith and Other Cotton Patch Sermons by Clarence Jordan* (New York, Ny.: Association, 1972), p. 71.

religion; it may even cost him his life at the hands of religious people with different scruples than he holds. But he will not join the religion of rebellion and violence that culture supports.

A religion of manifest destiny

The expression *manifest destiny* first appeared in 1845 during the campaign for the United States to take possession of all territory to the southern border of Alaska (which belonged to Russia). The concept of manifest destiny was nurtured by the feeling that Americans were superior to the British, French, Mexicans, and Native Americans, and by the fact that immigrants to America needed more room. For these reasons, most Americans thought the United States was clearly (manifestly) destined by God to expand to the Pacific Ocean.

Manifest destiny per se began in 1845, but the spirit of manifest destiny has been a feature of civil religion in almost every nation since nations existed. It is the belief that divine powers are assisting men in doing whatever is necessary to take control of the land, the people, or the resources they desire. In manifest destiny, religion stamps its blessing upon the exploits of carnal people. Manifest destiny defines man's dreams as God's will.

Manifest destiny defines man's dreams as God's will.

Ancient Babylon, so its priests said in its heyday, sat on top of the world because Marduk, god of gods, had decreed it so. Whatever Babylon undertook could not fail or be altered; she was destined to succeed. The king's word was immutable; the army's exploits were Marduk's will. The mere planning of a military offensive started the whole affair on its way to inevitable fulfillment. In times ancient and modern, civil religion has used the idea of manifest destiny to marshal public opinion and power to political causes.

Spain's general treasurer Sanchez claimed divine approval for Columbus' voyage to "discover and acquire certain islands and mainlands of the ocean sea." This expedition, Sanchez told Queen Isabella, "could prove of so great service to God and the exaltation of his Church" that to deny Columbus' request would be a grave reproach against God. Urged on by the alleged approval of divinity, the queen supported the voyage in God's Name for the glory and wealth of His blessed nation, Spain. Ten weeks later, a praying, Bible-reading Columbus landed on one of the Bahama islands and named it San Salvador (Holy Saviour).

Never mind that in the Name of this defenseless Jesus, the Spaniards had driven swords into thousands of Muslims in the eight hundred years before 1492. Never mind that they had persecuted and killed the Jews with abandon, and that in 1492 they also exiled over 100,000 Jews from their homes in Spain. Never mind that the Spanish Inquisition had ruled the country in holy terror, making it one of the purest Catholic enclaves in the world. The first cross planted in the New World was stained not with the blood of Christ but with the blood of men. Not only did the Spaniards overlook those and many other anti-Christian elements of their society; they actually claimed that those accomplishments were signs of God's approval. In Columbus' words,

> God made me the messenger of the new heaven and the new earth of which he spoke in the Apocalypse of St. John . . . and he

showed me the spot where to find it. . . . [This success is due] to the holy Christian faith, and to the piety and religion of our Sovereigns. . . . Thanks to our Lord and Savior Jesus Christ, who has granted us so great a victory and such prosperity. Let processions be made and sacred feasts be held, and the temples be adorned with festive boughs. Let Christ rejoice on earth, as he rejoices in heaven in the prospect of the salvation of the souls of so many nations hitherto lost.

But other nations cried foul. Surely God had not consigned the whole New World to Spain, their archrival. Portugal appealed to the pope, and he drew the Line of Demarcation to divide the unknown territories, giving the lion's share to Spain. Catholic France disregarded the pope's intervention and claimed possession of North America from north to south as far west as the Mississippi River, saying that God had called *them* to convert the miserable savages to the true faith.

England came late to the land rush, but under the same divine banner. In the 1580s, Sir Humphrey Gilbert urged Queen Elizabeth to put her trust in God and seize the opportunities for expanding England's power. "The safety of States, Monarchies, and Commonwealths," Sir Humphrey contended, "rests chiefly in making their enemies weak and poor, and themselves strong and rich." He proposed that a wise Christian policy would be to fight Spanish sea power in any way and any place.

Francis Drake believed in this theology with all his heart. He became England's most famous "sea dog" and mounted many daring, successful attacks on Spain's ships and New World settlements. He was one of the most feared pirates of his time. He considered himself a key figure in God's fight against Catholicism. He held worship services on his ships and provided Bibles, prayer books, and Foxe's *Book of Martyrs* for his sailors and soldiers. If any of them lacked courage, the awful stories about Catholic persecution of Protestants would revive a righteous wrath against Spain.

The doctrine of manifest destiny paved the way for the early North American settlers to displace the Indians (and opposing Europeans) and claim what they wanted in the new land. When people in England questioned the Puritans' right to simply take land, John Winthrop even found manifest destiny in the Bible. If Abraham was called to go out and take possession of other people's lands, the Puritans could do the same.

The Indians were viewed as mere savages who lived on the land without truly owning it. It was obvious that this land was destined to have property titles, permanent houses, farms, fences, and cattle. It was equally clear that by the Puritans' safe passage to America, God had called them to subdue any opposition to accomplishing this task, and He had sanctioned any violence necessary to achieve His goals. Manifest destiny denied the rights of others in order to establish the same rights for the newcomers. "Invoking the name of God," wrote John L. Ruth, ". . . for what is demanded at the mouth of a cannon has its own hypocrisies."[7]

Manifest destiny motivated both the Americans and the British in the Revolution. After the Revolutionary victory, this doctrine became practically an article of faith for millions of Americans. They believed that God had created a new man in America—northern European in heritage, Protestant in religion, democratic in government, and white in complexion—

---

7. John L. Ruth, *'Twas Seeding Time*, p. 150.

and this new man was destined to rule the continent from sea to sea, if not the world from pole to pole.

But not everyone approved the way this new man set out to accomplish his "God-given" task. After the Americans won the Mexican War in 1848, black abolitionist Frederick Douglass said,

> The joyful news is told in every quarter with enthusiastic delight. We are such an exception to the great mass of our fellow

Manifest destiny involved many things—civilizing the West, demanding control of much of Mexico's territory and the Oregon territory, and driving Native Americans off the land. In the minds of many Americans, God was leading them in triumph from sea to sea, as in this picture of an angel stringing a telegraph wire behind fleeing Indians.

countrymen in respect to everything else, and have been so accustomed to hear them rejoice over the most barbarous outrages committed upon an unoffending people, that we find it difficult to unite with them in their general exultation at this time. . . .

In our judgment, those who have all along been loudly in favor of a vigorous prosecution of the war, and heralding its bloody triumphs . . . have no love of peace. . . . Had they not succeeded in robbing Mexico of the most important and most valuable part of her territory, many of those now loudest in their professions of favor for peace would be loudest and wildest for war—war to the knife.

Our soul is sick of such hypocrisy. . . . We are not the people to rejoice; we ought rather . . . hang our heads in shame, and, in the spirit of profound humility, crave pardon for our crimes at the hands of a God whose mercy endureth forever.

Manifest destiny was inflated by the fact that America succeeded. In 150 years, a wilderness yielded rich farms, shabby villages became bustling cities, and an uncertain patchwork of colonial governments formed a unified republic. Based on these successes, many Americans believed that they could do anything. They considered themselves right; they believed that God had rewarded them with wealth and power; and thought that they were on the path to an even brighter destiny. But such thoughts did not first appear in this country; they are not unique to America. Horace, Cicero, and many another Roman thought of their empire in the same terms. They too built their manifest destiny on wrong theology—which in their case was idol worship.

In many cases, manifest destiny in America was even explained as an external force that simply moved the country like a pawn, thus absolving the people of any wrongs committed in the pursuit of their destiny. In Woodrow Wilson's words in 1919, America has "now been found to be compact of the spiritual forces that must free men of every nation of every unworthy bondage.... The stage is set, the destiny is disclosed. It has come about by no plan of our conceiving, but by the hand of God who led us into this way. We cannot turn back. We can only go forward . . . to follow the vision. . . . America shall in truth show the way."

The doctrine of manifest destiny stands in direct opposition to the Gospel message. From before the time of the Revolution, most Americans have not been able to accept the bad news about man that precedes the good news of the Gospel. Man's sinful nature, which can be redeemed only by repentance and faith in Christ, has been all but disregarded in American culture—along with the power of Satan and the reality of judgment and hell. How can Americans be under God's judgment when He has manifestly helped them to succeed in so many ways?

Crocuses in the winter of a fallen world

According to the book *Christ the Meaning of History*, a scene "such as an ambulance stopping all traffic because *one* wounded man must be transported" is a result of Christ's work on earth. But we must understand that such features of society are at best only token effects of God's work on earth; they do not indicate that any earthly culture has become the kingdom of God. "They are the crocuses," the author wrote, "in the winter of a fallen world."[8]

---

8. Hendrikus Berkhof (Richmond, Va.: John Knox, 1966), pp. 88, 181.

For true Christians seeking to be an influence for Christ in a fallen world, it is very important to understand that civil religion and true religion never have been and never will be the same. If we should spend our whole lives in trying to change or better civil religion, as many sincere people do, we would die exhausted in an impossible task. It is a hopeless cause to transform a nation's civil religion into true religion. How true is the testimony of a Muslim: "In the Koran, I can find nothing to teach us how to be a minority religion, while in the New Testament I can find nothing to teach Christians how to be a majority religion." Instead, the true Christian concentrates on influencing people for Christ, one neighbor at a time.

> **The best civil religion can never remedy or stop the relentless slide of morals in society.**

The best civil religion can never remedy or stop the relentless slide of morals in society. Even the loftiest moral precepts of civil religion inevitably have within them the seeds of moral decay. Civil religion avoids Christ's claims and recognizes no need of Him. In an article entitled "Sound Literature," N. Harvey Witmer wrote:

> Some years ago there was an article in a popular news magazine entitled "Civil Religion." Among other things, it stated that such things as going to church, honesty, and heaven are desirable, not because of what God says, but because they fit into the American way of life. If that were true, literature would be sound if it harmonized with historical facts or the ideas and ideals

of the average American mind. . . . Truly we need a better guide than that.[9]

Much can be said for the good that civil religion does. When people are respected, personal property is safeguarded, laws promote basic morality, and God's creation is protected—that is a great blessing to mankind. True Christians are grateful for these effects in society.

But none of those things indicate that there are a great many true Christians in the culture or that God is basically pleased with the people. Christ's principles have affected culture, but Christ specifically taught that He did not come to redeem culture. Instead, He came to save those who are willing to be outcasts from mainstream culture and even to be killed by that culture.

As the salt of the earth, true Christians are to be a preserving influence in a naturally decaying culture. Our work will not result in transforming culture, but in slowing the rate of decay and helping to save the few who are willing to make a commitment beyond the shallow, carnal ideals of civil religion.

---

9. Rod and Staff Newsletter, July 2010.

The kingdom of Christ is not of this world.
For this reason no true Christian
>> may administer cities and protect countries. . . .
That is what many false [Christians]
>> have undertaken to do in our time,
>> among them the Papists and Evangelicals. . . .
It is difficult for a Christian to be a worldly ruler. . . .
How long would his conscience
>> allow him to be a magistrate,
>> assuming he did not want to forsake the Lord Jesus Christ
>>>> and Christian patience, . . .
or at least that he did not want to sustain
some injury to his soul or Christianity?

>>>> —*Pilgram Marpeck (d. 1556), Swiss Anabaptist minister*

13

A Christian View of Civil Government

The Christian's relationship to civil government has been one of the most lively topics ever since the days of the early church. Christ commanded His followers to obey both God and Caesar in ways appropriate to each; the apostle Paul called for subjection to the tyranny of Nero; and the apostle Peter told his brethren to fear God and honor the king.[1] But Christians have debated just how to apply these teachings in different times and circumstances.

Even in the time of the early church fathers, right after the era of the apostles, many differing opinions arose on how to relate to government. From what those church fathers wrote about the struggles and varying opinions of their time, it is

---

1. Matthew 22:21; Luke 20:25; Romans 13:1; 1 Peter 2:17

evident that these problems are not unique to the present age. The two-thousand-year-old true church has outlasted every form of government, and in doing so she has experienced almost every imaginable blessing, question, and pitfall that the relationship between the two could produce.

This chapter discusses the New Testament view of government and some of the practical implications of that view, especially in North America.

Christ's view of civil government

Before and during New Testament times, the Jews constantly hoped to shake off the yoke of Gentile rule and to regain their sovereignty. Groups such as the Maccabees, the Zealots, and the Pharisees all wanted to restore their own civil government. The Jews' political-religious ambitions kept the country in ferment and the Romans on edge for generations. Finally in A.D. 70, the Romans under Titus destroyed much of Jerusalem and killed, enslaved, or exiled most Jews living in the area. Thus the aspirations for Jewish sovereignty largely came to an end.

So when Christ walked on earth, the main focus of several generations had centered upon the burning question of how to drive out the Romans and establish a righteous government for Israel. That is the context of Christ's simple statements about civil government.

When Satan offered Jesus all the glory of the kingdoms of this world, Jesus rejected the offer. He did not join the Sadducees in favoring the Romans, or the vast majority of His fellow Jews in hating the Romans. He wanted nothing to do with the union of church and state that characterized the

13 • A Christian View of Civil Government

Old Testament. He had no political agenda and could not be sidetracked into adopting one.

Jesus acknowledged that civil government has a place to fill in the sinful world, but He did not say that any government or state was righteous or in any sense equal to the kingdom of God.

One of the strongest challenges put to Jesus was to aid the Zealots. What teacher of righteousness would not support the cause of a godly state? What good Jewish leader did not want to see his people restored to their status as God's special nation, directly ruled by God? Jesus' teaching and the crowds He drew made Him a magnet for the Zealots, and they urgently wanted Him to use His natural advantages for their cause. His disciple Simon Zelotes had been a former Zealot, and some Bible scholars believe that likely more of His disciples had such connections as well, including Peter, Judas Iscariot, and possibly James and John, the sons of Zebedee.

Jesus acknowledged that civil government has a place to fill in the sinful world.

With that in mind, consider Jesus' teachings. The Beatitudes begin with blessings on the poor in spirit, the mourners, the meek, the merciful, and the persecuted. All these characteristics were the opposite of what the Zealots displayed in their drive to bring in an earthly kingdom of God. Jesus spoke of being a light to the world, not a sword-swinging deliverer. He denounced the Pharisees, those supposed paragons of virtue, as flagrant sinners. He told His followers not to nourish grudges but to make peace quickly with their adversaries; not to resist evil, but to give in to unjust demands. They were to go beyond the selfish publican love that greeted friends and despised others.

The emphases of Matthew 5 and 6 lead up to the crowning statement, "Seek ye first the kingdom of God" (6:33). What goes before is an explanation of God's kingdom to a people who were almost completely absorbed in trying to establish a righteous state, and it is just as applicable today to those who are trying to bring in morality or righteousness by means of civil government.

In Jesus' time as today, people taken up with that earthly goal miss the true meaning of His words. After several years of explaining what the kingdom of God really is, after fleeing when people tried to force Him to be king, even after He died and rose again, Jesus was asked by the eager disciples, "Lord, wilt thou at this time restore again the kingdom to Israel?"[2] True to Jewish form, all they could think of was an earthly, political kingdom.

How it must have grieved Jesus to hear this familiar refrain! Once more, He told His disciples that His kingdom is a kingdom of spiritual power from the Holy Ghost. And after Jesus ascended into heaven and the disciples had spent days in prayer, culminating in the coming of the Holy Ghost, they finally understood what He meant.

Christ still grieves today when people try to accomplish by law and "bringing in the kingdom" what can be accomplished only through repentance and the Holy Spirit. He is grieved when His own disciples think that God has lost control because a bad man is ruling, or they lose their joy because of an election.

---

2. Acts 1:6

13 • A Christian View of Civil Government

Jesus Christ is not on the side of the modern Zealots who try to save nations by putting upright men in office, passing good laws, or reforming external morals. He accepted the wicked Roman state as having a brief duty; He neither slandered it nor approved its awfully wicked condition. He was detached from it, and the church He was building had no particular relationship to it except to call people from it to a higher service. As the talk of creating a righteous government swirled around Him, as well-meaning people gave their lifeblood for that very cause, Jesus emphatically taught that those efforts would come to nothing.

In opposition to the Zealot desire to gain tiny Palestine for God, Jesus said that a man could win the whole world without gaining a thing. The only thing that would make any difference in the end was whether the man gained his own soul. When Jesus learned of an apparently outrageous act of Pilate's—mingling the blood of some Galilaeans with their sacrifices—He refused to comment on the political meaning of such a maneuver. Instead, he brought the focus right back to the salvation of the people gathered around Him. "I tell you... except ye repent, ye shall all likewise perish."[3]

Peter had discovered the kingdom of God at long last when he preached in Acts 2:40, "Save yourselves *from* this untoward generation"—*not* "Save this untoward generation."

Legitimacy of civil government

Civil government is legitimate by virtue of its existence. This fact is established by Christ's acknowledgment that certain things belong to Caesar, by Paul's statement that the

---
3. Luke 13:1-3

powers that be are ordained of God, and by Peter's command to honor the king. The Christian must accept the state as God's earthly agent over him; there is no other proposition in the Bible.

Christ and all the New Testament writers lived under exceedingly corrupt governments. Yet none of them taught that a government is illegitimate when it fails to support Christian principles, or even when it directly opposes them. As noted in chapter 4, Romans 13:1-7 does not teach that a government which imprisons Christians is a bad government and is therefore illegitimate in God's sight. Instead, the apostles taught obedience and respect to all governments.

Like the apostles, the early Christians saw no contradiction between the fact that their civil authorities were legitimate and that they persecuted God's people.

> Let the emperor fight heaven; let him lead it prisoner in his triumph; let him police heaven; let him tax heaven. He cannot. He is great just because he is less than heaven. The emperor gets his scepter where he got his humanity, his power where he got the breath of life. . . . Ceaselessly we pray for our emperors, for long life, for a peaceful empire, for a secure dynasty, for a tranquil world, for whatever, as man or Caesar, the emperor would wish.
>
> —*Tertullian (160-230),* Apology

> One who has faith in God ought not to dissemble or fear the powerful, especially those who use power for evil. . . . The words of the apostle—to obey the authorities that are over us (Rom. 13:1)—enjoin us not to obey human commands against our belief and God's law but to avoid doing evil while respecting authority in order to escape punishment as lawbreakers. For this reason it is

13 • A Christian View of Civil Government

said: "The ruler is God's servant" (Rom. 13:4) against those who do evil.

—*Hippolytus of Rome (d.236)*, Commentary on the Book of Daniel

"There is no authority," Paul says, "except from God" (Rom. 13:1). Someone may object: Indeed? And what of authority that persecutes the servants of God, fights the Faith, overturns religion: Does this power come from God?

Let us answer this objection briefly. No one is unaware that sight, hearing, and feeling are given by God. Though we receive these things from God, it remains in our power to use sight for good or bad. . . . In the same way, all authority has been given us by God "for the punishment of criminals and the recognition of the upright" (1 Pet. 2:14), as the Apostle says. . . . And there will be a just sentence of God on those who use the authority received from God unjustly. . . .

I find these words of Paul deeply moving: he calls earthly authority and human judgment the servant of God not once but repeats it two or three times. . . . The subject is a wide one, embracing such rulers as reign cruelly and tyrannically and such as make the kingly office the means of indulging in luxury and sinful pleasures.

—*Origen (185-253)*, Commentary on the Letter to the Romans and Against Celsus

Remember that the government in power over the apostles and early church fathers demanded things such as emperor worship. These rulers were cruel, tyrannical, and indulgent. Origen did not resist or condemn the state on that basis, but left it to God and the future: "There will be a just sentence of God on those." Sentence against the rulers was not his to pronounce, nor is it ours.

Christ, the apostles, and the early church fathers agree that the state is legitimate. It is an institution divinely ordained and willed by God in the sense that God makes use of it and ultimately controls it.

> ## "The Powers That Be [Good] Are Ordained of God"
>
> That is what men like Zwingli, Luther, and Calvin thought when they read Romans 13:1. These Reformation leaders used the state to force changes in the church. In order to get what they wanted, they pushed the Catholics aside or forced them to become Protestants. They also sent armies to the battlefront to settle disputes between Protestant and Catholic states, and they executed or exiled Anabaptists and others who would not participate in the prescribed worship. The Protestants could do these things because they believed that revolution against "heretical" government was their God-given right.
>
> The American patriots in Revolution times viewed Romans 13:1 in the same way, although their "right of revolution" theories were worded a little differently. Their concern was not whether the king of England was a heretic, but whether he gave them the freedoms they wanted. Their interpretation of Romans 13:1 went like this: "The powers that secure the personal property, wealth, and happiness of society are ordained of God." The patriots felt that God was calling them to break free from any king who did not support these ideals.
>
> The American Anabaptists and other nonresistant groups could not see any right of revolution in the Scriptures. They did not look to the state as the provider of happiness for mankind. They expected far less from their government than did the Reformation Protestants or the American patriots. They understood that the existence of any civil government showed that God had established it, whether it was good or not.

When we say that civil government is legitimate, we must remember what *legitimate* does not mean. It does not indicate that God is necessarily approving of what a government is

13 • A Christian View of Civil Government

doing, but simply that He is permitting it to rule a given part of the world at a given time.

The New Testament does not call any government wise. Paul wrote in 1 Corinthians 2 that the wisdom of princes will do foolish things (verse 8) and will come to nothing in the end (verse 6).

The New Testament does not call any government righteous. It does not give any basis on which a government may be considered godly. The state does not need to be Christian; in fact, it cannot be Christian.

Christians do not need to evaluate a government before they can live peaceably under it. They thank God for it, but they do not justify its sins; they know that God will judge all evil. They know that all governments will suffer the same basic fate in the end, though they recognize that God can recompense rulers "here and in eternity, for all the benefits, liberties, and favors which we enjoy under their laudable administration."[4] Christians simply call individuals—including government officials—out of the darkness of this world and into the light of the Gospel. They teach the truth and let it penetrate society in godly ways, without feeling any responsibility to reform the government.

Servants of wrath

The Anabaptists said that the government did things "outside the perfection of Christ," while the church was "inside

---
4. Dortrecht Confession of Faith, Article 13.

the perfection of Christ." A description by Peter Riedemann explains this Biblical view, in which God created two orders in this world—one as the arm of His wrath, and the other as the arm of His mercy.

> Thus no Christian is a ruler and no ruler is a Christian, for the child of blessing cannot be the servant of wrath. . . .
>
> The power of the sword has passed to the heathen, that they may therewith punish their evildoers. But that is no concern of ours; as Paul says, "What have I to do to judge them that are without?" Thus no Christian can rule over the world. . . .
>
> If rulers divest themselves of their glory as Christ did, and humble themselves and allow Christ, only, to use them, then the way to life would be as open to them as to others. But when Christ begins to work in men, he does nothing except what he himself did—and he fled when men sought to make him a king.

God uses the servants of wrath to maintain order on earth. Within this earthly order there is justice and injustice, right and wrong, although these concepts are never fully understood by fallen men. To maintain order, the servants of wrath use a broad array of penalties ranging from restriction of privileges to fines, imprisonment, and even death. How they punish offenders is entirely their decision.

It is out of order for a true Christian to advise the government on proper punishments for offenders. Civil government was not instituted as a channel for Christians to express their opinions and exercise their influence on earth. The Christian's wisdom is given by the Holy Spirit for edifying the church, not for administrating the halls of civil power. No one has explained this better than Pilgram Marpeck, a Swiss Anabaptist minister in the 1500s.

13 • A Christian View of Civil Government

But Saint Paul distinguishes this wisdom of the worldly magistrates from the wisdom of Christ when he says: It is not the wisdom of the rulers of this world (1 Corinthians 2:6). It is thus clear that worldly rulers have a special wisdom for their service. For Christian wisdom is not suited to their office nor will it serve them since it brings about only grace, mercy, love for the enemy, spiritual supernatural things, cross, tribulation, patience and faith in Christ without coercion . . . only through the Word of God. The wisdom of the office of the worldly rulers is designed to work through the external sword in vindictiveness, mercilessness . . . and similar things. It is therefore without foundation to say that no one can exercise worldly government better than a Christian. That would imply that he needed the wisdom of Christ for it or that Christ's wisdom is his wisdom of office. Christ's wisdom is merciful and will not serve him in his office because he is not merciful in his office but rather an avenger.

The civil government is a servant of wrath in that it makes those suffer who do wrong, but it is also a servant of wrath in that the government itself is under the wrath of God. Every type of civil government commits evils that call for God's judgment. As portrayed in Ezekiel 31, all nations are trees in God's garden, and they will all see each other in the eternal pit.

Then-Senator Barack Obama was right when he said in 2006 that the Sermon on the Mount is "so radical that it's doubtful that our own Defense Department would survive its application." Christ did not preach that sermon for the state.

When people try to produce a righteous government through religious efforts, what they have in the end is a sinful church. A secular government can serve God's purposes, but a secular church is heresy.

A separate kingdom

Many religious people feel that a Christian in civil government operates on different levels. In the church and in his home neighborhood, he is called to love his neighbor as himself, turn the other cheek, and give soft answers. In civil office he is called to sentence wrongdoers, shoot down enemies, and flip the switch of the electric chair.

In this view, both kingdoms operate in one man, and a man's spiritual beliefs are completely separated from his physical actions. Most Protestants inherited this view from Luther, Zwingli, and Calvin; and even some formerly nonresistant groups have moved into the Protestant camp. Explaining the mainstream Mennonite view, Paul Schrag wrote,

> We've decided that the division between the church and the world is not an unbridgeable chasm. We have become politically engaged, believing that Christians actually live in both kingdoms. Then we try to sort out the uncertainties and gray areas that come from having a foot in each.[5]

The New Testament removes the gray areas. It clearly shows that two kingdoms cannot operate in the same person. Here are a few of the many verses that teach this principle.

> Ye have heard that it hath been said, An eye for an eye, and a tooth for a tooth: but I say unto you, That ye resist not evil: but whosoever shall smite thee on thy right cheek, turn to him the other also. And if any man will sue thee at the law, and take away

---

5. *Mennonite Weekly Review*, May 11, 2009, p. 4.

13 • A Christian View of Civil Government

thy coat, let him have thy cloak also. . . . Ye have heard that it hath been said, Thou shalt love thy neighbour, and hate thine enemy. But I say unto you, Love your enemies, bless them that curse you, do good to them that hate you, and pray for them which despitefully use you, and persecute you; that ye may be the children of your Father which is in heaven (Matthew 5:38-40, 43-45).

I have given them thy word; and the world hath hated them, because they are not of the world, even as I am not of the world. I pray not that thou shouldest take them out of the world, but that thou shouldest keep them from the evil. (John 17:14, 15)

Jesus answered, My kingdom is not of this world: if my kingdom were of this world, then would my servants fight, that I should not be delivered to the Jews: but now is my kingdom not from hence (John 18:36).

Be ye not unequally yoked together with unbelievers: for what fellowship hath righteousness with unrighteousness? and what communion hath light with darkness? and what concord hath Christ with Belial? or what part hath he that believeth with an infidel? and what agreement hath the temple of God with idols? For ye are the temple of the living God; as God hath said, I will dwell in them, and walk in them; and I will be their God, and they shall be my people. Wherefore come out from among them, and be ye separate, saith the Lord, and touch not the unclean thing; and I will receive you, and will be a Father unto you, and ye shall be my sons and daughters, saith the Lord Almighty (2 Corinthians 6:14-18).

Love not the world, neither the things that are in the world. If any man love the world, the love of the Father is not in him. For all that is in the world, the lust of the flesh, and the lust of the eyes, and the pride of life, is not of the Father, but is of the world. And the world passeth away, and the lust thereof: but he that doeth the will of God abideth forever (1 John 2:15-17).

There is no position in the legislative, executive, or judicial branches of civil government that can be filled without resisting evil or loving and having fellowship with the world. It is not for us to say that no ruler is a Christian; we leave that with God to judge. But according to the Scriptures, we can certainly say that no Christian can long continue serving as a government official if he or she is growing in Bible understanding. It will not be long until the Holy Spirit leads a sincere Christian to the beliefs that render him or her unable to perform the duties of these earthly positions. A Christian devoted to obeying the Bible cannot survive indefinitely in two roles that are as opposite as day and night.

Government's "proper" role

From Romans 13 and other Scriptures, we can infer that the "proper" role of civil government is to punish evil and encourage good behavior. The state should serve justice without taking over responsibilities that belong to the church or the family. Stephen Russell put it like this: "Ideally, the state will interfere in the life of the individual only to the degree necessary to maintain this state of equity."[6] Certainly such an approach is the most comfortable for true Christians.

But we know that the entire New Testament was written under "improper" governments, and that true Christians in almost all times and places since Christ have lived with a great

---

6. *Overcoming Evil God's Way* (Guys Mills, Pa.: Faith Builders Resource Group, 2008), p. 83.

deal of government interference that had nothing to do with equity. Every concept or command given in the New Testament was given in the context of governments involved in the worship of man, the killing of Christians, and similar evils. The Bible does not anticipate that Christians will typically deal with governments that stay in their "proper" role. There is also no Biblical precedent for Christians to pressure the government to remain within a "proper" role as defined by the church.

As Christians, we might think that we understand the government's "proper" role, but in the real world many of our political ideas soon look foolish. To illustrate, the way that social services sometimes reaches into family matters can look very sinister. Christians are apprehensive that the government may outlaw certain Scriptural methods of discipline for children. Wouldn't a "proper" government stay out of home issues? That is one way to look at social services.

> As Christians, we might think that we understand the government's "proper" role, but in the real world many of our political ideas soon look foolish.

Another way is this: Who should deal with the man who beats his children in a drunken rage? What would you recommend for the family whose shiftless father does not hold a job? If the offender is jailed, who should feed his children? Should the children perhaps be taken from the irresponsible parents and placed in homes where they can learn better habits? And if they should, who is responsible to see that it happens?

Do you see where this is leading? Government authorities deal with many hard situations through no fault of their own, and God leaves it for them to decide how to handle such things. Even the "righteous" Puritan government in early America faced these things, strict as its laws were. The virtues of the government did not remove the sinful tendencies of the citizens. It is not true that the government creates all of the problems it faces.

A Christian who is faithful to the Bible can offer no social solutions outside of Jesus Christ. And since Jesus Christ cannot be legislated, He cannot become part of a government solution to any problem. The Bible gives Christians specific principles for dealing with social needs that they meet personally, but it gives no patterns for dealing with those problems from the standpoint of civil government.

To solve social problems, civil leaders may devise solutions such as passing laws against beating, which also outlaw spanking by default. True Christians know that the real problem behind child abuse is a lack of love and timely Biblical discipline; but the non-Christian state does not always perceive that. It is impossible to govern fallen man without also tramping on some Christian beliefs and practices. As David L. Martin noted in an article titled "The Darker Side of the Coin":

> Public officials have seen things that would sicken your stomach, and have sickened theirs. The outrage they feel over the outrages they have seen has led them to stiffen anti-abuse laws and to interfere more promptly and boldly where abuse is suspected. . . .
>
> The fact that the legal system sometimes threatens us is the indirect work of ungodly men, child abusers indeed, who have brought the wrath of the government down on their own heads. Had they not tempted the higher powers, the higher powers would probably never have been tempted. But now "the minister of

13 • A Christian View of Civil Government

God to thee for good" (Romans 13:4) is going from growl to roar and will not easily be placated. This is to our own discomfort and danger.[7]

Ideally, civil government would rule a moral, peaceable population. Ideally, it would not feel pressured to make weapons of mass destruction. Ideally, it would not need to make laws about vandalism, food safety, and sewage running across the highway. But government never existed in an ideal world. Christians must not expect that the theoretically proper sphere of government will ever be attained and maintained in any nation. Nor should we say that if civil leaders do not stick to their "proper" role, God will punish them.

Neither does the Christian condemn or interfere with government social programs. Rather, by his words and actions he will provide a good example for the town drunks, the irate parents, and the neglected children in his community. He is more likely to take a Thanksgiving dinner to a needy family than to write a complaining letter to the local newspaper.

The civil government is an institution that shifts with the times and theories of mankind. It tries to respond to the people's needs with the only tools it has—theories, power, and money.

No civil government has ever known the true meaning of love, peace, justice, truth, or deliverance. No government can be expected to look at society through Bible lenses or to always have a high regard for the truly Christian people within it.

Pray, pay, respect, and obey

The Christian obeys his government unless its commands are contrary to God's Word; he pays taxes; and he respects the

---

7. *The Christian School Builder*, August 2010, p. 3.

authorities regardless of their service or demeanor. The Christian prays both that his rulers may find salvation and that they will rule well.

In most free countries around the world, where citizens ought to feel the most thankful, the normal fare is habitual complaints about the government. Political jokes and wisecracks abound, and government bashing seems to be a national pastime. In almost any audience, Americans chuckle over one-liners like, "The District of Columbia is sixty-eight square miles surrounded by reality," and others much worse.

Appreciation for civil authorities is not based on how they do their job but on how God tells us to relate to them.

Saying that we must appreciate our government does not mean that everything they do is above criticism. But again we come back to a simple fact: Appreciation for civil authorities is not based on how they do their job but on how God tells us to relate to them. Whether we are under a good government, a bumbling government, or an outrageously wicked government, the following verses apply.

> Curse not the king, no not in thy thought; and curse not the rich in thy bedchamber: for a bird of the air shall carry the voice, and that which hath wings shall tell the matter (Ecclesiastes 10:20).

> Wherefore ye must needs be subject, not only for wrath, but also for conscience sake.... Render therefore to all their dues:... fear to whom fear; honour to whom honour (Romans 13:5, 7).

13 • A Christian View of Civil Government

> Honour all men. Love the brotherhood. Fear God. Honour the king (1 Peter 2:17).

> The Lord knoweth how . . . to reserve the unjust unto the day of judgment to be punished: but chiefly them that walk after the flesh in the lust of uncleanness, and despise government. Presumptuous are they, selfwilled, they are not afraid to speak evil of dignities (2 Peter 2:9, 10).

Christians also respect government because they realize that without government, the world would be far worse off than it is today. Government in free countries is not such a durable structure as many make it out to be. It is actually very fragile because it depends on respect for government and law. People who disrespect and hate the government do not realize that God is protecting them from terrible chaos by that very government, imperfect though it is.

Citizens or subjects?

We take citizenship for granted today, but it was not always easy to obtain. In Bible times and through much of the Middle Ages, citizenship was a high honor bestowed on people who had the right ancestry, the right merits, or enough money to purchase citizenship. Most people were simply subjects, without rights or privileges such as being able to own land, travel freely, and engage in the occupation of their choice.

We are thankful for our rights as citizens in free countries such as America, but we need to remember that this citizenship brings certain obligations. For example, every citizen is normally expected to render jury duty and to fight for his country. People generally believe that you do not deserve the rights of citizenship if you are unwilling to do these things. (Citizens of some free countries are fined if they fail to vote.) In America, people with religious objections have been excused from these duties, but this is more of an exception than the norm in the world.

It is better for Christians to view themselves as subjects than as full citizens. If we live in the United States, we are not Americans who happen to be Christians; we are Christians who happen to be Americans.

Adolf Hitler was right when he said, "One is either a good German or a good Christian. It is impossible to be both at the same time." The same could be said for any country in any time period.

A true Christian tries to be an asset to his country in every way that the Bible teaches. But he focuses on a Christian identity, not a national one. His world-view should be more like that of a Christian brother in India than like that of his unconverted next-door neighbor. As Christians we should freely use expressions like "what we believe," "the faith delivered to us," and "our goals" when speaking of ourselves and fellow believers. But we need to be very careful when using *we, us,* and *our* with reference to the country in which we live. It seems reasonable to speak of *our* president and *our* government, especially in the country where we are citizens. But how can a Christian refer to *our* elections, *our* policies, *our* military forces, *our* enemies, or the wars *we* have won?

Civil government was not instituted to keep true Christians from suffering. Political leaders consider allegiance and protection reciprocal. In 1777 all white males in Pennsylvania were ordered to declare allegiance to the patriot government, and the bill stated that anyone who refused to do so was not entitled to the benefits of protection. That is the attitude of all civil governments, although not all have forced these issues when they could have.

The civil government is not obligated to tolerate true Christians. In speaking about the church and the state, Christ said, "And ye shall be brought before governors and kings for my sake, for a testimony against them and the Gentiles" (Matthew 10:18). His words do not mean that a civil government *must* persecute the church. They mean only that the church must always remember that she can and sometimes will be persecuted by the state.

The embrace of the state is far more terrible than its frown.

The best that the church can hope for from civil governments is half-hearted tolerance. That is all she really wants, for the embrace of the state is far more terrible than its frown.

It is better to trust in the Lord
    than to put confidence in man.
It is better to trust in the Lord
    than to put confidence in princes. . . .
Put not your trust in princes,
    nor in the son of man,
    in whom there is no help.
His breath goeth forth,
    he returneth to his earth;
    in that very day his thoughts perish.
Happy is he that hath
    the God of Jacob for his help,
    whose hope is in the Lord his God.
        —*Psalms 118:8, 9; 146:3–5*

14

A Christian View of Officials

Trust in civil leaders and trust in God are mutually exclusive. We can place our trust in one or the other, but not in both.

"No man that warreth entangleth himself with the affairs of this life;" the apostle Paul told Timothy, "that he may please him who hath chosen him to be a soldier."[1] A Christian is called to live above politics; he can never become involved in supporting a civil leader with the loyalty that belongs to God. Nor does he become emotionally involved in a particular candidate's campaign or election; he realizes that the best of men are usually unable to fulfill all their campaign promises.

---

1. 2 Timothy 2:4

When Barack Obama was elected president of the United States in 2008, countries around the world hailed him as a savior. It did not take many months until that proved a hollow claim. Christians respect their rulers, but they do not see them as saviors. Such terms belong only to God.

Honor the king

When a judge makes a decision that seems foolish, when our senator supports a bill that favors immorality, or when the news is full of stories about a president's sordid actions—how do we respond? Some professing Christians seem to live by the slogan, "I paid my taxes, I voted, and I get to yell at any official who doesn't perform the way I think he should." Is that what the Bible says?

The "Operation Rescue" that organized to fight Clinton's campaign in the early 1990s declared, "A vote for Bill Clinton is a sin against God." If it was a sin to vote for him, was it also a sin to respect him when it became obvious that God had chosen him for the presidential office?

In Clinton's later years in office, he told a reporter that he fully understood why many Christians disagreed with his views. But what shocked him, he said, was how ministers of the Gospel attacked him and preached against him by name from the pulpit. Many of these ministers also mocked Mrs. Clinton in their sermons, and they published or sold anti-Clinton literature and media. Such things clearly violated the Bible command to honor and pray for leaders, and the Clintons knew it.

Which did more harm to the cause of Christ: the obvious sins of a secular man in high office, or the obvious sins of the secular "Christians" defaming him in the headlines, mocking him in the pulpits, and sneering at him in the cartoons? It is the worst possible witness to unbelievers when those who claim to be Christians do not follow Christ.

Sometimes, from a worldly point of view, a leader's actions earn him all the disrespect he gets. But God calls the Christian to respect the unworthy. God's command to respect officials has nothing to do with the respectability of the officials. The New Testament specifically condemns people who "despise government" and "speak evil of dignities," without saying anything about the character of the government or the dignitaries.

Our calm respect for leaders will draw a little of the poison out of the acrid political atmosphere.

Christians often meet acquaintances who ask, "What do you think of this leader? What he is doing is awful!"

An answer based on civil religion would run like this: "You're right, it is terrible! When leaders act so disgracefully, it encourages everyone else to do the same. Well, that's what a country comes to if it forgets God. People get what they deserve."

A true Christian's response might run like this: "Yes, it is sad. But do you know what Jesus taught us in the Scriptures? He said that the person who is without sin should throw the first stone at a sinner. Certainly civil leaders will need to answer to God for their sins, but it is more important for you and me to make sure that we are right with God. We should pray that the government leaders will hear God's personal call and will find Bible answers for their problems." Our calm respect for leaders will plant a seed of right thinking in the minds of people we meet, and will draw a little of the poison out of the acrid political atmosphere.

Our respect for leaders may also make our Christian positions more acceptable to those leaders when our beliefs clash with government values. Unwise statements have often had a poor effect for Christians caught in persecution or stressful political times. Michael Sattler, an early Anabaptist leader, once told someone that if fighting were right, he would rather fight against the "Christian" Europeans than against the heathen Turks who were threatening Europe. This remark was used against him at his trial.

During the American Revolution, nonresistant Mennonites suffered a number of times for speaking rashly. In May 1775, one young man in York County, Pennsylvania, could not hold his tongue when a militia captain announced that every man had to join the army, or he would be considered a British sympathizer. The young man contradicted the captain, argued against raising an army, and told him the day might come when he would repent for supporting the Revolution. The young man was hauled into court, where he barely escaped being tarred and feathered. In another case in the same month, a Mennonite who had been warned to be careful with his words "gave vent to his feelings in insulting Congress and its measures for instituting defensive warfare." The court record reads, "In accordance with the usual mode of punishing such delinquents, he was seized, and tarred and feathered, for his insulting speech."

A Peter Kraybill was accused of drinking health to the British monarch and cursing the American Congress; he answered in court for these misdeeds. In Berks County, Pennsylvania, the court records of August 1779 say that Isaac Kauffman was an "Enemy to the Liberties and Independency of the United States" and was "contriving to disturb the peace of the Commonwealth and to aid and abet the King of Great Britain." Isaac had told some soldiers who were demanding his horse, "You are Rebels, and I will not give a horse to such blood-spilling persons." Isaac was tried for treason, found guilty, and imprisoned for the duration of the war, along with having half of his assets seized.

The Mennonite and Amish churches officially did not approve this kind of talk; but it shows how strongly one can be tempted to show disrespect, especially in tumultuous times like the American Revolution. A good way to prepare for such circumstances is to practice complete respect at all times, even when officers treat us in ways that are illegal.

Honoring officials is honoring God; disrespecting them is disrespecting God.

Respect Preserves a Testimony

Lloy A. Kniss, a young Mennonite man from Johnstown, Pennsylvania, was drafted into the army in World War I and sent to Camp Greenleaf in Georgia. He had deep convictions on nonresistance, so he did not help in the war effort in any way, including wearing a uniform, drilling, carrying a gun, or even helping in the kitchen. For this stand, Lloy was kicked, beaten, and disgraced. Once he was taken to an open grave and told that others who did not refused to fight had been shot and buried there, and the same thing would happen to him if he continued to refuse.

Lloy could have reported the abusive officers to Washington, D.C., and those officers would have lost their positions. But he did not because doing so would have been an act of revenge. Actually, the officers felt safe in beating Lloy and others like him, because they knew that these men would not report them. Through it all, Lloy maintained his respect for the officers and the government,

> and years later he referred to the things that were done in camp as "not in any way worthy of or countenanced by our excellent government."
>
> When Lloy was finally released at the end of the war, he stepped off the train in Pittsburgh and was surprised to meet one of his officers from Camp Greenleaf. In tears, the officer said that he had heard that Kniss was coming home on this train, and that he had come there to apologize to him for the rough way he had treated him. Lloy assured him that he held no grudges about the mistreatment, and fifty-three years later he could still say that he felt the same way toward all the officers who had abused him.

In God's hand

God selects and places civil officials. From a worldly viewpoint, it appears that some win their positions by being the strongest and smartest, by happening to be in the right place at the right time, or by having the most money to support their campaign. But all of these are only surface reasons.

> Blessed be the name of God for ever and ever: for wisdom and might are his: and he changeth the times and the seasons: he removeth kings and setteth up kings: he giveth wisdom unto the wise, and knowledge to them that know understanding (Daniel 2:20, 21).

> This matter is by the decree of the watchers, and the demand by the word of the holy ones: to the intent that the living may know that the most High ruleth in the kingdom of men, and giveth it to whomsoever he will, and setteth up over it the basest of men (Daniel 4:17).

Jesus recognized the Caesar of His time as the legitimate ruler of the Jews. We might think that in the eyes of God, the wicked Romans were usurpers of the "righteous" Jewish rule. But Jesus did not believe, as the Jews of His time did, that a more righteous government was necessarily God's will.

That has implications for our time. The rulers whom God places in power are ruling under a divine mandate. We may not understand why God sets up wicked men to rule, but the Bible is clear that He does so at times.

> Jesus did not believe, as the Jews of His time did, that a more righteous government was necessarily God's will.

It is arrogant for Christians to presume that their thinking reflects the mind of God on politics. God has clearly told us that we do not know how to supervise a nation. Neither do we know who should lead a country, or how or why God moves the way He does in elections.

A Christian accepts the outcome of elections or other means by which leaders come to power, and he accepts the outcome when God puts men out of office. After the 2007 election in Kenya that resulted in severe fighting and hardship, Kenyan Tonny Shimali Sande wrote,

> The majority said the minority could be manipulating the results in their favor. The fear of the majority became true and the unexpected minority candidate was announced to be the winner of the presidential election.
>
> Quickly chaos broke loose in Kenya. There was fighting, looting, and torching of buildings and vehicles. All the evils from the devil had been unleashed. What seemed to be promising had become bitter gall for all who had put their trust in mortal men. "Cursed is the man who puts his trust in flesh" (Jeremiah 17:5).
>
> Christians should vote only on their knees. Regardless who is elected, Christians don't lose a civil election, because they don't

belong here. They know all authority comes from God, and they accept the verdict humbly as the will of God. As Christians, we know about our heavenly kingdom where God is sovereign. No one can threaten His sovereignty.[2]

It can be difficult to know who is ruling or should be ruling when intrigue and corruption foul an election process. But just as the Scriptures are clear that our respect for a civil leader does not hinge on his morality, so also our respect for him does not hinge on how he got into office.

I wrote most of this book while living in the Philippines. Some years ago the mayor of our town was Eduardo Roquero; and when his term expired, he had reached his legal limit of consecutive mayor terms. He won a seat in Congress; then a few years later he came back to our town and won the mayor position again. In so doing he ousted Mayor Angelito Sarmiento, who had served in the meantime.

Or so we thought. Mr. Roquero died in office in the fall of 2009. Soon afterward, the National Commission on Elections ruled that Mr. Sarmiento had won the last election, and that Mr. Roquero should never have returned to the mayor's seat. This led to a considerable fight by Mr. Roquero's vice-mayor, who now occupied the mayor position. But after weeks of troops, army trucks, and guns all over the town, the vice-mayor finally ceded the position and Mr. Sarmiento became mayor again. It was widely believed that Mr. Roquero had paid the election authorities to hide the truth about the election results.

---

2. *Beside the Still Waters,* November-December 2008, "Stolen Election," reading for November 4. Used by permission.

Such things and worse are reality in much of the world. Which was the right mayor for us to honor? According to the Bible, all that a Christian can rightly do is to honor the person who occupies the position.

A Christian respects officials because he obeys God, not because he agrees with the officials. Modern Christianity has this all backwards. It is not uncommon to hear that respect for a wicked ruler is sin, when in truth disrespect for any ruler is sin.

The basic reason for this is that modern professing Christians feel responsible to help God select leaders. They believe they know which man God would choose if He could, so they feel justified in disrespecting officials that they think God did not choose.

I have often been amazed at the peace and serenity of my brothers in Christ in the Philippines as they face the staggering corruption of their national government. In contrast, many Christians in America become confused, anxious, or discouraged over election issues, even though their political situation is far better than what Filipino Christians experience.

As I write these lines in 2010, the Philippines is preparing for a presidential election. One candidate near the top of the polls claims to own all the land where my local brethren live and where their church and school is located. Numerous local people believe that if he should win the election, he would drive everyone off this land and build a housing development there. Yet these Christians raise their families in their little bamboo houses and work their fields as peacefully as always since they found Christ. They hardly follow the polls, and only occasionally talk about the election.

When I feel knots in my stomach over their possible fate, and I ask them how they feel about things, they reply, "Whomever

God puts in office will be there. God gave us this land and we want to live here; but if He allows it to be taken from us, He will provide something else. At least we have an eternal home that no one can take away! Think of what that man will face in the Judgment for all the corruption he is involved in. We should pray for his salvation. Let's pray that God's will be done, and that He will provide a way for us to be faithful regardless of the circumstances."[3]

How can these Christians talk this way, especially in a setting where things happen like the ones described below?

- Within five years, three local municipal captains were shot over political differences.
- Face-offs (with deaths) regularly occur between the official army and Communist factions.
- A top senator, also an early candidate in the recent presidential election, later became an international fugitive for his crimes.
- At least three of the eight candidates for the presidency were allegedly involved in killings to remove political opponents, to hide embarrassing information, or for other purposes. The other five candidates were at the bottom in the polls.
- The candidates' immorality is seen as a trivial matter and hardly registers with the public.

What is wrong with these Philippine Christians? Are they nonchalant? Naïve? Cavalier? These brothers have far more reason than I to be concerned—and they are concerned. But they have faith, and their faith puts me to shame. If I cannot have respect, peace, and courage in the face of the relatively

---

3. Just before the election, this candidate's popularity declined rapidly, and he lost.

benign political scene in present-day America, I am ill prepared to face the inevitably tougher future. I have much to learn from believers in other countries about a truly Christian attitude toward politics.

Testimonies on Civil Leaders from Russia and Iran

A Christian brother traveling in Russia gave these insights into how the Russian Baptists related to a powerful but corrupt leader.

"In a discussion one day with one of the underground Russian Baptist leaders, I asked him, 'What do you think of Putin?'

"'God has appointed Putin,' he answered noncommittally.

"I asked the same question in another way, hoping to discover his views. Again he answered without really telling me anything.

"When I pressed him further, he finally said, 'We don't criticize political leaders. We are Christians, and the Bible teaches us that God sets up leaders and puts them down. It is not the church's business to comment on that process.'"

In America, Christians usually get their opinions about world leaders from the news media. They often view leaders of other nations in the same way that the United States government views them. Yet such opinions may be directly contrary to those of believers in a particular leader's country. For example, nearly any American Christian would have considered it a blessing to the Iranian church if Khomeini, the religious extremist who ruled Iran in the 1980s, had been deposed. But when "Brother Andrew" visited Christians in Tehran in 1981, they saw things differently.

"We consider Khomeini a blessing," they insisted, "because he is such an obvious tyrant. His intolerance and oppressive use of the police have exposed him as a hypocritical fraud. This 'holy man' of the Muslim faith has soured many Muslims on their religion."[4] Christians were meeting in the shadow of a huge mosque in downtown Tehran, basically ignored because of the chaos and confusion. They were even printing Bibles.

This viewpoint does not justify Khomeini's actions. It simply represents the feelings of Christians who were joyful for every opportunity to get the Word of God into their fellow Iranians' hands. Instead of bemoaning the condition of their leader, they were rejoicing in how God used Khomeini's radicalism as a way for Christianity to make progress in Iran.

---

4. Alan Millwright, *Brother Andrew* (Uhrichsville, Oh.: Barbour Publishing, Inc, 1999), p. 179.

Acknowledging officials

When I was a boy of eleven or twelve, a man and his wife brought a starter to my father's repair shop. The couple was well dressed, and the man introduced his wife to my father. He greeted the woman briefly and then began discussing the repair job that the couple had brought. Soon after they left, it suddenly struck my father who the lady was.

"Why, she is in the state legislature as the representative for this district!" he exclaimed. "And I didn't even acknowledge it." He regretted that he had not given more recognition to this representative. Later, when her husband returned to pick up the finished job, my father apologized for the oversight and asked the man to pass on the apology to his wife. This incident strongly impressed on me that we should properly acknowledge officials when we meet them.

That can be difficult when the official seems to find petty faults with our operation. When I started an auto-electric business of my own ten years after that encounter, the county fire marshal stopped by to inspect my premises. He asked me to place a fire extinguisher in my shop, to have it inspected or replaced annually, and to remove some boxes that I had stacked on high shelves, right up against the ceiling. I thought the fire extinguisher was a good idea, but removing the boxes rankled me. I was starting with borrowed money, and didn't think I could afford more shelving. Fire marshals never inspected my father's shop in Pennsylvania; why should they bother me in Wisconsin?

> **The question is not whether the rules are ideal but whether we will obey God, who calls us to respect authorities in everything that does not violate His laws.**

Well, I reasoned, I suppose I can take the boxes down to satisfy the marshal and put them back up after he leaves. After all, he will inspect my shop only once a year.

But after the man left, the Lord told me to consider this thing with a better attitude. Why should I assume that the marshal was out to interfere with my liberties and tramp on my rights? What he said made sense, and I would be wise to pay attention to his direction. He was working to prevent disasters like the ones he had seen others suffer. But regardless of his motives, he represented an authority over me, and my response to his direction would tell him something about the Christianity I claimed to promote.

Names such as the Environmental Protection Agency might give us an image of petty bureaucrats who do not understand the needs of businesses and farms. Emission regulations, waste disposal requirements, and manure management plans might seem like pointless restrictions. Sometimes the laws are such that one must do clumsy things to obey them, and sometimes they appear to be made by people who understand only one viewpoint. But as Christians, we ought to be careful to follow these rules as much as possible. The question is not whether the rules are ideal but whether we will obey God, who calls us to respect authorities in everything that does not violate His laws.

After living in the Philippines, I see more wisdom in laws that protect land and water from pollution. There, people have become seriously ill after eating fish from polluted rivers. Numerous deaths have occurred among people living beside rivers contaminated with chemicals from the steel industry. One such river is located a scant fifteen miles from where I lived, and it is ranked among the world's thirty worst chemically contaminated areas. Dozens of times I have walked across one of the bridges over the main river in Manila, and never could I see beyond the surface of the murky water.

Children playing in the streets of poorer sections in Manila can contract hepatitis from sewage running down the road during the rainy season. In many public places, the ground is littered with paper and plastic that people throw away. Heavy trucks rolled past our house in the countryside several times, carrying surgical wastes from another Asian country and reeking with a horrible stench. These wastes were dumped in a beautiful little valley a few miles away and were covered with a thin layer of soil, while someone filled his wallet from the lucrative transaction. In certain areas of some countries, it is fairly common to see children disfigured or handicapped due to the improper disposal of wastes or the careless use of chemicals.

Americans should be thankful that there are agencies appointed to keep water supplies pure and to keep wastes from causing widespread diseases. Complying with officials generally does not mean cooperating with a sinister force. Most of the time it is simply common sense.

A friend of mine was once stopped by a police officer for violating seat belt laws because his children were riding on the back of his pickup. For farm boys raised in the sixties and seventies it is hard to get used to the fact that our children cannot enjoy a truck bed ride on country roads. However, what caused the greatest mental struggle for my friend was that the officer was a woman. Out of her place according to the Bible, restricting his enjoyable family activity—such a scene has the potential to stir irritable feelings

An encounter with an official is also an encounter with God.

in any of us. But when we remember that God has appointed the officers over us—men or women, kind or unkind, gracious or belligerent—we can keep such feelings to ourselves, as my friend did, and let the Lord take care of them.

I am humbled with the way that Josef Tson, a pastor in Romania during the Communist years, spoke of his encounter with the abusive, dreaded secret police. A six-man interrogation team was assigned to confront and sentence him, and one of the men challenged Josef to obey Romans 13 and cooperate with the officials.

> "Sir," I interrupted, "would you let me explain how I see Romans 13 in this situation?"
>
> He smiled ever so slightly; maybe he was curious. "All right, go on."
>
> "What is taking place here is not an encounter between you and me," I began. "This is an encounter between my God and me."
>
> His expression grew puzzled.
>
> "My God is teaching me a lesson. I do not know what it is. Maybe he wants to teach me several lessons. I only know, sir, that you will do to me only what he wants you to do—and you will not go one inch further—because you are simply an instrument of my God."
>
> He did not like that interpretation of Romans 13, but I did! To see those six pompous men as my Father's puppets! They immediately consigned me to six months of interrogation, five days a week, sometimes up to ten hours a day.
>
> But in the end, I was right: I learned a great deal.

Josef needed this vision of his officials as instruments of his heavenly Father. Four years later, as two officers were questioning him, a general entered the room and dismissed the officers.

> He began to curse me and hit me, slapping my face and hitting my head with his fist, finally knocking my head against the wall.
>
> I screamed—intentionally. I shouted so the other detainees in nearby rooms would hear me. What the general was doing was clearly illegal. . . .
>
> He kept on for a while, then left without another word. The two officers came back and resumed the interrogation as if nothing had happened.
>
> On Thursday afternoon, the general returned. Again he motioned with his hand for the two to leave. I braced myself for a second round of beating.
>
> But the man sat down behind the desk and said, "Don't worry. This time I am calm. I have come to talk to you."
>
> Now the Lord has promised that when his people are questioned, the Holy Spirit within them will do the talking. I can testify to this truth. I myself was surprised as I said, "Mr. General, because you came to talk to me, I want first of all to apologize for what happened on Monday."
>
> He was very surprised.
>
> "Let me explain what I mean," I said. "On Tuesday . . . I had plenty of time to think. All of a sudden, it dawned on me that this was Holy Week.
>
> "Well, sir, for a Christian, nothing is more beautiful than to suffer during the time his Saviour and Lord suffered. When you beat me, you did me a great honor. I am sorry for shouting at you. I should have thanked you for the most beautiful gift you could

ever have given to me. Since Tuesday I have been praying for you and your family."

I saw the man choking. He tried hard to swallow. Then, somehow, he said, "Well, I shouldn't have done it. I am sorry—let's talk."

We talked many days after that. Eventually he said, "Would you put on paper all you have said to me? I want the president of the country to read it."

From this I learned that no one—not even a Communist—is beyond the reach of Calvary love. These are savable people, redeemable people like anyone else. They desperately needed to see Christ in me.[5]

It will be easier to respect officials if we remember the truth that Josef Tson pointed out. An encounter with an official is also an encounter with God. The way we relate to the official and to God in such encounters will be a powerful witness either for or against Christ. We will answer to God for how we think and talk about those whom He has called us to respect.

---

5. Josef Tson, "Thank You for the Beating," *Christian Herald*, April 1988, pp. 28-32. c.f. Dean Merrill, *Sinners in the Hands of an Angry Church*, (Grand Rapids, Mi.: Zondervan Publishing House, 1997), pp. 102-105.

Submit yourselves to every ordinance of man
    for the Lord's sake:
    whether it be to the king, as supreme;
    or unto governors,
    as unto them that are sent by him
    for the punishment of evildoers,
    and for the praise of them that do well.
For so is the will of God,
    that with well doing ye may put to silence
    the ignorance of foolish men:
    as free, and not using your liberty
    for a cloke of maliciousness,
    but as the servants of God.

—1 Peter 2:13–16

15

A Christian View of Laws

The rule of law in many nations today is a great blessing. For much of history, civil leaders were viewed as the law or as being above the law. When leadership changed, no one knew what to expect. The laws could change overnight.

Of all people, Christians ought to be the most careful to obey laws, because that obedience is part of their submission to God and their testimony for Him. Also, they ought to be the first to understand the weakness of laws. True Christians have reached the end of their efforts to change themselves through good intentions to keep laws, and in desperation they have come to the Lord Jesus Christ for a new heart. More than anyone else, they know the inability of law to truly change a person or a culture.

The divine origin and purpose of law

In the Garden of Eden, God gave man several simple laws. After Adam and Eve sinned, God communicated more spiritual truth and concepts of civil law to them and their children. Apparently these rules were clear and specific. Abel was righteous and Cain was wicked, and they both knew why. They both understood that their choices affected their relationship with God. Cain knew that because he killed Abel, other people would want to kill him.

It appears that God communicated through oral history, through nature, through the conscience, and through teaching by godly people such as Abel. Noah walked with God and preached righteousness for hundreds of years before the Flood.

After the Babel dispersion, due to the language barrier, there may have been little cross-cultural sharing of information for hundreds of years. Yet in nearly every civilization, similar values prevailed. Concepts such as civil authority, respect for life, the importance of truthfulness, and the family unit were dispersed to all places as men spread over the world. Though not all people followed these concepts, they appear to have been present as standards in mankind's conscience.

God provided civil law for the entire 2,500 years of world history before the time of Moses. The Mosaic law was not the beginning of civil law. But Israel's laws were the clearest communication of divine law in ancient times.

15 • A Christian View of Laws

God designed civil law to keep order in humanity. Laws tell us what society expects of us and restrain man's natural bent toward evil. The majority of laws in every civilization, regardless of the religion(s) of that civilization, are a reflection of the laws of God.

The weakness of law

Most of the Old Testament is the story of "what the law could not do, in that it was weak through the flesh" (Romans 8:3). The apostle Paul also described the Old Testament law as "weak and beggarly elements" (Galatians 4:9). These verses specifically describe the Mosaic Law, but they illustrate a problem with all civil law. If God's laws themselves were unable to accomplish a great change in man, how much less can modern civil laws accomplish such a change?

Civil law can warn people, it can restrain people, and it can turn them away from courses they might otherwise take; but it cannot change the condition of their hearts.

Laws tell society what is allowable and what is not, but often are not a true picture of what God says is right and wrong.

Laws are weak because they are poor at telling people right from wrong. Laws tell society what is allowable and what is not, but often are not a true picture of what God says is right and wrong. The bulk of civil law deals with things like speed limits on highways, which in many cases are not necessarily right or wrong in relation to divine law. And when civil law does deal with things that are definitely right or wrong according to divine law, such as abortion, the laws in most countries are lower than God's standard.

While civil law in all countries of the world is based on God's concept of law, it has never served as a divine revelation from God in the way that the conscience, the Holy Spirit, or the Bible can do. When viewed against God's standard for Christian behavior, civil law in all times and places has had serious inconsistencies and major omissions.

Laws are weak because they can deal with only surface issues in human conduct. Laws can control crimes such as murder, theft, public drunkenness, and false legal testimony much of the time. But even a list as basic as the Ten Commandments mostly contains commands that are impossible for any civil government to enforce, such as the following:

- Making sure everyone worships only the one true God
- Verifying that no one has a physical idol
- Eliminating profane or blasphemous speech
- Seeing that everyone keeps the Lord's Day holy
- Making sure children honor their parents
- Eradicating covetousness

Any government can make laws that apply to such matters, but the simple fact is that no one except the Holy Spirit can actually make these things happen. There are many more such areas, including selfishness, lust, immoral relations between consenting adults, witchcraft, divorce, gluttony, and private drunkenness.

To illustrate the difficulty of establishing laws to control such things, suppose we wanted to pass a law against violent expressions of anger. Surely that would be politically acceptable.

Legal definitions would need to be set, especially for the word *violent*, since lawyers would defend clients on the basis

15 • A Christian View of Laws

that their actions were not actually violent; they were only emphatic or forceful. The illegal words, facial expressions, gestures, and actions would need to be described in detail.

The person who provoked the anger may need to be indicted for aiding and abetting the wrong expressions. Perhaps he should be punished even more severely than the person who reacted in anger, especially if it can be proved that he intentionally did something to make the accused angry.

If the accused had a late night the evening before, was suffering financial stress, or was having any kind of family trouble, those things would lower his "boiling point" and should reduce the penalty, especially when it can be determined that the contributing factors were outside his control. Also, the class of people involved would need to be considered. Male or female? Parent or child? First-time or repeat offender? Minorities should be treated more gently, especially those who are recent immigrants.

Can you see where we are heading?

"There ought to be a law against that," we sometimes say, but most of the time there isn't. The reason is simply that laws cannot regulate matters of the heart.[1]

Laws are weak because they cannot necessarily create a conscience. Romans 13:5 explains that there are two kinds of submission to law. "Wherefore ye must needs be subject, not only for wrath, but also for conscience sake." Fear of punishment makes many unbelievers obey law. But for the Christian, the voice of conscience is stronger than the fear of punishment. God has told

---

1. The ideas in this section and on pages 310 and 311 were inspired by Dean Merrill's explanations in *Sinners in the Hands of an Angry Church*, (Grand Rapids, Mi.: Zondervan Publishing House, 1997), pp. 113-116.

the Christian to obey law, and his love for God creates a greater force than fear of punishment can produce. That is why, when a civil law conflicts with a Bible precept, the Christian can disobey the law without feeling guilty. His conscience is under the law of God as well as all laws of man that are right to obey.

Generally, if a person grows up in a home that teaches respect for God and law, he will develop a conscience for obeying law because it is law. But if he grows up without learning these things, he generally will obey only for fear of punishment. The existence of civil law alone cannot generally create a conscience against law breaking.

> **Christians seeking to influence the world for Christ are wasting their time if they try to do it through enacting better laws.**

In Romans 7, Paul explained that he was raised in an atmosphere of deep respect for the law and its teachers, and when he fell into sin, he was overcome with guilt. On the other hand, Eli raised his sons with little respect for God or law. He honored his sons above God; and though they knew the Old Testament Law, they apparently had neither conscience against law breaking nor fear of punishment.

Laws are weak because they cannot necessarily change public opinion. This has been illustrated numerous times in history. For example, in 1973 the United States Supreme Court declared that a woman has the right to have an abortion. That year, 68 percent of surveyed Americans agreed with this statement: "It is against God's will to destroy any human life, especially that of an unborn baby." In 1998, studies of opinion polls by the American Enterprise Institute and the Roper Center

15 • A Christian View of Laws

Ladies sing hymns in front of a bar. Sometimes they entered the saloons, prayed, and asked the owners to stop selling alcoholic drinks. Such efforts took place in 23 states, and resulted in the closing of thousands of saloons across America.

concluded that despite the hard work of both abortion and anti-abortion forces, the American people's opinions on abortion remained basically the same as in 1973.

Also consider that the per capita number of abortions in the United States in the 1860s was nearly the same as today, even though laws against abortion were in place at that time.

These facts do not mean that abortion laws are neutral. The anti-abortion laws of earlier years were good; the present laws that allow abortion are a serious departure from moral principles. But the unchanged opinions do illustrate that many factors besides civil laws affect a population. Christians seeking to influence the world for Christ are wasting their time if they try to do it through enacting better laws.

Other examples could be cited. In Rome, abortion, homosexuality, and divorce were outlawed most of the time, yet they flourished by common consent. The laws were good, but they were also helpless. There is no better example of this than the campaign against alcohol that culminated in the eighteenth amendment to the United States Constitution.

The Prohibition failure

For centuries, Europeans drank beer, wine, hard cider, and other alcoholic drinks. Early American colonists continued this tradition. By the early 1830s, it is estimated that the average American drank 6 to 7 gallons of pure alcohol annually, in the form of beer, wine, and liquor. Many people became concerned because drinking to this extent caused poverty, health problems, and moral depravity. Women were especially active in the movement against drink, and they united under banners such as "For God, home, and native land." They worked hard to have communities where it was safe for women to walk the streets, where their sons would not lose their lives to the bottle, and where their daughters could marry "dry" men.

The campaign against alcoholic drinks was called the temperance movement. By convincing people to stop or to reduce their drinking, this movement cut the consumption of alcohol in America to less than half by the mid-1800s. The temperance movement slowly gained strength in the following

15 • A Christian View of Laws

decades, and it finally had enough support that lawmakers passed the eighteenth amendment to the Constitution. This measure banned the making, selling, transporting, importing, or exporting of alcoholic drinks, and it went into effect in January 1920. The amendment and the efforts leading to it represent one of the noblest, grandest efforts to stop one of the oldest scourges known to mankind.

How did Prohibition work?

For several years there was a drop in the amount of alcohol consumed in the United States. Liquor was available only on the black market and therefore expensive. But by 1927, consumption levels were climbing rapidly.

People learned to make alcoholic beverages on their kitchen stoves, in their barns, and in shacks in the woods. They bought alcohol at drugstores for "medical reasons," and soon the demand for "medical alcohol" soared over one million gallons per year. Secret, illegal bars called *speakeasies* sprang up. Men organized into gangs of bootleggers, and crime flourished as the gangsters fought and murdered each other to gain control of the black market in various cities. Other rings smuggled in drink from Canada and other countries. Many of the 1,550 federal agents assigned to enforce the Prohibition took bribes and looked the other way while people broke the law.

In *Having Our Say*, 103-year-old Sadie Delany recalled, "From 1920 to 1933, prohibition was going on, and you couldn't drink legally, but that didn't stop anybody."[2]

A poignant glimpse into these times is given in *The Man Who Moved a Mountain*, the story of Bob Childress. Bob was a mountaineer from a rough, backcountry area in southern

---

2. Amy Hill Hearth (New York, Ny.: Dell Publishing, 1993), p. 188.

Virginia. Most of his family and neighbors were involved in making home brew for sale. They felt this was the only way they could make a living, and they did not stop during Prohibition. But Bob had become a Christian, and though he did not understand Bible doctrines such as nonresistance, he turned away from fighting and drinking, and tried to help his fellow mountaineers lead better lives. He closed his blacksmith shop and offered to help the county sheriff.

> The next day—June 4, 1919—he was sworn in as a deputy sheriff, pledged to uphold and enforce the laws against drink and shooting. The court that week had a busy calendar: seven mountaineers for miscellaneous shooting scrapes, ten for felonious shooting and murder, not to mention twenty-six misdemeanors, mostly for "U.M.A.S."—unlawful manufacture of ardent spirits...
>
> The sheriff was glad to have such a mountain of a man as Bob Childress, so quick to move, so sure of tongue. He immediately sent Bob after a boy in liquor trouble who said he'd shoot it out before he'd be dragged to jail. Another deputy had refused to go. Bob talked to the boy from outside his cabin, finally persuading him to come quietly to town. A few weeks after that, Bob trailed and caught a fugitive in North Carolina, disarmed him, and started home, riding awhile himself, then letting his prisoner ride. Twice the man tried to charge the horse over him. . . .
>
> It wasn't long before Bob began to feel prohibition was futile, especially the way it was carried out. He discovered that most times the sheriff and his deputies would find a still, smash it, arrest the man, and then and there—along with the prisoner—get drunk on the evidence. In most cases, the sheriff had no intention of making arrests. Bob felt foolish for not having guessed it earlier. On one of

15 • A Christian View of Laws

his last raids the posse surprised a moonshiner and five of his sons at the still—a fine man except for the liquor, Bob knew. There was considerable shooting, though no one was hit. Taking out after the moonshiners in the dark of the forest, Bob scrambled over rocks, slid down fallen logs, and stopped beside a big chestnut log to catch his breath. Then he decided to give up and go back to the still. There he found his fellow deputies all drunk. He wondered what he was doing on their side.

Later, after federal agents had imprisoned the moonshiner and his boys, Bob visited them in prison, bringing gifts. . . .

"Bob," they said, "do you recollect our battle, when you got separated and was a-restin' by the side of that chestnut log?"

"I sure do," Bob said, "for all I could think of was how disgusted I were at myself."

"Bob, you were in a bad fix then, wuss than you know."

"How's that?"

"All six of us were a-lyin' t'other side of that log with our guns a-pointin' at you. If you'd a-looked over it, we were all a-goin' to shoot."

"I wouldn't a-blamed you much, neither."

Two years as a deputy was long enough to convince Bob that the law would never conquer the proud people of the Blue Ridge. The killing and drinking would go on and on, no matter how tough they made the law. He turned in his badge, went back to his home, and opened the smithy again.[3]

Bob Childress found a better way to help his fellow mountaineers gain freedom from the violence and vices that had

---

3. Richard C. Davids (Philadelphia, Pa.: Fortress Press, 1970), p. 42-44. Used by permission.

plagued their lives so long. He became a minister and taught them the ways of the Lord.

Government officials found it impossible to control liquor during Prohibition because so many people opposed the amendment, there were such large profits in the black market, and many officials were either drinkers themselves or were unwilling to deal with other drinkers. The overall effect of the Prohibition was to increase drinking, create official corruption, and overburden the legal and judicial systems. Eventually, some states hardly did anything to enforce the laws.

One of Prohibition's most serious effects was the eroding of respect for the rule of law, which had been highly prized in England and America. There was a widespread belief that law and order were breaking down. Many people feared that this would lead to disrespect for all law and that anarchy and corrupt government were just around the corner. In the late 1940s Eleanor Roosevelt had a question and answer column in the *Saturday Evening Post*. A reader asked her why her husband, Franklin D. Roosevelt, had repealed the Prohibition law. She answered, "Our nation was fast becoming a nation of lawbreakers."

Al Capone, one of the most famous, powerful, and violent gangsters in the history of the United States, was actually treated like a celebrity in the 1920s. Capone was the kingpin in Chicago's liquor, prostitution, and gambling activities. However, he bought protection by bribing politicians and police. When at last he went to jail in 1931, it was on the charge of income tax evasion, not for all his other crimes.

The supporters of Prohibition had claimed that the eighteenth amendment would make the United States safer, more prosperous, and more productive—but it made things worse, not better. By the early 1930s, the tide of opinion had changed, and Congress ended Prohibition in 1933.

The supporters of Prohibition had made several serious mistakes.

They tried to get the government to do the work of the church. One of the main goals of the temperance movement was to gain political power and to sway public opinion against alcohol. While they also tried to influence society in other ways, which were actually more effective, their real goal was to legally ban strong drink. But when they reached their goal, the whole plan backfired. If the temperance movement had united its forces to bring people to Christ, they would have had greater success against alcoholism. But they traded that great goal for a lesser, political one, and in so doing they lost the impact they might have had.

Moral legislation is rarely effective unless it results from a change in culture; it cannot produce cultural change.

Prohibition promoters thought that morality could come through law. They did not realize that moral legislation is rarely effective unless it *results* from a change in culture; it cannot *produce* cultural change. Dr. Samuel Johnson said it well.

> How small of all that human hearts endure
> That part which kings or laws can cause or cure.

Should nations follow the Old Testament civil law?

In promoting morality in the public arena, some Christians talk like this: "Christ taught a broad way and a narrow way, and He said that only a few people will enter the way to eternal life. So we do not expect many people to become true Christians. But in order for nations to be blessed, they should at least follow 'the righteousness of the law.' The more closely any nation follows the pattern of the Old Testament Law, the more God will bless that nation and the more prosperous it will be. Galatians 3:24 says that the law is a schoolmaster to bring us unto Christ. Surely more people from such a culture will be truly saved as opposed to cultures that give God's Word a lesser place or that deny it altogether, such as Muslims and Communists."

This kind of reasoning contains a little truth but is mostly based on false assumptions. The New Testament does not speak of a level of righteousness that can be attained through civil law. The Old Testament definition of righteousness meant fulfilling the whole law—ceremonial, religious, and civil. When the New Testament speaks of the righteousness of the law, it is referring to that comprehensive Old Testament definition.

This reasoning assumes that the "righteousness of the law" can be extracted from the setting of Old Testament Israel and applied anywhere in the world with similar results. But Paul said in Romans 10:4, "For Christ is the end of the law for righteousness to every one that believeth." Numerous similar Scriptures make it very clear that today God does not want us to think that following the Old Testament will bring special blessing.

Most of the time, Israel herself could not achieve the blessings God intended for the nation—not because the Law was at fault, but because they did not follow the Law. Based on

15 • A Christian View of Laws

Romans 8:3 and similar Scriptures, it is fair to say that Israel *could not* follow the Law in the manner necessary to receive God's full blessing. There simply was not enough spiritual power in the Law to make a nation follow it. God used the enormous failure of the Law—again, not His failure but Israel's failure—as a compelling example to all peoples of what law cannot do.

The Old Covenant was not a set of "timeless universal principles" dropped from the sky for all peoples and all times. It was first and foremost a relationship with Israel—a relationship intended to demonstrate the glory and power of the one true God to the world. Israel's work was not to turn all other countries into nations similar to herself. God would deal with those nations in His own way and time. Israel's task was to be faithful to her God.

That is still true for Christians today. Our task is not to make the world turn out "right" by promoting Old Testament patterns for modern nations. When we promote such things, we actually promote some severe contradictions to New Testament principles.

> **The Old Covenant was not a set of "timeless universal principles" dropped from the sky for all peoples and all times.**

Civil governments that have tried to enforce the First Commandment have generally persecuted true Christians. The one true God, as defined by a carnal mind, is the God of civil religion with all its violence, war, and manifest destiny. He is not the God of the New Testament believer, but rather the God of the Catholics and of Luther, Zwingli, and Calvin—who imprisoned, drowned, decapitated, and burned many true Christians.

If we wish that government would institute Old Covenant civil laws, are we remembering that this will allow for divorce, polygamy, and slavery?

In *Biblical Pacifism*,[4] Dale Brown tells the story of an old nonresistant grandmother who was confronted with the question of whether we should obey the command in Leviticus 20:9 to execute anyone "that curseth his father or his mother." The devout grandmother answered instinctively, "But Jesus would not want us to do that!"

Leaving the questions of civil government with the government, the grandmother returned the focus for the child of God to where it belongs: What does Jesus Christ want you and me to do?

Can Good Laws Maintain Morality?

When Christians try to keep a society "Christian" by maintaining external pressures instead of preaching the saving Gospel of Jesus Christ, the results may be some great cultural contradictions instead of an improved morality. For example, the strong Catholic influence in the Philippines has helped to maintain the anti-divorce laws of that country. This influence has also been largely successful in keeping birth-control education out of public schools, and it has defeated numerous legislative attempts to provide government-sponsored contraceptives.

In the Western world, divorce, sex education, and state-sponsored family planning have often been blamed for the culture's low moral condition. Are morals any better in the Philippines, where these things are currently illegal?

Common-law arrangements are popular among Filipinos. Married people who want to get out of their relationship simply leave. The fact that they cannot legally divorce does nothing to keep them from moving on to another partner.

---

4. (Nappanee, In.: co-published by Herald Press and Evangel Publishing House, second edition, 2003), p. 95.

15 • A Christian View of Laws

On one occasion, I served as a witness when a common-law couple went to the local municipal office to be married. A number of couples were getting married in a joint ceremony that day, and the official who solemnized their vows lectured them before the ceremony. Part of his speech illustrated just how immoral a no-divorce society can be. The official asked each couple if they had lived together before deciding to be married. (Five out of six had.)

"This is very important," he emphasized, "because the Philippines does not allow divorce. You should experience life together before deciding to get married so that you can be sure you are the right people for each other." He joked about sacred things and about how many children (of the couples to be married) were present at the ceremony. It is obvious that regardless of the anti-divorce laws, marriage in the Philippines is no more stable and the homes are no happier than in countries where divorce is allowed.

The strongly religious yet immoral nature of the Philippine culture hosts many other contradictions as well. Near where we lived, one of the public transportation vehicles had a large picture of Jesus Christ on the driver's door, and the remainder of the side of the vehicle was covered with a painting of gross impurity. It is not unusual to see such a vehicle sporting a religious message such as "God bless our journey" or "Lord, guide us" along with immoral displays.

Visitors to the Philippines from countries such as America often note that the outdoor signs are much more immodest than what they are used to seeing. Even in homes, many Filipino families display large posters or calendars with very indecent pictures. Young people are often extremely loose. One young Christian man handing out Gospel tracts in a marketplace had to leave the building because of the immoral comments of some of the women tending the market booths.

Reflecting on how to help his children grow up in purity, a Filipino Christian told me, "It seems like we are living in Sodom." Christians around the world have similar evaluations, even though the laws and religions of their respective countries vary widely. We are thankful for the effects good laws have, but it is apparent that laws alone are powerless to curb lust, and that bad laws alone are not the source of immorality.

A Christian who spends his time in trying to improve laws or in decrying poor laws is squandering his God-given talents on an effort that will yield few if any results. Attempts to Christianize a culture may actually work against the kingdom of God, as Leslie Weatherhead's comment so aptly explained: "The trouble with some of us is that we have been inoculated with small doses of Christianity which keep us from catching the real thing."

"Christian" laws or cultural expressions may be alive and well while sincere discipleship is practically nonexistent. Religion can win the day while true Christianity loses. Christians cannot change people or create a Christian nation through law. Instead, they create a secular church.

The basis for American laws

Many people in mainstream American churches emphatically say that American laws do have and must have a base in the Bible—a Judeo-Christian base. These people declare that when new laws are passed or existing laws are changed, everything must be done on an enduring foundation of righteousness.

True Christians can identify with that wish, but it is only a wish. Like laws in many other countries, American laws do reflect God's principles to a large degree. However, humanism and other carnal influences have also clearly influenced American lawmakers since colonial times. When more people respected the Bible, more Bible principles tended to find their way into law. But compared with the Ten Commandments or other aspects of the Old Covenant civil law, there have always been huge gaps in American law.

Article I, section 7 of the Constitution does *not* read "Every Bill which shall have passed the house of Representatives and the Senate, shall, before it becomes a Law, be evaluated to determine its harmony with Judeo-Christian ideals, as represented by the Bible." What it does say, in brief, is this:

> Every Bill which shall have passed the house of Representatives and the Senate, shall, before it becomes a Law, be presented to the President of the United States; If he approve he shall sign it, but if not he shall return it, with his Objections to that House in which it shall have originated, who shall . . . proceed to reconsider it. . . . In all such Cases the Votes of both Houses shall be determined by Yeas and Nays. . . .

15 • A Christian View of Laws

> Every Order, Resolution, or Vote to which the Concurrence of the Senate and House of Representatives may be necessary . . . shall be presented to the President of the United States; and before the Same shall take effect, shall be approved by him, or being disapproved by him, shall be repassed by two thirds of the Senate and House of Representatives, according to the Rules and Limitations prescribed in the Case of a Bill.

The American system of laws is only what the majority of the representatives will vote for, the president will sign, and the Supreme Court will allow to stand. It is a system based on the values of the majority. The godly or ungodly implications of a particular issue do not usually carry much weight, even with the religious people in public office.

We are thankful that in America the law has generally allowed Christians to practice their faith, but that does not mean that American law is uniquely based on God's will. The laws of other countries also reflect divine principles. All civil law systems have strong points and weak points. All legal systems are earthly; none of them can bring the worldling to Christ or keep a repentant sinner away from Christ.

"Be careful, little tongue, what you say."

Then what can a Christian say about law and government? He can recognize that because a government exists, it has been permitted by God and is to be obeyed as long as it does not require disobedience to God. He can be thankful for the order that government provides. He should say kind and respectful things about law officials. He should compliment the government when its laws reflect God's moral principles. If a Christian goes beyond these simple New Testament standards, he becomes hopelessly tangled in contradictions.

In the debates that surround changes in law, Christians should not leave the impression that they believe laws are the answer to society's problems. Let us also beware of the mindset that certain laws are necessary for the cause of Jesus Christ to succeed. In the time of the New Testament, laws were enacted to repress Christianity, but there is no record of Christians in that time trying to change law for the sake of human rights or religious toleration. They accepted the fact that the world was a foe to grace and faithfully won souls for Christ in enemy territory.

Let us beware of the mindset that certain laws are necessary for the cause of Jesus Christ to succeed.

Christians in free countries experience many blessings because of the present laws that tolerate true Christianity. But even while we enjoy these blessings, we may forget our mission as disciples of Christ, as Jonathan Erb wrote in an article entitled "Patriotic and Political Influences."

> With most political issues, Biblical principles indicate which option would be for the most good. . . . [But] the church and its peoples, cannot take it upon itself to dictate or advise the affairs of the kingdoms of this world. And so . . . we dare not become entangled in unbecoming thoughts, words, or actions about these issues. . . .
>
> As we live in America, we are participating in the American dream. . . . It is quite easy to become enraptured with these blessings. We can become more opinionated about them than

about Christian realities—the reality of the value of a soul, the reality of the mission of the church, and the reality of Christian service opportunities. While we chase these butterflies, people perish.[5]

When the church tries to control society through law, it is like a blind man at target practice. He tries to aim in the direction of the target, but he always ends up missing the bull's-eye, shooting holes through unintended objects, and wasting ammunition. But the Christian's weapon, the Word of God, is "quick, and powerful, and sharper than any twoedged sword, piercing even to the dividing asunder of soul and spirit, and of the joints and marrow, and is a discerner of the thoughts and intents of the heart."[6]

---

5. *The Christian School Builder*, October 2010, p. 62.
6. Hebrews 4:12

American people
   think this U.S. is great
   and that [its] honor
   is something great to be preserved.
What does it amount to in the sight of God?
>*—Stanley Martin*

Honor seeking, pride, and pleasure
   are the three great evils
   in the United States today.
>*—Benjamin Baer*

Extortionate prosperity
   is leading humanity away
   from the true Gospel principles.
>*—C. R. Strite*

Comments on American culture by Mennonites of Washington County, Maryland and Franklin County, Pennsylvania, 1917[1]

---

1. *Building on the Gospel Foundation,* pp. 395, 406. Used by permission.

16

A Christian View of Culture

Culture is the fabric of beliefs, behavior, and traditions that make up society. Because cultures consist of people created in God's image and influenced by God, all cultures of the world have the potential for good in them. And because all cultures consist primarily of unrepentant people, all cultures also have much evil in them.

We need to understand cultural issues in the context of God's Word and history.

Knowing the past

Bible passages such as Psalm 44 and Hebrews 3 show that knowing history is a huge advantage to faith. In C. S. Lewis' book *The Screwtape Letters*, the devil Screwtape instructs younger devils on corrupting people by keeping them ignorant of the past and getting them to focus only on the present. "Since we cannot deceive the whole human race all the time," Screwtape says, "it is important to cut every generation off from all others." Where knowledge flows easily across the ages, he explains, there is a danger that people may learn about their errors by observing people in the past.

Certainly, many people who do not remember the past are doomed to repeat it. And just as certainly, a wrong view of history saps the Christian of spiritual energy and makes him question God's faithfulness. I recall a friend who literally trembled as he told me the "secret" that there would be a Muslim takeover of America if Barack Obama were elected president of the United States. "Don't you know," he said fearfully, "that he is planning to be sworn into office with his hand on the Koran?" If you and I are to remain calm as the "heathen rage, and the people imagine a vain thing," we need to see past the issues that are roiling the religious media this month.

Understanding past cultures protects us from wrong theories about history. For example, historians may use quotations like George Washington's prayer at the end of the Revolutionary War to show that early America was a Christian nation. This prayer was sent to the governors of the states in 1783.

> I now make it my earnest prayer, that God would have you, and the State over which you preside, in his holy protection . . . that he would most graciously be pleased to dispose us all to do justice, to love mercy, and to demean ourselves with that charity, humility, and pacific temper of mind, which were the characteristics of the Divine

Author of our blessed religion, and without an humble imitation of whose example in these things, we can never hope to be a happy nation.

In a similar vein is Benjamin Franklin's description of America for Frenchmen who considered making the new country their home. The French population of that time rejected much about religion, was very immoral, and probably included more atheists than any other European country.

Bad examples to youth are more rare in America, which must be a comfortable consideration to parents. To this may be truly added, that serious religion, under its various denominations, is not only tolerated, but respected and practised. Atheism is unknown there; infidelity is rare and secret; so that persons may live to a great age in that country without having their piety shocked by meeting with either an Atheist or an Infidel.

Certainly these are good sentiments; they portray a respect for the principles of Christianity that is often missing these days. If we did not know that Washington rarely spoke of the Bible or of Jesus Christ, we might conclude that he was an orthodox Christian. If we did not know that Benjamin Franklin seldom attended church, that he said religion is useful primarily for the weak and ignorant, and that he thought eternal punishment was a myth, we might conclude that he was an ardent Episcopalian, Puritan, or Anglican.

Consider the aged Benjamin Franklin's oft-cited words as he called for prayer at the Constitutional Convention.

The small progress we have made after four or five weeks' close attendance . . . is, methinks, a melancholy proof of the imperfection of human understanding. . . . How has it happened that we have not hitherto once thought of humbly applying to the Father of Lights to illuminate our understandings?

This quotation often appears in Christian articles and books as an expression of the faith of the Founding Fathers when they established the United States government. But for some reason, most writers do not say what was done with Franklin's suggestion. The delegates discussed it and then dropped it without a vote.

We need not teach our children all the wrong things that the Founding Fathers did or believed. But if our children grow up thinking that these men were venerable Christians or that their beliefs were much like those of the early church or the Anabaptists, we have erred seriously. We have prepared our children to mistake civil religion for true religion and to be manipulated by those who misrepresent history.

If our children grow up thinking that the Founding Fathers were venerable Christians, we have prepared our children to mistake civil religion for true religion.

It is indeed wonderful that the patriots prayed at some of their gatherings and that many of this nation's early leaders saw Christianity as one of the best supports of morality. It is commendable that the Supreme Court of olden days made many judgments based on Christian values, that the first McGuffey readers used the Scriptures liberally, and that almost every college in America was founded on religious principles. But it is equally important for us to realize that nearly all of this was taught or done in the context of a "Christianity" that required no personal response to the call of Christ. Many early Americans thought they were saved without repentance and obedience to Jesus Christ, and they despised the demands of Christian discipleship. These attitudes resulted in a continual erosion of Bible principles.

Understanding past cultures also corrects wrong assumptions about the present. Much that seems certain in the modern world is merely a fleeting notion. Many present political concepts, such as the importance of personal freedom and a government by the people, are not common rights in the history of mankind.

C. S. Lewis once said that a person who has lived in many places is likely to recognize some errors in his native village. Because a history student tries to understand culture in many times and places, he "is therefore in some degree immune to the great cataract of nonsense that pours from the press and the microphone of his own age."[2] Christians often equate contemporary ideals, such as capitalism, with Christianity. But when we understand the historical sources and effects of such ideas, we can more easily identify what actually comes from God's Word and what comes from the minds of men.

Cultural myths

Early America represents a "golden age" that can offer solid solutions for the ills of modern America. This claim is based on selected facts about the influence of Bible principles when this nation was founded; but it fails to consider that as a whole, the government

---

2. C .S. Lewis, "Learning in War-Time" in *The Weight of the Glory and Other Essays* (New York, Ny.: Macmillan, 1980), pp. 28, 29.

This drawing was published in England in 1832 in the book **Domestic Manners of the Americans.** *It compared decadence in Roman times to decadence in America by showing a Roman reclining with his lyre, being served wine, and an American drunk with whiskey with his feet on the table.*

was based on a patchwork of Christian and Enlightenment ideals (including concepts that reached back as far as Rome and Greece). Those humanistic ideals deliberately scorned great Bible truths such as the divinity of Christ and the power of the Gospel, which provide the only solid solutions to anyone's ills.

This claim also fails to recognize that true Christians in early America often felt much the same about their culture as we feel about modern culture. Nor does it consider that none of our African-American friends would enjoy turning back the clock to those times.

More importantly, such a claim does not consider that as a matter of Bible principle, the Christian considers the future the only "golden age." If we speak lightly about the "good old days" and how much easier life was back then, we simply reveal our need to study the Bible and history. As one old gentleman pointed out, "When I was young, the times we know now as the 'good old days' were called 'these trying times.'" True Christians in every era have sensed that "the whole world lieth in wickedness" and have "looked for a city which hath foundations, whose builder and maker is God."[3]

America is a special nation to God. This idea has been widely held ever since the Puritans tried to build the new Israel on the shores of Massachusetts. Prayers like the following are common religious fare.

> We are humbled when we think of the courage and faith of our pioneer forefathers. We ask for Your help that we might carry on the traditions that they established. Lord, it was their faith in You that made our dreams come true.
>
> We are aware of our place in Your grand scheme as we look around at the beauty and success of America. When we acknowledge You as the Master and Creator of the universe, we can truly appreciate Your special love for our land.

Since America is rich and strong, many religious people think it is quite obvious that she is special to God. But this kind of thinking is based on faulty ideas of manifest destiny, not on any special favor that actually exists.

The first five chapters of this book show that the Bible gives no grounds for thinking that any modern nation is special

---

3. I John 5:19; Hebrews 11:10

to God. Consider too that if America is great because she is special to God, what are we to say about the numerous other nations that have experienced similar greatness and power? What about the periods of power and wealth in Egypt, China, Assyria, Babylonia, Persia, Greece, and Rome? In relation to their times, some of these nations experienced more wealth and power than America has, for more years than the United States has existed. Many Christians do not realize how inconsistent their ideas are, simply because they consider only their own nation or their own time.

We must reclaim America for Christ. This statement is often made in words like these: "America is a prosperous world power because its government was founded on Christian principles. But we may soon lose that because sin has taken over the nation." Then comes the inevitable last line: "If you want to preserve your family's future, send a donation now to ———." Christ never taught such things or tried to gain support for His kingdom in such a fashion.

Christ did not give His followers the task of preserving the nation. Rather, we have been assigned to teach that we cannot hope in this world's systems and that we cannot halt the world's decline. We are on a sinking ship directing people to the lifeboat.

We cannot reclaim America for Christ when America never lived under the lordship of Christ. The Christianity of America in every era held values directly opposed to New Testament principles.

Does God Always Bless "Christian" Cultures?

In the latter half of the 1500s, dedicated Anabaptists known as Hutterites flourished in Moravia. These nonresistant Christians probably numbered between fifteen and thirty thousand souls in their peaceful period, which lasted from about 1554 to 1595. They were deeply spiritual people with a strong evangelistic zeal. They spread the Gospel in dangerous places and led converts on hazardous journeys to freedom in Moravia.

The Hutterites in Moravia lived under Protestant lords who prided themselves in their religious toleration and appreciated the economic contributions of the Hutterites. Some of these ruling families had provided protection for other religious sects, such as the followers of John Huss, for over a century before the Reformation. At least one lord of Nikolsburg was a member in a church that taught some Anabaptist beliefs, under the leadership of Balthasar Hubmaier.

But beginning in 1593, wars between the great European powers shattered the Hutterite communities and the power of the Moravian lords to tolerate them. The *Hutterite Chronicle* contains terrible stories of killing, raping, and wanton torture in which horrible, lewd acts were committed against the Hutterites by soldiers on both sides of the conflicts. Some of the most appalling persecution in the history of God's people occurred during this period. By the early 1620s, only a few thousand Hutterites were left. These destitute people straggled into Hungary, where a few years later they numbered less than one thousand. By the late 1600s they were nearly extinct.

Today it is said that if a country is Christian—at least in a general sense—God will honor that country and bless it with prosperity and freedom. It is also said that God will bless a country if it values and protects its Christian citizens, and that these are the citizens who actually make a country great. How do these claims compare with the Hutterite experience?

From a human viewpoint, it appears that God's kingdom would have made much greater progress in the world if He had not permitted the devastation of these "Christian" lords' domain. But He did allow it, even though one of the few havens available to true Christians in Europe was destroyed, and a group of true Christians was almost obliterated. We do not know His reasons, but these are historical facts that should keep us from swallowing the political-religious myths that are so easily formulated in times of peace and tolerance.

The theory that God will always bless "Christian" cultures leads to several non-Christian assumptions. It gives Christians the right to condemn a nation that mistreats them, although Jesus Christ and the apostles never suggested such a thing. It assumes that God's Word provides a definable level of righteousness by which men can be assured of earthly blessings such as military might and prosperity—an idea directly opposed to New Testament teaching. It also assumes that God will destroy or humble a modern nation that fails to treat His children well, though the facts do not support that idea. An outstanding example is Switzerland, where many of God's children were killed in Reformation times and where nonresistant people are barred because of the universal military conscription. Yet Switzerland is the most trusted banking stronghold in the world today.

Another example that casts doubt on the oft-repeated assumptions is the history of Rome, the original "Christian nation." Rome was greatest and strongest when she was pagan. She was declining when Constantine publicly recognized Christianity in 313. Christian principles gradually became more and more influential in Rome after this, until in 379 the emperor Theodosius I made Christianity the state religion and restricted heathen worship. But these actions had little effect on Rome's decline, and the Western Roman Empire fell in 476.

According to modern theories, Rome's history should have improved after 313. If there ever was an opportunity for the kind of nation that God supposedly wants, it would have been the emerging empire of "Christian" Rome. But for some reason, God saw that it was better to let the world go through the Dark Ages than to have a "Christian" government rule the world.

A culture of freedom

Probably the most deeply cherished common value among Americans is personal freedom. The inscription on the Liberty Bell reads, "Proclaim Liberty throughout all the land unto all the inhabitants thereof."[4] The full name of the Statue of Liberty is "Liberty Enlightening the World," and the Declaration of Independence holds that God gives people "certain unalienable Rights, that among these are Life, Liberty, and the pursuit of Happiness." Freedom has been a god throughout American history.

The Revolutionary desire for freedom from the restraints of European governments has been carried over many times to new issues. The ideal of freedom for the white, Protestant American slowly translated into freedom for the African slave, for the immigrant European Catholic, for other immigrants of all nationalities and religions, and eventually for women to vote and hold public office.

---

4. Leviticus 25:10

The pace of emancipation has increased in the past century. Freedom for families has become freedom for individuals. Freedom of religion has become freedom to be irreligious or anti-religious. Freedom for children has become freedom from parental rule. Personal freedom has become freedom from God, from one's first husband or wife, and from financial debts. Today many Americans consider it their right to be free to do whatever they think will make them happy.

The Biblical view of freedom is that true liberty is found only in submission to Jesus Christ. We are delivered from the tortured slavery under Satan to become love-slaves to Jesus Christ. The New Testament teaches the Christian not to expect the "rights" touted by the Declaration of Independence. He may be called to give up natural life for eternal life or to be physically bound because of his freedom from sin; and he is always called to give up the selfish pursuit of happiness so that he can attain true joy. The only right that the New Testament gives Christians is the right to salvation.

> **The only right that the New Testament gives Christians is the right to salvation.**

The Declaration of Independence has given true Christians some blessings, but it also poses some significant snares. For everyone outside of Christ, the pursuit of life, liberty, and happiness is a naturally decaying process. The view of freedom in the Declaration of Independence is secular; it appeals to carnal instincts, not spiritual convictions. It is based on the desires of unconverted people.

A paradox today is that the emphasis on tolerance and freedom is what gives both the Christian and the alternate-lifestyle person the freedom to live as they do. American society tolerates a Christian who practices Biblical child discipline, knows little about modern cultural icons, does not vote or accept jury duty, does not go to college or war, does not buy insurance, and goes shopping with six to twelve children in tow. However, many people consider him exceedingly odd, likely ignorant of some basics, and perhaps even irresponsible. Christians tend to think they are tolerated because they are a great asset to the nation; but for the most part, that is not how the world thinks about them.

The Scriptures never picture the kingdom of God as a weak entity that requires favorable cultural conditions to succeed.

If a Christian says that society should be tolerant of his personal "weirdness" but should restrict things that offend him, he is building his own guillotine. Certainly, a Christian must not accept everything that is legal. He witnesses against all sin, whether it is legal or not. But he does not try to bring about a cultural revival by pressuring the government to restrict the freedom to sin.

A secular culture

Culture is always comprised mostly of secular people; therefore, culture is always basically secular. Jesus taught that only a few will enter the narrow way and that the secular majority can be expected to persecute the spiritual minority. His words describe the world as it stands and will stand.

Christ said these things not to discourage us but to give us a sense of urgency about helping to save souls. He also wanted to keep us from being disheartened by the way things are in this world. We are to keep laboring even if few are saved, culture keeps decaying, and some believers fall away. Such things do not mean that God's kingdom is losing ground. We should not think that American culture must be saved to preserve the cause of Christ. We should not speak of the war for America's soul—as if America had a collective soul. God sees all the hundreds of millions of her citizens as individual souls.

Because they try to save culture instead of saving souls from the evils of culture, many religious people are discouraged and overwhelmed. They tend to see Christianity as a cause presently lost. They feel that God used to control the world and that He will regain control in the future. But in the present He seems to have lost His grip.

Like the philosophy of a deist in the 1700s, this view suggests that God created the world but then left it to run on its own. "It seems as if God can't handle what He started," the reasoning goes, "and Christians, who are apparently left in charge of His program, are failing. Christianity doesn't stand a chance if society is not controlled by good government. When people become so wicked, they become impervious to the Gospel."

If we want people to believe what God says, we must live as if we believe what He says.

As sincere as this reasoning may be, it flatly contradicts the Bible and what is happening today in the world. The Gospel can never be overwhelmed and buried in obscurity. Paul said that Christ has "spoiled principalities and powers" and is openly triumphing over evil since His death on the cross.[5] He also taught that where sin is abundant, grace is much more abundant.[6] The Scriptures never picture the kingdom of God as a weak entity that requires favorable cultural conditions to succeed.

Indeed, many things have changed in the past one hundred years; but if we could return to culture before that time, we would not experience any advantage for the kingdom of God. Culture has always been secular. The world has always been a foe to grace. Hundreds of years before people dressed in scanty clothes, watched immoral movies, or attended irreligious schools, Christians spoke of the vast difference between the world and the church. Consider the words written around 1577, likely by Peter Walpot, an Anabaptist bishop in the Hutterite church.

> Between the Christian and the world there exists a vast difference like that between heaven and earth. The world is the world, always remains the world, behaves like the world and all the world is nothing but the world. The Christian, on the other hand, has been called away from the world. He has been called never to conform to the world, never to be a consort, never to run along with the crowd of the world, and never to pull its yoke.

This description is true of the entire sweep of American culture and every culture in the world. The cause of Christ cannot be disturbed, defeated, or destroyed by culture. Christ always reigns above culture. If we want people to believe what God says, we must live as if *we* believe what He says.

---

5. Colossians 2:15
6. Romans 5:20

How Much Help Does the Gospel Need?

Christians who live in free countries tend to feel that religious freedom and government support for things such as school prayer help to keep society in touch with God. The sentiment is often expressed that if the Bible is not freely circulated, God hardly has a foothold in a culture. But reports from countries where Christianity is prohibited or discouraged show some surprising facts.

Before 1949, thousands of churches and other Christian institutions were active in China, representing a wide variety of denominations from North America and Europe. Seventy-five percent of the Christian pastors in China were on the payroll of foreign organizations. Much of the work of these organizations was social improvement efforts such as schools and hospitals, with little emphasis on Christian discipleship.

When the Communists came to power in 1949, they drove foreigners out of the country. But they soon realized that Christianity was still a significant force. To bring the churches under their control, they forced them to register with the government and began to monitor them. These registered churches became little more than puppets of the government.

Some dedicated pastors, realizing what the government was doing, refused to register their churches. So those pastors were imprisoned or sent to labor camps, their churches were broken up, and the members had no choice but to meet secretly in groups of two or three families. Christians were watched so closely and persecuted so severely that when two of them met on the street, they could not show recognition of each other for fear of retribution. Some Christians were crucified on the walls of their churches or dragged to death on ropes behind horses. This phase of persecution continued from about 1950 to 1966, but the church prospered.

The leader of China was Mao Zedong, and in 1966 he and radicals in the Communist party put China back on the path to revolution. Under Mao's plan, called the Cultural Revolution, young people formed military associations and were permitted to destroy anything that was valued in China before 1949. Antiques, old art, and old books were put to the torch; and far worse, thousands of people were destroyed.

The mobs of radical youth killed pastors, teachers, and older folks who held on to anti-Communist ideas. Competing Communist groups also fought each other through this time. The Cultural Revolution disrupted society so greatly that China was set back many years in economic and social terms, and Zedong finally used military force to halt the effects of his own plan.

In the 1970s and 1980s, China again opened her borders to foreigners, and people in the West began to learn what had taken place since 1950. The secret, persecuted church in China had grown astoundingly. There had been about one million Chinese Christians in 1949, but the estimated number around the year 2000 was from fifty to eighty million. Though legally denied Bibles and Christian literature, many of these people had a devotion to Christ that dwarfed the commitment of Christians in free countries.

These Christians must operate so secretly that it is hard for foreigners to communicate with them. Many of them need instruction in discipleship matters such as marriage and the Christian home, to counteract the effects of liberal religious teachers. For years, concerned Christians have been secretly printing Bibles and discipleship literature within China and also smuggling these things into the country. But the field is huge and growing, and much more could be done.

The story of an elderly Chinese Christian is typical of many. This man was a dedicated Christian youth who dropped out of university studies because that environment was hostile to his faith. He was a pastor of a Christian church during the Communist takeover. He refused to register his congregation with the new government, because he believed this would be an act of compromise. As a result, he sat in prison for over twenty years with little knowledge of what was happening to his beloved church outside the gray walls of his cell.

After the Cultural Revolution had killed off many younger Christian pastors, the Chinese authorities decided to release the elderly pastors whom they had imprisoned in the early 1950s. No one would listen to old men today, they reasoned; but just to be sure, they put this man under house arrest for another ten years. When that time expired, they continued to watch him closely, convinced that they could detect and stop any influence he might try to exercise.

But the truth was that after these elderly pastors were released, they secretly provided valuable leadership for the underground church that had lost so many pastors in the Cultural Revolution. The old man's wife summed up the story like this: "If my husband had been out of prison all those years, he would surely have been killed by the forces of persecution. God had a plan for him. He was saved for the church in a crucial time, and God brought him out of prison at the right moment."

Many accounts from China disprove the idea that Christianity needs favorable cultural conditions to grow. Christianity actually prospered the most when freedom and foreigners and their money were cut off. There are many similar cases in history, where the numbers of believers multiplied in adverse cultural conditions but showed only mediocre growth or actual decline in so-called good cultural conditions. God can make marvels happen in countries where His Word is banned.

The Christians in such circumstances often have different perspectives than outsiders about their situation. A Christian from a free country once told a Chinese house church leader that he had been praying for years that the Chinese Communist government would collapse so that Christians there could live in freedom. The Chinese Christian responded,

> This is not what we pray! We never pray against our government... Instead, we have learned that God is in control of both our own lives and the government we live under. Isaiah prophesied about Jesus, *"The government will be on his shoulders." Isaiah 9:6.*
>
> God has used China's government for his own purposes, moulding and shaping his children as he sees fit. Instead of focusing our prayers against any political system, we pray that regardless of what happens to us, we will be pleasing to God.[7]

In Iran, Muslim extremists have controlled the country since Ayatollah Khomeini took over the government in 1979. By law the death penalty applies to those who reject Islam. In the late 1970s and early 1980s, it seemed obvious to outsiders that the situation in Iran was getting worse for Christianity, not better. But since that time, the opposite has proven true. In the most adverse circumstances, many Iranians are searching for truth, and evidence of Christ's power has blossomed. One mission newsletter reported,

> With one of the highest rates of drug addiction in the world, the suffering of many in Iran has led to a great spiritual openness. Through the power of the Gospel, we continue to experience dramatic change in the lives of those who have repented and turned to God. Such transformation is a very powerful witness in Iranian society.[8]

A historian adds another startling revelation. "More Iranians have come to Christ in the last 16 years [since the 1979 Revolution] than in the last 1,000 years."[9] As mentioned in chapter 14, some Christians in Khomeini's time testified that they considered his fanatic ways a blessing. He was so radical that he soured many Muslims on their faith. Many people who saw him as a hypocrite began going to other religions, especially Christianity, for answers to life's questions.

But why should these revelations surprise us? God has always specialized in this sort of victory. He used the pagan nation of Egypt to preserve His godly people, through whom He could send His Son Jesus Christ to die so that He could triumph openly over Satan.

---

7. "Brother Yun" with Paul Hattaway, *The Heavenly Man* (London, UK.: Monarch Books, 2002), pp. 286, 287.

8. As cited in Grace Press Newsletter, October 2009, from Elam Ministries' newsletter.

9. As cited in ibid., from Zarin Behravesh Pakizegi, *History of the Christians in Iran.*

> When we cannot understand how God will use a situation for His glory, we must remember the words of Joseph. Sold into slavery far from home, he remained faithful to God even though he never expected to see his family again. Later Joseph told his brothers, "Now therefore be not grieved, nor angry with yourselves, that ye sold me hither: for God did send me before you to preserve life . . . to preserve you a posterity in the earth, and to save your lives by a great deliverance. So now it was not you that sent me hither, but God."[10]

The view from the sky

We need to better understand God's view of the world, the view from the sky. This view takes in much more than the rabble and rubble here on earth. It is the view described in Maltbie D. Babcock's familiar hymn, "This Is My Father's World."

> This is my Father's world / O let me ne'er forget
> That though the wrong seems oft so strong, / God is the Ruler yet.
> This is my Father's world! / The battle is not done;
> Jesus who died shall be satisfied, / And earth and heav'n be one.

Did Mr. Babcock think this way because his world was righteous and idyllic? Not at all. He spent the last fifteen years of his life serving churches in Baltimore and New York, cities where immorality was rampant. From 1899 to 1902, the United States was at war in the Philippines, trying to hang on to the spoils of the Spanish-American War. Because of the cruelty of the United States troops against civilians in the Philippines, many Americans opposed this war, making it the equivalent of the Vietnam War in that period. Babcock died in May 1901, at the height of the military conflict. No wonder that to him, wrong seemed so strong. In spite of such circumstances, however, Mr. Babcock wrote the following.

---

10. Genesis 45:5, 7, 8

> Be strong!
> Say not, "The days are evil. Who's to blame?"
> And fold the hands and acquiesce—oh, shame!
> Stand up, speak out, and bravely, in God's Name.

It is inspiring that many of our cherished hymns of trust and comfort were written in very poor political circumstances.

"A Charge to Keep I Have" and "Am I a Soldier of the Cross" were written in England when groups that dissented from the Anglican Church, such as the Methodists, faced heavy persecution. The Anglicans inflamed mobs against these Christians and charged their ministers with blasphemy. The public stoned and beat some Methodists, chased others with bulldogs, broke into their homes, and boycotted their businesses to the point that some were forced to close shop. Passersby could pick out these Christians' homes because of their vandalized condition.

In such conditions, one could imagine the "on-fire-for-God" religious people of modern America composing songs about God's judgment on those who forget Him and about the loss of power and prosperity certain to come to countries that mistreat Christians. Remember, England in the 1700s was running on just as much "Christian capital" as America had at its beginning, and it occupied a high position among the world's powers.

But those persecuted Christians apparently did not spend much time in making threats. Instead, they used themes right out of the Bible, singing of the charge *I* have to keep and of making sure *my* soul is not lost. They sang of their calling in the present age—not to bring England "back to God," but to give a personal account at the judgment. They asked themselves whether they would be able to testify for the Lamb in spite of persecution. They challenged themselves to own God's cause and to bear the pain, even though the vile world was a foe to grace.

"A Shelter in the Time of Storm," written in the late 1830s, gained great popularity in the American and British revivals after the Civil War. Thousands of people in that era could identify with their world as a raging storm and a weary land, where ills abounded, fears alarmed, and foes frightened. They knew all about the religious confusion of those times, and about the senseless discrimination in the South that the Civil War and equality laws seemed helpless to root out. They were aware of the immorality in the cities, the social unrest, and the labor problems in their day. Those revivals had few long-term effects on American society, but it is obvious that many hearts in that time did cry out to the Rock Jesus Christ as an answer that culture could never provide.

There is an inspiring story behind Bill and Gloria Gaither's song "Because He Lives." The couple wrote this song in the late 1960s, when American culture was in turmoil from the effects of teen rebellion, drugs, the Vietnam War, and the "God is dead" theory. Bill and Gloria's third child was on the way, and they were quite dejected. "What an awful time," they thought, "to bring a child into the world."

But after their son was born, the Gaithers were encouraged by a new thought: Despite all the world's problems, "this child can face uncertain days because Christ lives." Their song has become very meaningful to thousands of people, especially in difficult circumstances such as the death of a loved one. It is an example of what a Bible truth can do for us in spite of culture.

Patience, not weakness

To put the struggles of modern culture in perspective, think of Christ's death two thousand years ago. In the minds of His disciples, if there was ever a victory in Satan's program, Christ's crucifixion was it. What *could* God do now? The disciples had believed, right up until Christ's last drops of life blood seeped into the sun-baked soil, that He really could do something wonderful for the Jewish nation. But when He died, these hopes evaporated.

Today, looking back at Christ's crucifixion with the whole Bible in our hands and with two thousand more years behind us, we can easily agree that "surely the wrath of man shall praise thee."[11] Now, having witnessed the devil's greatest ploy turn into his ultimate defeat, can we trust that God can also turn the wrath of man today into His praise? Can we have faith that the last part of this verse—"the remainder of wrath shalt thou restrain"—is also true? Will God really restrain any wrathful action of man that cannot or will not be turned into His glory? That is what the Bible says.

The fact that God is patient doesn't mean He is weak.

Jesus Christ has told us, "All things are delivered unto me of my Father," and "All power is given unto me in heaven and in earth." He is described as "the head of all principality and power," the "prince of the kings of the earth," and the "Alpha and Omega, the beginning and the ending . . . which is, and

---
11. Psalm 76:10

which was, and which is to come, the Almighty." [12] God was in control, is in control, and will always be in control. The fact that He is patient doesn't mean He is weak. The fact that He doesn't use a loudspeaker when people refuse to heed His still, small voice, does not mean that He is unable to reach our generation.

It was confidence in that divine control which gave Paul the courage to stand in Athens, a city almost wholly given to idol worship, and insist that God was the One in charge. "He made everything," Paul preached, in essence. "He gave you life, breath, and everything you have. He made you like everyone else on earth, determined where you will live, and gave you the opportunity to seek Him. He is close to you, and you need to repent. He is going to judge the whole world, including you, by Jesus Christ."[13]

Today, instead of using terms like the apostle Paul's, many people speak in the language of war when they describe cultural conflicts. "We must overcome the evil powers in America's culture war," they cry. "Christians must act before it is too late." Many religious people seem to wish that God would strike down every blasphemer, atheist, or abortionist.

That whole picture is wrong according to Luke 9. As Jesus and His disciples were traveling to Jerusalem, they wanted to stop in a Samaritan village, perhaps for rest and a meal. But no one there would receive them. Two of Jesus' disciples, James and John, were greatly offended. "Lord," they asked, "wilt thou that we command fire to come down from heaven, and consume them, even as Elias did?"

James and John hoped Jesus would prove to these Samaritans that as the Son of God, He would not put up with such

---

12. Matthew 11:27, 28:18; Colossians 2:10; Revelation 1:5, 8
13. Acts 17:22-31

treatment. If these people would not respond properly, they would need to become an example of what happens to unbelievers. Wouldn't such a display of power bring the whole Jewish nation over to Jesus' side? James and John were eager to play a part in the judgment, and they even prescribed the punishment. If Jesus would just give the word, they were ready to burn up these people in a moment.

But Jesus rebuked those zealous disciples. "Ye know not what manner of spirit ye are of," He told them. "For the Son of man is not come to destroy men's lives, but to save them." Christ is still speaking like that today. "I love these people, and I want you to be a reflection of my love and truth. I am working to bring these souls into the kingdom, and I want you to witness for me."

What God can do with cultural change

Is it possible that God can work in spite of, or even because of, cultural changes such as banning public prayer and Bible reading in government schools? Some people think that such changes have caused millions of children to be deprived of the truth. "The Supreme Court kicked God out of public education," they say.

What is this view missing?

Concerning his school experience in Philadelphia, one Christian said: "When I was a boy in public school, every day started with a prayer. Yet that prayer made little if any difference in the students' lives and conduct. Most of the time, people simply ignored God and His moral principles in spite of the prayer."

Many others have echoed this sentiment. The majority of teachers and students did not know or care about the meaning of these exercises. The routine prayers, repeated in a vacuum of discipleship, were not a significant force for godliness in the schools. Still, stopping the prayers was a step away from God.

But stopping the religious exercises did not bar heaven's influence. No one can kick God out of anywhere. God is still in the public school, the liberal university, and the inner city slum. The idea that mere mortals can remove God from anywhere is wrong. Invited or uninvited, God is present.

> **No one can kick God out of anywhere. Invited or uninvited, God is present.**

Far from being defeated by changes in the public schools, God actually used these increasingly irreligious schools to accomplish a significant revival across America. To understand this, let us take a brief look at American school history since the Revolution.

When the United States began to promote education, it did so with the secular, humanistic bent of the Enlightenment. Often the rhetoric included religious terms, but it freely stated that schooling should have civic duty as its chief objective. The following paragraphs describe the scene after the Revolution.

> The general American public was ready for the new state-sponsored, tax-supported free education. They were caught up in the patriotic cause and liked the idea of freedom in democracy and the ability to vote. Most of them were not religious anyway. The 1790 census reveals that only 6 percent were members of a church.

> The population was already largely secular, and the new doctrines of democracy gave them a cause to live for. . . .
> The whole experience was a grand mixture of good and bad, God and godlessness, the Bible and secularism.[14]

By the mid-1800s, the Christian content in school curriculum was down to about 50 percent of what it had been in the early 1800s; and by 1900 it was down to about 25 percent. In 1918, the United States Bureau of Education published the *Cardinal Principles of Secondary Education*, which promoted developing ethical character but was silent on religious training.

Separated Christians like the Anabaptists felt uncomfortable with government schooling as far back as the 1830s. But they gradually succumbed to state pressure and accepted the government schools. Over the years they paid a heavy price for this as many of their youth, attracted by worldly friends, lifestyles, and beliefs, chose to join the world.

Gradually Christian parents came to realize that they could do something about the way American public schools were undermining their efforts to raise Christian families. The Amish and Mennonite movement for private schools began in a small way in the 1920s and 1930s, and since the 1960s it has mushroomed.[15]

The Anabaptist groups did not have the largest religious school movement in the 1960s. Many other denominational schools also opened in that period. Also, homeschooling

---

14. Lester E. Showalter, *The History of Christian Education* (Crockett, Ky.: Rod and Staff Publishers, Inc., 1997), pp. 54, 58.

15. The Amish were the most active in establishing Christian schools in the beginning of this movement. They suffered fines, court trials, and jail sentences, and some families had their children taken from them for a time. But because of the staunch Amish convictions, most of the states eventually relented.

increased dramatically since the 1970s; and by some estimates today, a million or more students are being taught at home, mostly for religious reasons.

The patrons of many religious private schools, as well as many homeschoolers, did not oppose all the secular trends of American culture. But they were concerned about the irreligious atmosphere in the schools that was counteracting their denominational efforts. They had some good convictions, like those expressed by T. Robert Ingram in 1961 at the Christian School Seminar in Winona Lake, Indiana.

> Christian schools are at last burgeoning in a widespread recovery of sanity and order. The Christian people of all denominations in all parts of the country are becoming more and more aroused and more and more accepting their lonely responsibility in the matter. The remedy, as with all things Christian, is not to be found in political action. It does not come from simply repealing compulsory school attendance laws. . . . It lies in the direct and heroic procedure of establishing a church school. . . . That parent who assumes the financial and moral obligation to put his child in a Christian school has taken back to himself control over that child's learning. . . .
>
> Nobody but Christian people and Christian churches can possibly assume the responsibility and initiative of establishing Christian schools. . . . It is impossible for the government to have Christian schools. It is absurd to think that anyone would establish a Christian school who was himself possessed with a zeal for some philosophy or false religious system.[16]

---

16. When Mr. Ingram made these observations in 1961, the Supreme Court had not yet ruled that schools cannot compose official prayers for students to recite (*Engel v. Vitale, 1962*) and that required daily Bible readings are prohibited (*School District of Abington Township, Pennsylvania v. Schempp, 1963*). Many religious people felt very uneasy about the public school system long before those rulings.

Might God have permitted the public schools to decay so that He could bring many children out of that system and save a much larger remnant for Himself than would otherwise have happened? There had been over one hundred years of losses in many Christian denominations, partly because of the public schools; yet before the 1950s and 1960s, few people realized what was happening. How many more things has God allowed as means of promoting His ends, which we tend to see as weakening His cause?

> We are not clinging to the last piece of driftwood; we are standing on the Rock of Ages.

It is entirely possible that through the secularizing of education, far more families have been moved toward the kingdom of God than would have been the case if state education had continued on its quasi-religious course. Thousands of families who began home schooling then had their eyes opened to other Bible teachings such as home order, which they may never have seen otherwise.

God's plan for you in your culture

Recently a Christian brother almost seventy years old surprised me. "I thank God," he said, "that He gave me life in this time, from the 1940s to today. I have seen remnants brought out of failing churches, schools started to help our children stay with the church instead of following worldly school chums, and a movement of people in the world such as homeschool families that are regaining some godly values. We have also had religious freedom for my entire lifetime, and an economy that enabled Christians to send the Gospel to many other lands. If I would have had to pick it myself, I couldn't have chosen a better time in which to live."

That testimony reminds me of Mordecai's words to Esther: "Who knoweth whether thou art come to the kingdom for such a time as this?" (Esther 4:14). Mordecai could have pitied Esther for all her misfortunes. Both her parents had died, and a heathen king had torn her away from the hope of every Jewish maiden—a happy, upright home with a kind, godly husband. If only this poor girl had been born back in the "good old days" when Israel was free and when families went on regular trips to the temple in Jerusalem! But Mordecai dried his tears and rose to the responsibility of loving and guiding his orphan niece. He was faithful to God in the time and circumstances where he lived, and he encouraged Esther to do the same.

Now it is your turn and my turn to do our part in our culture, in our time. We are not clinging to the last piece of driftwood; we are standing on the Rock of Ages.[17] God placed us here to live a godly life, to encourage others, to live in hope, and to maintain the view from the sky.

---

17. In the 1920s, Fundamentalists were sometimes described as people who talked of standing on the Rock of Ages, but acted as though they were clinging to the last piece of driftwood.

> We Christians should have
>> a special love for each other
>> because we are brothers in Christ,
>> but we should also love all men
>> as brothers in Adam.
>
> The Jews and Muslims love
>> only their brothers in Adam
>> who look and sound as they do;
>> theirs is a tribal love.
>
> We Christians are called to go
>> beyond that natural kind of love
>> and love even our enemies.
>
> However, our love will also become
>> a tribal love
>> if we work for nationalistic interests.
>
>> —*Stephen Russell,*
>>> Overcoming Evil God's Way, 2008[1]

---

1. (Guys Mills, Pa.: Faith Builders Resource Group, 2008), p. 241. Used by permission.

17

A Christian View of Foreign Cultures

We tend to be strongly influenced by what our government or our culture thinks of foreign cultures. But to accept our earthly country's international views will usually compromise the values of the New Testament.

The myth of worldly equality

Every culture tends to alienate itself from other cultures. Nearly every culture considers itself the cream of the crop. For example, Americans tend to think that they know best and their country is superior to others. That idea has hindered many American Christians in their evangelistic efforts, as Stephen Russell describes in *Overcoming Evil God's Way*.

> The second problem with nationalism is the disconnection it makes among men. The Lord wants unity in Jesus among all the different races and nationalities and communities. Of course this is possible only in Christ, but many American Christians risk losing this ideal and alienating brothers and sisters in Christ from other nations by our participation in politics that often seems to be attempting to realize the kingdom of God in the United States through the American political system. The New Testament knows nothing of this.[2]

Many times in the history of the United States, the ideals that Americans claimed to hold were abandoned in the quest for land, resources, or international political support. We are thankful for the many ways that Bible teachings on equity, justice, and mercy have influenced civil leaders, but no government can reach these ideals consistently. The talk about equality and the rights of all mankind can be quickly reduced to so many empty syllables in the compromising world of politics.

We are the most comfortable in our native country, but we must not think something is the best simply because it is the most familiar.

The world's concept of equality says that everyone is equal; but secretly or openly, many people despise other cultures because they are different. Christians should openly recognize that cultures have differences, and love others regardless of these differences.

He who knows but one culture, the saying goes, knows no culture. It is easy to think of our own ways as the best ways

---

2. Ibid., 226.

and even as the only ways. But thoughtful Christians find both positive and negative aspects in their own culture as well as any culture they encounter. It is carnal to view anything foreign as inferior. We are the most comfortable in our native country, but we must not think something is the best simply because it is the most familiar.

The Gospel for every culture

God separated the sons of Adam into different cultures.[3] He made "all nations of men for to dwell on all the face of the earth, and hath determined the times before appointed, and the bounds of their habitation."[4] Aside from people deported by war and slavery, most people live among their culture-mates. This helps to avoid cultural tension.

But the church was designed for cultures everywhere, including where several cultures live together. In fact, the church was introduced to the world in an area ruled by Romans and inhabited by Jews and Samaritans. Jesus preached the Sermon on the Mount to people living in cultural tension. Later He commanded His disciples to go into the entire world and preach the Gospel.

And the church grew far beyond the boundaries of Judaism in its first year. Acts 2 describes the devout men at Jerusalem at the time of Pentecost as hailing from "every nation under heaven . . . Parthians, and Medes, and Elamites, and the dwellers in Mesopotamia, and in Judaea, and Cappadocia, in Pontus, and Asia, Phrygia, and Pamphylia, in Egypt, and in all the parts of Libya about Cyrene, and strangers of Rome, Jews

---

3. Deuteronomy 32:8
4. Acts 17:26

and proselytes, Cretes and Arabians." These people carried the Gospel back to their home towns.

The Jews had a central role in the early years of Christianity; but about forty years after Christ's death, Jerusalem was razed and that role ended. After that, Christianity had no geographical headquarters.

The church was designed to work anywhere in the world. It does not require particular political conditions or local customs. It thrives equally well in Eastern or Western cultures, under socialism or capitalism, and under monarchies or democracies. Christianity creates its own godly subculture in any worldly culture.

"And who is my neighbour?"

Jesus' teaching introduced a new standard for how God's people look at different cultures. The story of the Good Samaritan in Luke 10 is an example of this. After reminding a lawyer of God's command to love your neighbor as yourself, Jesus told the story of a certain man, most likely a Jew, who lay wounded along a dangerous highway between Jerusalem and Jericho. Two high-class Jews, a priest and a Levite, passed by the man and left him to die. But a Samaritan picked up the man, took him to an inn, and paid the bill for his care.

There is more to this story than meets the eye at first reading.

The Jews and Samaritans had hated each other for centuries before Christ. The Samaritans were a people of mixed blood and pagan origin. Even though some of them were mostly Jewish through intermarriage, the Jews despised them, publicly cursed them, and treated them like dogs. The Samaritans in turn spited the Jews.

17 • A Christian View of Foreign Cultures

In the story of the Good Samaritan, Jesus was telling the proud Jews, "Those Samaritans are normal people with the same desires and feelings that you have. You will never see the kingdom of God as long as you allow your culture to tell you how to relate to different peoples. To love God, you must love other Jews, the Samaritans, and even the Greeks and Romans."

In Matthew 5:44, Jesus told us, "Love your enemies, bless them that curse you, do good to them that hate you." It would be just as wrong for us to describe Muslims as our enemies as to describe the Swiss, Canadians, or Australians that way. Christians are often tempted to look at a certain people as enemies because that is the way their country views those people. But the simplistic views of propaganda are carnal. Christians cannot accept at face value the allegations of their civil rulers about other people and cultures at any time, and especially in wartime. In some of the world's most terrible moments, propaganda and cultural dislike convinced thousands of people who called themselves Christians to become servants of evil.

In World War II, most Mennonites in Germany and Prussia were swayed by the propaganda of German superiority and became fully involved in the war efforts of the Nazis. There is no record of any German Mennonite who refused military service in World War II. Mennonite newspapers

> **In some of the world's most terrible moments, propaganda and cultural dislike convinced thousands of people who called themselves Christians to become servants of evil.**

This picture, called "The Breath of the Hun," was published in the New York Herald in March 1918. Through the first few years of World War I, many Americans did not want to become involved in a European war. These anti-war feelings were still strong in 1918, and hampered American efforts to prepare for war. America entered the war on April 6, 1918, while government propaganda helped to convince many Americans that the Germans were vicious killers.

German immigrants in Minnesota who did not want to return to their homeland to fight were an example of this problem. It hurt them to hear their kinfolk called "man-eating Huns." In the town of New Ulm, citizens held a meeting to express their loyalty to the United States but also to ask the government to not send their young men to fight their relatives. People all over Minnesota called these citizens traitors, and the town's mayor was removed from office. The Minnesota legislature created a Commission of Public Safety, which led people to watch their neighbors for signs of disloyalty. With bullying and mob violence, "traitors" were punished, and no one stopped the aggressors.

17 • A Christian View of Foreign Cultures

carried advertisements for recruitment agencies and expressed gratitude to God when Nazi forces prevailed. Many Christians of many denominations were convinced that Hitler was right, even though Hitler himself declared that his program was not Christian.

On the other side of the Atlantic, Millard Lind told the story in 1952 of a young Bible student who professed nonresistance before World War II. But when America declared war on Germany, he was one of the first to enlist. When asked why he changed his mind, he opened a map of Europe on the table.

"There's the reason," he declared as he traced the expanding borders of Germany.[5]

In 1994, a horrible genocide took place in Rwanda, Africa's most "Christian" nation. At the time of this genocide, as many as 90 percent of Rwandans claimed to be Christian. Before this time, the nominal Christian world had considered Rwanda an outstanding mission success. In the 1930s, a vigorous Catholic mission effort had succeeded in gathering the Tutsi people into the church, and in the following years nearly all the Hutu people were "converted" as well. But these "Christian" Tutsis and Hutus became inflamed against each other, and in the genocide "Christians" hacked each other to death, often with machetes, with no respect for old or young, woman or child, neighbor or stranger. There were some Christians among them who understood Christ's way of peace and were martyred for their stand, but they were a small minority.

Middle East propaganda often portrays the Jews as having the main right to Israel and the Palestinians as hot-blooded, radical Muslims who shoot for the thrill of it. But the history of

---

5. *Answer to War* (Scottdale, Pa.: Mennonite Publishing House, 1952), p. 45.

the Middle East is a long, twisted story of intrigue and maneuvering by the local powers as well as by European countries and America. Even a brief study of the lying, deception, killing of innocents, and cold-blooded brutality of both Zionists and Palestinians would make any sincere Christian want to avoid being identified with either group. The teachings of Jesus Christ provide clear instructions for relating to such conflicts.

As I walked through the streets of Manila in the Philippines soon after the terrorist attacks on September 11, 2001, I realized that not every country viewed the terrorist conflict like "my" country did. American propaganda was saying that they needed to bomb the terrorists' home countries to make the world safe for democracy. But in Manila, a different propaganda group was declaring that the purpose of America's recent wars was to grab oil and oppress the poor people of helpless countries. Other countries had their own explanations for these conflicts.

Who was right? Was anyone right? There was no way of knowing, but it didn't really matter. The important thing for Christians is that we hold all propaganda in question so that we do not start believing things that compromise the teachings of our King. We have no responsibility to pass judgment on the affairs of this world. If we begin to advocate our nation's views on such matters, we only destroy our witness and lead our families astray.

Accepting the theology of the holocaust, a genocide, or a "holy war" is not impossible in American Christianity. Any form of Christianity that is allied with political, economic, cultural, or ethnic causes is susceptible to mindlessly destroying its neighbor.

17 • A Christian View of Foreign Cultures

Examples from the Middle East

To illustrate some contradictions that we fall into if we accept the Western powers' views of cultures, consider the conflict in the Middle East. Large numbers of sincere Christians believe that modern Israel is at the center in the fulfilling of Bible prophecy. Many have concluded that if they do not support Israel, they are opposing God's plans. Because the Western powers are also supporting Israel,[6] such believers may feel a common bond with the political agenda of those powers. And tragedies such as terrorist attacks only strengthen the beliefs and stereotypes.

I want to say clearly here that as a nonresistant Christian, I serve a King who calls me to live above earthly wrangling. I have no opinions to offer on who is right (if anyone is) in worldly conflicts like that of the Middle East.

I share the following stories because I have been shocked at how many sincere Christians have an overt bias about the souls involved in the Middle East conflict. God wants us to love every person in the world with exactly the same love—the love that flows through us from Jesus Christ who died "that whosoever believeth in him should not perish, but have everlasting life."[7]

> **God wants us to love every person in the world with exactly the same love.**

Andy van der Bijl, the tireless Bible carrier from Holland commonly known as Brother Andrew, often met with

---

6. As I write this, the long-time Western ties to Israel are strained. Like any other matter of the world's politics, the support of certain countries for others can easily, rapidly change.

7. John 3:16

opposing forces as he worked in the Middle East. He believes that literal Israel has a special place in prophecy, but he was often called anti-Israel simply because he treated the Palestinians as friends. Once as Andrew discussed the conflicts with a senior member of Islamic Jihad, the man asked, "Maybe you can explain this to me. Why do the Christian Zionists support Israel so strongly? I would like to understand."

Andrew tried to explain the reasons, and the two discussed Scripture for a while. The following excerpt describes the scene after the Palestinian left.

> We sat in stunned silence. Finally, Al [one of Andrew's companions] commented that he was amazed at the man's openness.
>
> "Why?" I asked.
>
> "He's a thinker. He seems to be genuinely searching."
>
> "You are surprised that he is a human being like you and me? Perhaps it is easier to think of him as a mindless terrorist. That will do nothing to help solve the problems of the Middle East."
>
> Later as I lay on my bed, a ceiling fan trying listlessly to move the hot, humid air in my stuffy room, I thought about how Al's response was typical of many western Christians. The news media rarely put a face on Islamic fundamentalist groups in Gaza and West Bank. Therefore few people stopped to think that these men, like people everywhere, had families, dreams, and fears. Abdul was married, and he'd told us that he had seven young children. I could imagine him at home, sitting on his sofa with a toddler snuggled up to him on each side. This wasn't how most of us chose to think of a senior member of Islamic Jihad. I wondered how many of his colleagues were also struggling to figure out the meaning of life. For many, their only source of enlightenment was Islam. . . .

17 • A Christian View of Foreign Cultures

The next day when he picked us up for our meeting with Sheikh Al-Shami, Abdul told us that he had already read half of *God's Smuggler*, and he asked us if we could get him any more books about Christianity. Eighteen months later, we met him again and gave him three more Christian books in Arabic, plus an Arabic Bible. He said both he and his oldest son had read *God's Smuggler* and he had visited the Bible bookshop in Gaza city.[8]

On another occasion in 1982, a Lebanese Christian discussed with Andrew how western Christianity's decadence and views of Israel make a problem for Christians trying to follow Christ's commands in troubled areas of the Middle East.

There are many groups that are angry with the West in general and the United States government in particular. They resent the West for its cultural invasion, economic exploitation, political manipulation, military superiority and intimidation, and imperialistic greed. And they are specifically angry at the United States government for its unconditional support and overt bias toward Israel, which is poised right now to invade Lebanon, because the United States government allows it. Israel is viewed as an ambitious nation that would like to be the superpower in the Middle East, dominating its politics, resources, and affairs. These sentiments affect us and our ministry because many equate our version of Christianity with the West. . . .

Many here in the East assume that [we] . . . are following a Christianity that was imported from America. Also, community and religious leaders as well as regular God-fearing people resent the products, movies, magazines, lifestyles, music, advertisements,

---

8. Brother Andrew and Al Janssen, *Light Force*, (Grand Rapids, Mi.: Fleming H. Revell, 2004), pp. 19, 321. Used by permission.

and TV shows that the West exports. They connect them to the culture of the Christian West.[9]

This testimony, along with many similar ones, gives convincing evidence that conservative Anabaptist churches are in a unique position to penetrate the Islamic world. Most Muslims are repulsed by the barefaced, decadent Christianity that much of America represents. However, they are attracted to the spirit of an obedient, New Testament believer who abstains from the political smearing of the day and truly follows Christ.

Many western Christians seem oblivious to the fact that there are Arab Christians. After September 11, one Christian Palestinian in the United States noted that Americans assume all Arabs are Muslim terrorists. "When you say that you're an Arab Christian," he said, "they look at you funny, like you just said the moon is purple."

In reality, the area of Syria, Lebanon, Jordan, Israel, and the Palestinian territories was predominantly "Christian" from the time of Constantine until the Crusades in the early 1000s. The Crusaders killed Christians along with Muslims, which started the long decline of Christendom in the Middle East. About 13 percent of the indigenous population belonged to Christian denominations by about 1900, and today that has dropped to less than 2 percent. The Christians who practice Jesus' teachings such as forgiveness and nonresistance are a tiny fraction of that. But they do exist, the salt of the Middle East among both Jews and Arabs.

---

9. Ibid., 52, 53.

17 • A Christian View of Foreign Cultures

In 1988 Andrew visited a Palestinian woman in a hospital; she was caring for her grandson, a victim of Israeli-Palestinian violence. He had a shattered hip and two bullets in his leg, and the doctors thought he would never walk again. The woman seemed to be sincerely seeking God's will. Andrew asked her,

"Are you able to keep your faith in God in the midst of these hard times?"

The woman looked into my eyes, perhaps wondering how honest she could be with this stranger. "Christianity is a daily commitment," she answered in a steady voice. "But it is a daily struggle to forgive my enemies. How can I forgive those who want to kill me and my brothers and sisters and who would deny me my homeland? But I must forgive. Every time I pray the Our Father, I struggle with the words 'Forgive our trespasses as we forgive those who trespass against us.' I want to say, 'God, I forgive my enemies.' I picture them; I see what they are doing every day. I see the dead bodies, the suffering, the blood. I try to forgive, but I cannot. So I pray, 'God, You must help me forgive, because I cannot!'"

Most Muslims are repulsed by the barefaced, decadent Christianity that much of America represents. However, they are attracted to the spirit of an obedient, New Testament believer.

I was deeply moved by this woman's honesty. As Bishara [another Palestinian] and I walked to his car, I said to him, "I think God is more impressed with that woman's prayers than He is with all the silly, foolish ones that attempt to clean the slate with one easy swipe: 'God bless all our family and friends. Amen.' That woman is struggling with issues the magnitude of which most of us in the West have never imagined."

Bishara agreed: "She's serious about forgiveness. I understand her struggle. I've gone through it and continue to do so."[10]

Hundreds of stories like this can be told. The book *Blood Brothers* tells about a Palestinian family, the Chacours, and their fellow villagers. They were deceived and driven from their homes in the Israeli takeover in the late 1940s. The family was forced to live in a razed village on what pickings they could find. One day soldiers arrived and took all the men and older boys from the ruined homes, shouting at them that they were Palestinian terrorists and that their families would never see them again. After hours of traveling, the village men were released near Jordan as the soldiers fired bullets over their heads. Three months later, Michael Chacour and his oldest sons straggled back to the razed village from which they had been kidnapped. His son—who wrote the story—was amazed at his father's calmness and lack of resentment as he led them in prayer after their family was reunited.

> "Father," he prayed, "they are treating us badly because we are the children of Ishmael. But we are true sons of Abraham—and your children. You saved Ishmael from death in the wilderness, and you have saved us. . . ."
>
> Early in 1950, as the cold spring rains swept the hills, flooding the wild wells and driving our meagre flocks of sheep and goats into sheltering grottoes, more heart-stopping news reached us.

---

10. Ibid., 125.

17 • A Christian View of Foreign Cultures

Plans were under way for a new kibbutz, an experimental, agricultural community set up by the new government for settlers from Europe and America. It was to be located just across the fields from our still-empty homes, and strangely, it would be called Biram also. [The villagers were still under the deceptive impression that they could soon return to their village, Biram.] More startling was the news that some of the fertile land surrounding Biram had been sold to new landlords who had emigrated from foreign countries and were living in nearby Jewish towns. Now we understood why the soldiers had stayed on in Biram to "protect" it from our return.

Most painful was the word that Father's fig orchard had been purchased from the government by a well-to-do settler as some sort of investment.

At this news, Father's face furrowed with grief. I was terrified that he would weep. He was still, his eyes shut, his mustache drooping above a faintly trembling lip. He had planted those fig trees himself one by one, straining with heavy clay jars of water up the steep slopes, caring for each sapling until it was strong enough to survive on its own. They were almost like children to him.

And in the same moment, I wished that Father would rage. Perhaps fear had numbed my anger before this time. Now as I watched Father's pain-lined face, I shook with a horrible feeling. Wardi and my brothers squirmed. None of us could bear to see Father—dear, gentle Father—in such agony of spirit.

When he spoke in a few minutes, his voice was barely above a whisper.

"Children," he said softly, turning those sad eyes upon us, "if someone hurts you, you can curse him. But this would be useless. Instead, you have to ask the Lord to bless the man who makes himself your enemy. And do you know what will happen? The

359

Lord will bless you with inner peace—and perhaps your enemy will turn from his wickedness. If not, the Lord will deal with him."

I could scarcely believe it! His life's work had just been torn from his hands. His land and trees—the only earthly possessions he had to pass on to his children—were sold to a stranger. And still Father would not curse or allow himself to be angry. I puzzled at his words to us.

Inner peace. Maybe Father could find this strength in such circumstances. I doubted that I could.

I am certain that Father had a strong voice in what happened next. Immediately after the distressing news, the remnant of our village elders convened and decided to submit a petition to the new Israeli Supreme Court of Justice. In short, the petition welcomed the settlers to the new Biram. What had been taken could be considered as a gift from our people. However, they asked, could we return to our homes in the old Biram to live peacefully beside our new neighbors and farm the remaining land?

Father's other response to the sale of his land was more of a wonder to me.

In a few weeks we heard that the new owner of our property wanted to hire several men to come each day and dress the fig trees, tending them right through till harvest. Immediately, Father went to apply for the job, taking my three oldest brothers with him. They were hired and granted special work passes, the only way they could enter our own property.

When she heard what Father had done, Mother stared at him incredulously. "How can you do this, Michael? It's so awful. So wrong."

Father replied simply, "If we go to care for the trees, we'll do the best job. Someone else won't know what they are doing.

17 • A Christian View of Foreign Cultures

They'll break the branches and spoil the new growth." This was something Father could not bear to think.

These villagers were never able to return to their homes. The soldiers invited them to come back on Christmas Day in 1952, ostensibly to return to their houses. When they came within sight of their village on Christmas morning, they found it encircled by Israeli military equipment. As soon as the people came in sight of their village, the soldiers opened fire on it and destroyed it in five minutes of shelling.

> Then all was silent—except for the weeping of women and the terrified screams of babies and children.
>
> Mother and Father stood shaking, huddled together with Wardi and my brothers. In a numbness of horror, they watched as bulldozers plowed through the ruins, knocking down much of what had not been blown apart or tumbled. At last, Father said—to my brothers or to God, they were never sure—"Forgive them." Then he led them back to Gish.[11]

The only people who can obey Christ's teachings in such situations are those who accept their fellowmen regardless of their culture. Ephesians 2:11-22 says that Christ Jesus brought both the Jews and the Gentiles into His kingdom and broke down the wall between them. This is no abstract theory; He is our peace! He abolished the enmity between the cultures, made one man out of two, and reconciled them. He gave both groups access to the Father, made them fellow citizens,

---

11. Elias Chacour with David Hazard, *Blood Brothers* (Grand Rapids, Mi.: Chosen Books, a division of Baker Publishing Group, 2003), pp. 68-71, 89, 90. Used by permission.

and uses them both to build a holy temple where God dwells through the Spirit.

Regardless of our views on prophecy, if we do not believe what Jesus says about His work between cultures and what He can accomplish in the present time, we have little to offer the world.

An example from China

In 2009, Christian brethren from North America traveled to the troubled province of Xinjiang in the northwest corner of China, where killings and riots had recently taken place. These brethren wanted to encourage true believers in that area and learn of ways to help them. The local contact person was a believer by the name of JG (fake initials). Here is their condensed story.

> Approximately half of the people in Xinjiang province are of Turkish descent and are called Uyghurs. There are over thirty different people groups in Xinjiang, and twenty-three of those are primarily located only in this province. Many of these groups have no Scriptures in their language and no exposure to its teaching.
>
> We were in a city with a population of five million. One million were ethnic Uyghurs. Another million consisted of twenty-five to thirty different ethnic groups. The remaining three million were the Han Chinese.
>
> Around 1800 the Uyghurs had fought for liberation from the Russians, only to fall into the control of the Chinese. Years of strife and difficulty had followed, but the Uyghurs had been basically left alone. Then in 1949 the Communists came into power; and in the early 1960s huge amounts of natural resources, including oil, had been discovered in the Northwest. The Communists wanted these resources for their growing industrial plans.

17 • A Christian View of Foreign Cultures

Fearing that the local Uyghurs would try to claim and control the resources, the Communists moved in hundreds of thousands of Chinese (called the Han in this region) from other sections of the country. Trainloads of military personnel, farmers, and businessmen were shipped to the region. Many came because of the glowing promises the Communists provided. Soon young women were imported to become wives for the new settlers. The methods that were used to convince the great numbers to move west and the disappointments many of them faced is one of many incredible chapters in Chinese Communist history.

The Uyghurs never accepted the Communist rule, and the Communists never overcame their fear of the Uyghurs. Rebellion and fear—what a dangerous combination! The Communists had the power and therefore they ruled, but it was an uneasy rule.

Hoping to placate the brooding Uyghurs, the Communists made a few exceptions for them. Uyghurs were allowed large families; the Han were forced to follow China's official one-child policy. Uyghurs were allowed to carry their traditional weapons, lancets and knives; the Han were not allowed to carry weapons. The Han chafed under these unequal restrictions. For years, tensions simmered as each group vied for advantage.

The Central Communist Party in far-off Beijing tried to balance the uneasy state of affairs. They installed a Han as party secretary for the city, but in a bid to keep peace, they installed a Uyghur mayor. It is all so typical of man's attempts to keep peace. Politics, negotiations, compromise, cajoling—all without acknowledging the Prince of Peace.

When the initial riot broke out one evening at eight o'clock, the Uyghur city mayor made no move for a couple of days. During this time a mob of 20,000 Uyghurs surged through the streets, killing any Han they met and any fellow Uyghur who dared to challenge them. With bricks, rocks, and knives, the mob petrified the city. Hundreds of residents fled to the surrounding hills.

As JG drove us around the city, he told us of the awful violence. "Right here," he suddenly said, "on this street, right here, one of the church brothers witnessed twenty people attacked and murdered two nights ago." We could not imagine the terror of such sudden and violent attacks. We gazed at the burned-out buildings and charred vehicles. The Uyghurs would stop a crowded bus, allow only fellow Uyghurs to get off, and then torch the bus with the remaining Han passengers. Only God knows how many lost their lives. Finally the Han banded together.

"Get out of the way," they told the police. "We'll do what we have to do."

More blood flowed; both adults and children were murdered indiscriminately. On the third day, the military finally arrived and soon brought the situation under control.

"How are the Christians faring in all this? Were any of your people killed?" we inquired.

JG shook his head. "No, not one," he replied. One Korean lady, a believer, JG thought, had stepped out for an evening walk; she had never returned. But not one believer from their churches had been slain.

"Are there many believers here?" we asked. The answer surprised us. There are approximately 2,000 house churches, or small groups of believers. They used to gather in larger groups, but persecution forced them to split into smaller fragments.

The most heartwarming thing we learned about their groups is that they do not separate the Han from the Uyghur. They were one! The church was the only organization that could keep peace between the ethnic groups.

17 • A Christian View of Foreign Cultures

"I wanted you to visit one of our pastors, a Uyghur man, an hour or two outside the city," JG explained, "But it's too late. Just a few days ago, the police imprisoned him. It's too risky to go to their place just now."

At one checkpoint, military men with machine guns ordered us to stop. We all groaned. JG and the interpreter, both Chinese pastors, were in the front seat. What if the armed men would recognize one of them? The interpreter opened his window and greeted them courteously. They searched the interior. When they saw us three Americans, they chuckled and waved us on through. "Had we been Uyghur," the two in the front explained after we left the checkpoint, "they would have dragged you from the car." Another time, we saw security guards separating Han and Uyghur people from riding in the same vehicle.

But in the church, they were one. Only the Gospel had the power to break those walls of partition. Nowhere else in that city did such love exist between ethnic groups.[12]

Is this power evident in our lives? Unless it is, people will not believe on Jesus Christ. In John 17, as Jesus foresaw the church comprised of both Jews and Gentiles, He asked the Father that all these people might become one. He was not describing a surface unity but a heart change in how people looked at others. Jesus asked for unity like that of God the Son with God the Father. There can be no greater unity. There can be no greater testimony.

---

12. Adapted from *Five Loaves Ministry Newsletter*, October 2009, "Special Feature—Xinjiang Province, China." Used by permission.

And who, according to the average modern man,
> should reorganize society so that it would finally become what it should be?

The state, always the state.

Morality, like values, resides in the political realm.

We want to attain justice, liberty, and even—
> through science and information, truth. . . .

The average man's attitude toward these goals . . .
> [is] that the state can and must accomplish all this. . . .

Yet in these domains we are facing
> the most tragic illusion of our day.

It is certain that politics can solve administrative problems,
> problems concerning the material development of a city,
> or general problems of economic organization—
> which is a considerable accomplishment.

But politics absolutely cannot deal
> with man's personal problems, such as good and evil,
> or the meaning of life, or the responsibilities of freedom.

> —*Jacques Ellul*, The Political Illusion, 1967[1]

---

1. (New York, Ny.: Alfred A. Knopf, Inc.), p. 186. Used by permission.

18

A Christian View of Political Action: Part 1

Political action gives people a sense of power, a feeling of accomplishment, and a cause to live for. Winning a victory over the opposition is just as exciting in politics as in sports. John F. Kennedy spoke for many when he said, "The political world is stimulating. It's the most interesting thing you can do. It sure beats following the dollar."

But how does political action fit with New Testament Christianity? Does it bear eternal fruit? Can a Christian be true to his Lord and to a political cause at the same time? In this chapter, we will look at some of the main characteristics of political action and see how they fit with Christian faith.

I do not believe that all political action is worthless. Even the wrath of man can bring praise to God, and the apostle Paul rejoiced when Christ was preached, whether the preacher spoke in pretense or in truth.[2] If God chooses to do so, He can utilize the efforts of people to change culture, law, and government for good. Christians should not despise efforts to improve morality in nations or communities. But neither should they get sidetracked from church building to nation building. The focus of this chapter and chapter 19 is to understand political action in light of the New Testament standard for Christian living.

Political action follows worldly priorities.

The history of most American churches in the period before the Civil War illustrates the danger of Christians aligning themselves with political causes. In that time, slavery took precedence over every other issue in the churches even as those churches became increasingly overwhelmed with worldliness.

While the Mennonites and Amish also faced many struggles with worldliness in that time, they did leave a good example of how to relate to the slavery question. Few of them had slaves, and few of them lived in the South. But their anti-slavery feelings were not simply a reflection of abolition sentiment. They believed in purifying themselves of worldliness rather than trying to reform society.

The Anabaptist groups did not follow the Protestant example of making the church a forum for society's great issues. All around them, slavery was an urgent social question for nearly forty years, but there is no record of the Anabaptists trying to influence the question in any public way. Yet they were acutely aware of the issues of their times.

---

2. Psalm 76:10; Philippians 1:18

Their public silence was not because they disregarded society's questions, but because they did not follow society's priorities. To them, personal faithfulness was most important. They understood that slavery was an evil, but they also realized that unsaved Northerners and Southerners were both headed for the same judgment. They did not see the Civil War as a blood payment for sin that would cleanse the nation in God's sight, as many Protestants did.

To be faithful to God, Christians must be able to maintain Biblical priorities in times of burning social issues. The great political questions of culture, moral or not, are not God's greatest focus. Nor should they be the Christian's greatest focus.

The great political questions of culture, moral or not, are not God's greatest focus.

This does not mean that none of the world's issues are important. Some of them, such as how to treat people, are very important. But the main focus of the church is to save souls from the world and bring them into the church, where those issues can be resolved in a Biblical way.

Political action is built on compromise.

All successful politics is founded on compromise. Whenever Christians become excited about or deeply involved in what the world considers an important issue, they inevitably compromise.

How can a Christian seek "first the kingdom of God, and his righteousness" while focusing on politics?[3] In Matthew 4, when Satan showed Jesus the kingdoms and glory of the world, Jesus told him, "It is written, Thou shalt worship the Lord thy

---
3. Matthew 6:33

God, and him only shalt thou serve." Serving God is the opposite of serving the world.

Many people fully intend to be faithful to their principles when they go into politics. But they always face hard reality sooner or later. We can choose politics and compromise, or we can choose faith and absolutes, but we cannot have both.

A conservative United States senator, heading a conference on recommendations for public schools, worded some of his recommendations like this:

- It is better to earn something than to steal something.
- It is better to tell the truth than to tell a lie.
- Families are better than promiscuity.

He did this because he knew it would not work to recommend prayer, Bible reading, and prohibiting sex education in the schools. And his position worked. It won strong support in that day, even from people who held anti-Bible views. Compromise works in politics.

A Christian in that situation would have promoted God's Word with language like this:

- "Let him that stole steal no more: but rather let him labour, working with his hands the thing which is good" (Ephesians 4:28).
- "Lie not one to another" (Colossians 3:9).
- "Mortify therefore your members which are upon the earth; fornication, uncleanness, inordinate affection, evil concupiscence, and covetousness, which is idolatry: for which things' sake the wrath of God cometh on the children of disobedience" (Colossians 3:5, 6)

And what would have happened? The conference would have erupted in argument and opposition, and it would likely have ended in failure. The true Christian's inability to compromise makes him exactly what God wants him to be: a rock-solid testimony for truth in his community. But it makes him of little use if he tries to govern society on those principles.

According to the New Testament, it is wrong to remarry while the first partner is living. But those who believe that are considered people who do not understand the real world. Recent polls suggest that most Americans would reject a presidential candidate who was married three times, but being married twice presents little obstacle for political ambitions.

When Christians go into politics, they settle for less than the best.

True faith knows no compromise. Christians should settle only for the best—the Word of God. The great temptation for Christians is to at least put "good" or "better" principles into government, since the public will not accept the best. But as Oswald Chambers wrote in *My Utmost for His Highest*, the good is the enemy of the best. When Christians go into politics, they settle for less than the best, compromise their personal faith, and betray the principles of the true church.

Christians who settle for less than God's will also confuse the world's understanding of what the Bible means for their personal lives. Some people argue that we should try to put the fear of God into America's laws. Even if Americans refuse to follow Christ, they say, we should at least try to convince them to honor God in superficial ways so that America can be great and prosperous. "After all," the reasoning goes, "God honors those who honor Him, and history is clear that any nation that does not honor the true God will quickly be destroyed."

Certainly God has said, "Them that honour me I will honour, and they that despise me shall be lightly esteemed."[4] God said this to the house of Eli, His chosen priest. A direct parallel in our time would be to apply this verse to an erring Christian. This verse and others like it give us no authority to tell the world that if they superficially honor God, He is bound to bless them.[5] How can you and I, as servants of the God who has said that "all our righteousnesses are as filthy rags" pretend that we know just how many filthy rags it takes for God to honor a country?[6] On what basis could we claim that the honor of which God speaks here is simply a superficial recognition of right principles without a heart of true worship and obedience? Did God tell Cain that if he would only bring the right items to offer, he would be respected regardless of his heart condition? No, He said, "If thou doest well, shalt thou not be accepted? and if thou doest not well, sin lieth at the door."[7]

At times in history it seems that God did honor superficial obedience, and at other times it seems that He did not. He may or may not do so; that is His prerogative. But you and I are under strict New Testament orders to preach Jesus Christ to this generation. Regardless of how "good" people are, they need a complete heart and life change to be saved from the wrath to come. The New Testament gives no compromised,

---

[4]. 1 Samuel 2:30

[5]. Another verse often used to promote this is 2 Chronicles 7:14, where God promised Solomon that if the Israelites would be faithful to Him, He would heal their land. New Testament Christians, who have been told to expect war, persecution, spreading corruption, and a deteriorating earth, have no authority to take such Scriptures out of their specific Old Testament context.

[6]. Isaiah 64:6

[7]. Genesis 4:7

halfway principles to teach when people choose to disregard the salvation message.

Telling the world to superficially honor God so that they can experience some superficial blessings tells them that they can serve God without being saved and be a Christian without being a disciple. And it shows the biggest worry of many American Christians—somehow, America must remain "good" enough to be the world's top superpower, or God (and our lifestyle) will have a major backset!

When Christians are uncompromisingly faithful to calling people to repentance, worldly people might see them as being out of step with the "live and let live" spirit of democracy. But here is one of the differences between true faith and worldly faith.

True faith loves sinners and accepts that the world will always be as God describes it: sinful, corrupt, and decaying. Yet true faith does not accept sin within the church. True faith compassionately calls the sinner from his helpless position under the devil to new life and freedom in Christ.

In contrast, worldly faith tries to force the sinner to be good without giving him the power to do so. That is very discouraging, and it often bears fruit in hateful, angry relationships between "Christians" and sinners.

Political action is based on non-Christian attitudes.

After the list of moral sins in Colossians 3, Paul listed sins of the personality. "But now ye also put off all these;" he wrote, "anger, wrath, malice, blasphemy, filthy communication out of your mouth. . . . Put on therefore, as the elect of God, holy and beloved, bowels of mercies, kindness, humbleness of mind, meekness, longsuffering."[8]

Compare political action with these lists. Political activists are not well known for mercy, kindness, humility, and meekness. They do not "study to be quiet, and to do [their] own business."[9] Many of them are out to crush their opponents, not to win them. Lamenting conservative losses in the 2012 elections, one activist stated, "We aren't generating enough angry white guys to get the job done."

Even children can discern these attitudes. An evangelical minister once said that as a young boy in Northern Ireland, he sat on the edge of the podium steps in a crowded church while a minister-politician preached a powerful sermon. After the sermon, the minister turned with a smile to the people near him and said, "To hell with the pope."

Several people around the preacher laughed, but the boy was bewildered. He had often heard that phrase in school and on the street, but never from a minister. How could a minister hope someone would go to hell? The boy knew that God doesn't want anyone to go there.

When Christians become involved in the culture war, they tend to see their opponents as enemies whom they are determined to overcome. They tend to become fearful people, and fearful people do not love. Because of these attitudes, many people have expressed the idea that "I don't want anything to do with the Moral Majority, the Christian Coalition, or the Religious Right. The Bible doesn't support the way they act. If

---

8. 3:8, 12

9. 1 Thessalonians 4:11

you want to talk to me about God, you won't get anywhere by identifying with them."

Arrogance and anger destroys Christian witness. Many people today who reject the Religious Right would be more favorable toward Christ if they saw His will lived out in happy, peaceful Christian families. It may be that some of them are rejecting "Christians" instead of consciously rejecting Christ. If given the opportunity, these people might respond positively to the Christ of love and meekness who never stoops to political mud-slinging. Christ and His church are out to save people, not fight people.

A certain evangelical minister believed that Christians should not become involved in politics, and he refused to let his church become involved in voter drives, marches, and similar activities. There was a local campaign to overturn a law protecting homosexuals; and when the effort failed, religious people began accusing this minister of being a gay sympathizer and being soft on all moral issues. He and some of his members received letters full of anger and hatred. In reflection, the minister remarked that he was thankful he was not gay. Seeing how rudely "Christian" people treated him, he could not imagine the hatred that a homosexual must feel from them.

Christ and His church are out to save people, not fight people.

How can we expect to present the truth of our Saviour in tones of strident superiority and with better-than-thou attitudes? Were we drawn to the truth that way? Is it a coincidence that Jesus Christ reserved His gentlest tones for some of the "worst sinners" He met in His ministry?

People for the American Way, founded by Norman Lear, is often viewed as a major threat to Christianity in America. Cal Thomas, a conservative reporter, once interviewed Lear. Among other things, Thomas asked Lear what he would do if he were accidentally named the head of a Religious Right organization.

> *Mr. Lear:* I would bring together . . . those leaders in the Religious Right movement who, despite political disagreements, really are lovers.
>
> *Thomas:* Lovers?
>
> *Mr. Lear:* Lovers! People who love—seriously love—people. I don't believe Pat Robertson when one second he calls me "anti-Christian" and the next is saying how he loves everyone. . . . You can't love that way. But I think it would be a great benefit to bring together those people who do love that way, who disagree with me but clearly would love me. . . . I couldn't love Falwell or Robertson because I detect too much insincerity and too much animus. . . . It would be wonderful to bring all those people together to talk about differences of opinion—prayer in school, for example—all of these things from people who basically are capable of truly loving one another as God's children, as Christ would have it, as the Sermon on the Mount would have it. I mean, who would wish to live any other way—if a human being could accomplish it—than to seriously resonate with the Sermon on the Mount? . . .
>
> Jerry Falwell called me the most dangerous threat to the American family in our generation, or something like that. At that time I was getting a number of death threats. But I got a couple of death threats from one source that really brought me up short. . . . I hired

Gavin DeBecker, who's now a major name in the security field... DeBecker found the [culprit] . . . and he had a room full of things on his wall, including that Jerry Falwell quote, with a target around it...

Pat Robertson wrote me at one point and said, . . . "Norman, though I am a former Golden Gloves boxer, I dislike fights. I seldom fight, but when I do I seldom lose. But regardless of my personal action, I want to warn you with all solemnity in the words of a Negro spiritual, 'Your arms are too short to box with God.' The suppression of the voice of God's servant is a terrible thing! God himself will fight for me against you—and He will win."[10]

It is fascinating that Lear, whom the Religious Right depicts as a God-hating monster, would actually say such things about love and the Sermon on the Mount. Certainly, Lear's organization has supported some positions that stand against good principles. But he is still a person whom God loves. He would be deeply touched by Christians who truly showed love and who lived by the Sermon on the Mount. In all his contact with religious people, he has yet to see just one who sincerely loved him and lived according to the teachings of Jesus Christ. Anemic Christianity is a much greater problem in America than liberal politics.

What would happen to Lear and millions of people like him if they had just one Christian neighbor who studied to be quiet, loved all people, and *lived* the truth instead of trying to *flaunt* the truth?

Political action identifies Christians with unbelievers.

To get anywhere in politics, you need a crowd. That is why political action always involves being in league with

---

10. Cal Thomas and Ed Dobson, *Blinded By Might* (Grand Rapids, Mi.: Zondervan Publishing House, 1999), pp. 246, 247. Used by permission.

unbelievers. For political action needs power, and there is no political power without numbers.

With his godly demeanor and goals, a Christian does not fit with any political group, even on issues like abortion. In that issue, the fight against the pro-abortion side is often termed a "war," and the anger of war is usually apparent in both camps.

Anti-abortionists have barricaded the doors of abortion clinics. They have marched tirelessly in the street, waving placards, and have spent huge amounts of time and money to remove pro-abortion people from civil office. A few have gone to such extremes that they bombed abortion clinics or murdered abortion providers.

Certainly, not all pro-life people hate abortionists. But while few pro-life people would murder or destroy property to oppose abortion, many of them apparently do not realize that bitter statements against their political opponents could inspire murder in the name of life. Much of the rhetoric heard in political sparring over this issue is not Christian. And it can produce drastic consequences.

Can we be true to Jesus Christ and join forces with millions of people who do not practice discipleship as Jesus Christ taught it? Can we, for any political cause, join with those who live by the Old Testament standard of loving their friends and hating their enemies?[11] "Whosoever hateth his brother is a murderer."[12] When we join an effort that contains anger and bitterness in its statements, we have destroyed our Christian testimony.

After the Nickel Mines school shooting, a news commentator wrote, "The so-called Christian Right should look closely

---

11. Matthew 5:43-48
12. 1 John 3:13-15

at the Amish lifestyle for lessons in what is wrong with their approach to faith and politics." He went on to praise the fact that the Amish do not try to impose their values on the world by law or force. Instead, they live their faith, and for that reason they have far more impact on the world than those who simply flaunt faith. Through the Nickel Mines incident, professing Christians around the world were forced to consider the question, "What does it mean to live a truly Christian life?"

The Christian goes through the painful process of thinking about things the way the Bible teaches that he should, and he finds himself in the Christ-following minority for his pains. With Jesus Christ, he realizes that he is outside all the political categories of the world and that he fits only into the heavenly kingdom.

Political action uses secular power.

Secular power is the opposite of spiritual power. Spiritual power and secular power cannot operate in the same person at the same time. Christians can fight only with the sword of the Spirit. When they try to use that sword in politics, they reduce the Gospel to just another force competing for worldly power.

Since political action depends on secular power, every "Christian" political organization compromises Bible principles to maintain access to power. An example is the Moral Majority, who supported Ronald Reagan when he won the White House in 1980. (Never mind that he was divorced and remarried.) One month into his presidency, Reagan nominated Sandra Day O'Connor to replace retiring Justice Stewart Potter on the Supreme Court.

The Moral Majority did not like this because O'Connor had a questionable record on abortion. But Reagan called

Jerry Falwell, the Moral Majority's top leader, and asked him to back off and trust the President's judgment. Desperate to keep his good relationship with Reagan, Falwell agreed. Thus he compromised greatly on a value he claimed to hold, just to keep access to the halls of power. In the years that followed, Justice O'Connor often provided swing votes that decided case after case in favor of abortion.

For all political groups, maintaining power will always be more important in the end than maintaining principle. When that happens, the Gospel is bound by a political agenda. Such efforts, however well intended, become part of the very system they are seeking to change.

That is one of the greatest tragedies of the politically active church. A church that associates with politics is at once at the service of the monster she thought she would change. She will bless a dictatorship, a monarchy, a republic, or a democracy—whatever the case may be. That may sound outrageous, but it is the pattern of history. Every church that ever courted political power has blessed the tactics of political power.

For all political groups, maintaining power will always be more important in the end than maintaining principle.

That is why there were Russian and Chinese churches that became tools of Communism. That is why there were German churches that served Hitler's Third Reich. The reasoning that enabled churches to work with these regimes is the same reasoning that enables mainstream American churches to become tools of American political parties.

The Christian's goal is not power but faithfulness. That is the pattern that we see in the life of Jesus Christ. God could have used His power to crush Satan, but He chose instead to use His love and the faithfulness of Christ to make a voluntary way of redemption. Compulsion is not God's way of working.

> ## The Fight Against Saloons at Berne, Indiana
>
> The following story illustrates that Bible principles such as not going to law, abstaining from all appearance of evil, nonresistance, and similar teachings are often violated by those who use the weapons of unbelief in the fight against sin.
>
> The town of Berne, Indiana, was named after Bern, Switzerland, and it was populated almost completely by people of Swiss stock, including Mennonites. Like their fellows back in Europe, they drank wine and beer. Among people such as the Mennonites, there were a few who totally abstained from strong drink, but most of them drank in "moderation." Drunkenness was uncommon among them.
>
> As more and more people favored total abstinence from strong drink, some religious people of Berne (including Mennonites) formed a temperance society in 1886. The goals of the society were to monitor the town's four saloons to make sure they complied with the laws of Indiana, and to promote temperance in general society. Most of the Mennonites and other religious people opposed the society at first, but the group worked quietly and steadily in the community. Gradually the public sentiment turned against drink.
>
> By about 1900, one of the saloons had closed even though the population of the town had doubled since the mid 1880s. Meanwhile, Fred Rohrer, a Mennonite printer in Berne, had become one of the most deeply involved persons in the temperance movement. He was the editor and manager of a local newspaper, The Berne Witness, which he used to support the temperance cause.
>
> In 1902, an oil boom brought numerous oil field workers to Berne. These men were heavy drinkers who lived from hand to mouth, and they tended to disregard law and order. The leaders of the temperance society brought concerned citizens together, and they decided that the only way to keep their town reputable was to pass laws making Berne a "dry" town.
>
> In order to pass these laws, the temperance society needed to gather enough signatures of Berne residents on a petition against saloons. Then the society needed to obtain a court injunction against anyone who applied for a license to sell liquor. According to state law, the court would have to refuse the saloons' annual licenses if the petition carried enough signatures. Eventually the temperance society obtained enough signatures to take the matter to court.

In November 1902, the temperance leaders and the saloon men fought out a stubborn court battle, with lawyers hired for each side. The temperance society won, and the county was forced to deny the renewed liquor licenses. For several months the fight dragged on, with the saloon men trying to get the cases retried without their opponents present. But the temperance society was vigilant, in some cases keeping observers in the courthouse for days at a time to make sure that their case would not be overturned on a whim. Finally the saloon men gave up, and the temperance society thought they had the liquor under control.

But less than a year after the saloons were forced to close, several saloon-keepers began clubs. (One was actually called the "Dry Town Club.") At these clubs, the members bought liquor together by the barrel and contributed money to pay for what they drank. This was not illegal, for the law only forbade operating a saloon as a business; it did not prohibit private clubs. Each member had a key to a clubhouse, and the temperance society could only guess what happened behind the locked doors. However, the clubs lasted only a few months before they ran out of money.

Some time later, the county court began giving licenses to Berne saloon keepers. The county board had a new member, and now a majority of the board favored saloons. So the county court set itself above the law, and the temperance society was forced to take the cases to the circuit court. As the process wore on, the saloon keepers and their county allies kept postponing their trials as long as they could, with the result that the saloons in Berne stayed open. Mr. Rohrer kept up legal fights against the saloon keepers even though he was physically beaten and his house was dynamited. In March 1904, Rohrer and his allies again thought that they had won the victory, for the courts finally ruled against the saloons.

But the saloons stayed open. They simply operated without a license, which meant that they no longer had to obey the laws about business hours or selling to minors. They locked their front doors but kept their back doors open. The legal fights dragged on and on, with both sides using every opportunity to get ahead in what they called their "war" with each other. At one point Mr. Rohrer hired detectives to track down the person who had dynamited his house. At another time, when a man came to beat him, Mr. Rohrer and several workers knocked the man to the floor and held him down until the town authorities came after him.

Mr. Rohrer signed papers for arrests and search warrants, and he compelled the sheriff to break into locked rooms in saloons and roll out barrels of illegal brew. He became involved in trying to get "good" men voted into local office, even printing sample ballots "properly" filled out to help the many Germans in the area who could not read English. His sample ballots appeared so similar to the originals that he was accused of trying to stuff the ballot box. For this he was indicted and kept under arrest for almost a year before the court finally acquitted him.

On one occasion, Mr. Rohrer deliberately got drunk in order to prove that an allegedly nonalcoholic drink was actually intoxicating. For this, his Mennonite deacons asked him to make a confession in church. Mr. Rohrer's story illustrates the disunity that the congregation must have been experiencing at this time.

As a rule when a member of the Mennonite church becomes intoxicated or commits any other grave offense, he is disciplined, and the deacons, Fred Sprunger, C.W. Baumgartner and C.A. Neuenschwander, made no exception in this case. Fred Sprunger, an uncle of Samuel Sprunger, the man who was running the [saloon], thought I did wrong not only in drinking hop cream to excess, but in using the law at any time against saloon keepers. . . . He thought, in place of forcing them out of their nefarious business we ought to "love" them out.

To satisfy these deacons and the wet members of the congregation, I arose before the whole congregation on Sunday morning, March 24, 1907, and made the following confession:

"I am sorry that liquor has been sold in Berne for a long time under the name of "hop cream," and which had very likely been bought right along by some of our own church members, and was relished by them as a perfectly harmless and non-intoxicating beverage, failed to be such when I drank it. I confess to having taken so much of it, that it made me drunk, and I promise to drink no more of it knowingly."

Then the whole congregation arose, signifying thereby that they have forgiven me. After they were seated the pastor of the church, Rev. S.F. Sprunger, made the congregation arise once more (there were 800 or more people present) and made them confess to me that if every member of the church had done his or her duty, we would not have had this long and bitter war against law violators, and there would have been no occasion for my becoming intoxicated.

Finally in 1907, the temperance society gained so much power that Berne was forced to prohibit strong drink for a number of years. At the end of his story, Mr. Rohrer pointed out that since the town had been "dry," business had boomed as never before. He concluded with these words:

Verily, it pays to be fearless in the right, not only morally, but financially as well. And, remember, had God not been in this movement against the saloons in Berne, I would never have lived through it to tell the story. Therefore, praise the Lord, O my soul...

Let us now do the same [as the Civil War] with the liquor question and fight it out to the finish now, instead of leaving it to our children to settle. God will help us to do it.[13]

---

13. Fred Rohrer, *Saloon Fight at Berne, Ind.* (Berne, In.: The Berne Witness Company, 1913)

Political action cannot deliver on its promises.

Political activism promises to bring significant changes to the world, but the good that it achieves can never come close to the results of true faith. There is no better illustration of this than the failure of the Moral Majority.

The Moral Majority was the brainchild of three conservative religious men: Howard Phillips (Jewish), Paul Weyrich (Catholic), and Jerry Falwell (Baptist). They believed that with proper organization they could elect Christians to the government of the United States and beat back the liberals and "infidels" who were controlling it.

Their strategy seemed to work at first. Moral Majority leaders followed an incredible schedule, flying over the United States and often appearing in a number of cities in one day to give speeches, debate moral issues, and encourage Christians to vote for Republicans. They were able to marshal millions of dollars and votes in the 1980 election, and they are credited with getting President Reagan elected and returning the Congress to Republican control.

During this time, thousands of churches became involved in politics in a greater way than ever before. After the election, scores of churches placed large posters of Reagan beside pictures of Jesus Christ, or they displayed large photographs of their pastor shaking hands with the President. One observer noted that Christ often seemed to take second place to Reagan on a pastor's wall or desk. Cal Thomas was deeply involved with the Moral Majority at the time, and he described the euphoria they felt.

We were on our way to changing America. We had the power to right every wrong and cure every ill and end every frustration that God-fearing people had been forced to submit to by our "oppressors," whom we labeled secular humanists, abortionists, homosexuals, pornographers, and "liberals." We opposed them all with the righteous indignation we thought came directly from God. We opposed them because we knew they were the reason America was in decline. And we had been raised up by God himself to reverse that decline.

The election was proof that God was on our side and that he was well-pleased. We believed that we could restore "moral sanity" by might and by power, with the Spirit of the Lord upon us. Victory and success, money and access to the White House, to Congress, and to the media—this was all the proof we needed of God's approval and blessing. Anyone who disagreed with us was a liberal, an atheist, a compromiser, or a member of the National Council of Churches (or maybe all four).

We sang the hymn "Victory in Jesus" in church, and we believed that theme in the long run. But we also believed in victory in Ronald Reagan for the short haul and we knew he believed in us. Heaven was a long way away, and we needed something to help us make it through the political night. In Reagan we trusted...

If any political movement should have been able to change the country by implementing its agenda, it was the Moral Majority. We had the nation's attention. We were mobilizing the nation's largest demographic unit (it has often been noted that there are more people in church on Sunday than watch NFL football games), and we had a President in the White House friendly to our objectives. For six years we also had a Republican-controlled Senate. . . .

We were advancing. Liberalism was retreating. It was just a matter of time before our nation would be restored to what we wanted it to be. Those who doubted or questioned our power were dismissed. Those who warned of danger ahead were ignored, ridiculed, or condemned.

That was twenty years ago, and today very little that we set out to do has gotten done. In fact, the moral landscape of America has become worse. The Moral Majority folded in the late eighties, giving way to the Christian Coalition and other organizations that have taken up its agenda, using, with minor variations, the same strategies to achieve the same ends we failed to achieve.

Two decades after conservative Christians charged into the political arena, bringing new voters and millions of dollars with them in hopes of transforming the culture through political power, it must now be acknowledged that we have failed. We failed not because we were wrong about our critique of culture, or because we lacked conviction, or because there were not enough of us, or because too many were lethargic and uncommitted. We failed because we were unable to redirect a nation from the top down. Real change must come from the bottom up or, better yet, from the inside out. . . .

Politics was a better means to noble ends than the hard and often invisible efforts mandated by Scripture. Who wanted to ride into the capital on the back of an ass when one could go first class in a private jet and be picked up and driven around in a chauffeured limousine? Who wanted the role of a servant when one could have the accolades given to leaders? Who wanted the pain of Good Friday when one could have the acclaim of the masses on Palm Sunday? . . .

18 • A Christian View of Political Action: Part 1

The impotence and near-irrelevance of the Religious Right were demonstrated on the day William Jefferson Clinton was inaugurated. Clinton's first two acts as president were to sign executive orders liberalizing rules against homosexuals in the military and repealing the few abortion restrictions applied under presidents Reagan and Bush.

With a few pen strokes, Bill Clinton erased the little that the Moral Majority had been able to achieve during its brief existence. The tragedy was not the failure to succeed, but the waste of spiritual energy that would have been better spent on strategies and methods more likely to succeed than the quest for political power.[14]

When Clinton came to power, many Christians reasoned that by this election, God was judging America and giving it the kind of president it deserved. A better conclusion may be that the election was instead a judgment on "Christian" politics, to show Christians how little they can accomplish by political power.

The fact is that if all the laws that Religious Right organizations have wished for were passed today, the results would be negligible. Nothing would be changed in the hearts of Americans. These organizations have worked strenuously since the 1980s to accomplish their aims, but they will never accomplish much because their methods are wrong according to the New Testament. They believe that structural change equals real change, but that is a delusion. They advocate changed policies instead of changed hearts. They are content to put Band-Aids on the chest of a heart attack patient.

---

14. Cal Thomas and Ed Dobson, *Blinded By Might* (Grand Rapids, Mi.: Zondervan Publishing House, 1999), pp. 22, 23, 26, 27. Used by permission.

To set this discussion on political action in perspective, we should remember that God may utilize such efforts for His own purposes. We should not despise the efforts of political groups to bring about change for the better. We are thankful for any good effects such efforts may have, even if they are temporary or seem superficial. But it is very important that we view these efforts in light of the principles of the New Testament. That is the only stance that will keep us faithfully separated unto God in our time.

Resting in God's timing and justice frees us from the urge to try to set the world right.

Why political action is appealing

People are tempted with political action when they become impatient with God's timing and justice. It is easy to doubt the power of prayer when it looks as if God's work is not making progress. But God is still sovereign, and history is still moving toward a conclusion. When God says that Jesus Christ has lighted every man who comes into the world, that world events are in His control, that vengeance is His, and that every knee shall bow to Him, He knows what He is talking about.

Resting in God's timing and justice frees us from the urge to try to set the world right. It frees us from selfishness. It opens our hearts to be spent on saving souls for eternity. Someone described the Christian's viewpoint well when he said, "Never look for justice in this world, but never cease to give it."

People are tempted with political action when they feel like victims of evil. Many a Christian has been drawn into political action simply because he could no longer endure the world's attitude toward Christianity. "We shouldn't have to be considered foolish and outdated," say the political-religious people. "After all, this is *our* Christian country, and it was founded for *us*! You need to listen to us!"

Welcome to the real world. America is not paradise or the Garden of Eden. But that does not mean Christianity is a victim of sinful society. Christ's cause is openly triumphing over evil since His resurrection. Do not let the victim mentality lead you into discouragement. The Conqueror of all is leading His children!

People are tempted with political action when they desire the government's approval. Mainstream American Christians seem to need the government to support their values in order to feel significant. Many of them react in fear when a non-Christian idea influences the civil government. But such fear is not from God.

Christians in many parts of the world feel that they have an urgent, fulfilling work, even under oppressive regimes that are trying to stamp them out. The believers in these countries do not try to change the government; they are working to build Christ's church in the hostile world He has said we should expect.

> **We do not need to be politically visible in our community or have our faith recognized in Washington.**

Do not pity yourself if American culture or government does not seem to appreciate you as a Christian. We do not need to be significant in the world's eyes. We do not need to be politically visible in our community or have our faith recognized in Washington. Nor do we need high-profile converts to prove what our faith can do.

Be content to labor behind the scenes. Be content to witness quietly instead of shouting from a political stump. Be content to sow the unnoticed seed that sprouts in good soil. Be content to grow as the wheat among tares. These are powerful Christian activities that can produce a harvest of souls for the kingdom.

People are tempted with political action when it appears that certain individuals or organizations are responsible for the decline in the world. However, battering and blaming politicians or institutions generally has very little effect. If you push politicians, they will push you right back. If you fight them, you intensify their desire to win their goals. Christians only weaken their own cause when they act in these ways.

The real problem, as Jacques Ellul has pointed out, is that too many religious people are unwilling to live the Christian life and to witness of it themselves. Hence they want the government to represent their values for them.

> Because I am incapable of doing good in my own life, I insist that the state must do it in my place, by proxy. Because I am incapable of discerning the truth, I ask the government to discern it for me; I thus free myself of an onerous task and get my truth ready-made. Because I cannot dispense justice myself, I expect a just organization to exist which I only have to join to safeguard justice... This becomes a true flight from oneself, from one's own destiny, one's personal responsibilities....
>
> This... means that nobody is truly responsible or has any real obligation with respect to justice, truth, or freedom, which are the affairs of organizations—a collective affair.... If our values are not attained, if things go badly, it means the organization is bad. ... We will then accuse... the state power, because state power

must provide all just organization and the elimination of the pernicious enemy. This strenuous flight from the personal obligation to accomplish, oneself, what is good and just is often accompanied, in the case of intellectuals and Christians, by a corollary vice, that of insisting on universal responsibility. . . . What characterizes this attitude is impotence in the face of reality: I really cannot do anything about these things except sign manifestos and make declarations or claim that I act through political channels.[15]

At the least, blaming the state is wasting energy on the brick wall of politics. At the most, it is simply throwing up our hands and saying we can accomplish no good, because someone else is not doing what he should.

Further, blaming the state for the world's condition makes us just like everyone else. Many people do not want a careful, accurate evaluation of why things are the way they are; that would bring the blame too close home. Instead, they want a villain to punch in the face; and in their minds, one of Washington's chief purposes is to parade these villains. But the New Testament gives Christians no permission to think of government in that way.

In a Philippine government office one day, I waited in line for an official to stamp my papers. As he worked, the man was laughing and joking with several women co-workers, openly making crude and profane remarks. When it was my turn at his desk, he asked me if I was a missionary. I replied that I was, and he continued the conversation.

"The problem with the Philippines," he said, "is that this nation's leaders do not follow the Word of God. If the leaders

---

15. *The Political Illusion*, pp. 187-189. Used by permission.

were Christians, God would heal our land, and our economy wouldn't be in shambles. We would have a clean government. We would not have gotten such typhoons as we had this year."

Obviously, this man had accepted the false idea that Christianity produces prosperity and trouble-free living. More troubling, he was a married man openly violating God's Word; yet upon sight of a missionary, he could give all the reasons why the Philippines was not prospering—and not one of those reasons included his own sins. The whole problem lay with "them," not with "me." "They" were not obeying God's Word, and the "government" needed to be clean, though that apparently did not include the official I was conversing with. I am reminded of the satirical definition a man once wrote for the word *Christian*: "One who believes that the New Testament is a divinely inspired book admirably suited to the spiritual needs of his neighbors."

> **The New Testament does not say that people are living in sin because some king, policeman, or judge failed to do his job properly.**

When I challenged the man about his personal life, he laughed it off. Blame is easy; conviction is hard. It was the same for the Jews of Jesus' day. If Jesus had blamed the Romans and supported Jewish national renewal, He would have been a hero. But He spoke of personal regeneration, of willingness to suffer and sacrifice, with never an offer of hope for earthly nations—and He was crucified.

We cannot bring anyone to Christ today by making an issue over a Supreme Court decision fifty years ago. The New Testament does not say that people are living in sin because some king, policeman, or judge failed to do his job properly. Rather, "every one of us shall give account of himself to God."[16] When Christians blame politics, they only contribute to hardening unsaved souls against finding deliverance from sin.

---

16. Romans 14:12

Our people should keep themselves
> apart from all party matters in political things where
> brother votes against brother and father against son.

What poverty is this throughout our congregations
> that we want to help rule the world
> we who are chosen out of the world by God.
>> —*Amish Bishop Jacob Swartzendruber, 1865*

19

A Christian View of Political Action: Part 2

This chapter discusses examples and stories that show the dangers of Christians becoming involved in political action. It also explores why most conservative Anabaptists avoid the voter's booth, one of the simplest forms of political action.

"Christian" political actions that backfired

When Thomas Jefferson was campaigning for the presidential election of 1800, some churches predicted that his election would lead to the demise of Christianity in America. They charged him with being a deist (which he was) and an atheist (which he was not). The Jefferson party made counter charges, saying that Alexander Hamilton (who opposed Jefferson early in the campaign) was an adulterer and that John Adams and Charles Pinckney (the team running against Jefferson) were not orthodox Christians either.

The churches that were fighting Jefferson made such vehement and radical charges that they turned the election toward him instead of away from him. Regardless of what the truth was about Jefferson, opposing him became associated with the extremism of these churches, and many voters did not want to be identified with that. John Adams later reported,

> With the Baptists, Quakers, Methodists, and Moravians, as well as the Dutch and German Lutherans and Calvinists, it had an immense effect, and turned them in such numbers as decided the election. They said, let us have an Atheist or Deist or any thing rather than an establishment of Presbyterianism.

After the election, the ministers who had so viciously opposed Jefferson limped along with seriously damaged reputations. They had violated many Gospel principles in their fight to preserve a "Christian" America, and now it became a favorite sport to take shots at them. The Congregational, Presbyterian, and Episcopal churches suffered lost prestige and their reputation for integrity. Through that experience, one historian concluded, these churches lost the potential they might have exercised for good if they had been more charitable.

In the period before the Civil War, ministers and activists on both sides of the slavery issue spoke in fiery rhetoric. David Walker of Boston made some typical statements when he preached that the continued toleration of slavery would doom and ruin the entire United States. "Almighty God," he cried,

THE PROVIDENTIAL DETECTION

In this drawing, religious people remind the public that God was against electing Thomas Jefferson for president. Here God and an American eagle attempt to keep Jefferson from destroying the U. S. Constitution on the altar of "Gallic despotism." Jefferson's alleged attack on George Washington and John Adams in the form of a letter to Philip Mazzei falls from his pocket. Satan, the writings of Thomas Paine, and French philosophies are supporting Jefferson.

"will tear up the very face of the earth!" Such inflammatory preaching contributed directly to the actions of Nat Turner, a thirty-year-old slave and preacher of Southampton County, Virginia. Fired with apocalyptic zeal, Nat imagined that he was the long-awaited instrument of God's justice on earth.

In 1831, Turner and sixty to seventy other slaves led a rebellion that resulted in the deaths of about sixty whites. Turner was captured and hanged, along with about twenty of the slaves that had helped him. Angry whites also killed about one hundred innocent slaves in retaliation for Turner's rebellion. The belligerent, flamboyant oratory that roused Turner to his rebellion was not in the pattern of New Testament preaching, and it produced terrible results.

In 1925, as evolution was becoming accepted across America, a young schoolteacher named John T. Scopes agreed to be the "guinea pig" in a court case in which the American Civil Liberties Union sought to overturn Tennessee's law against teaching evolution in public schools. The entire trial was set up, as one of its reporters said later, as a lark on a monstrous scale. Scopes and his violation were not the focus. Instead, this was a court battle to test whether fundamentalists or modernists would win in the legal world. William Jennings Bryan, who assisted in the prosecution, stated, "The case is . . . a battle royal between unbelief that attempts to speak through so-called science and the defenders of the Christian faith, speaking through the legislators of Tennessee."

The fundamentalists won, and Tennessee's law was upheld. But it was a hollow victory. The news coverage of the trial depicted Tennessee as a stagnant backwater, creationism as gross ignorance, and the trial itself as a farce. A major news-

19 • A Christian View of Political Action: Part 2

paper claimed that the creationist side was characterized by "bigotry, ignorance, hatred, superstition, every sort of blackness that the human mind is capable of. On the other side was sense."

One wonders how different the results might have been if Christians of that day had refused to be drawn into a trap set up to portray them as ignorant, dark-minded people. Had they chosen to follow the ways of God in dealing with a secularizing society, they might not have looked so foolish in the end.

If the fundamentalists had realized that the truth has greater power when spoken through faithful lives than through the legislators of Tennessee, they might have won the case in more of America's hearts, where the real battle was being fought. Had they realized the powerful witness of a faithful, believing church, they might have concentrated on cleaning up their own ranks instead of trying to force the world to accept the truth. Franklin Littell has pointed out how devastating it was to American Protestant churches when they involved themselves in the political struggle surrounding Prohibition and the anti-evolution laws. The churches' efforts, he stated,

> ... diverted Christian energy from more important matters, [and] were fatal mistakes in Protestant action. They were wrongly conceived and wrongly executed, and above all they rested on a false presupposition: that America was still a Protestant nation and the Protestant churches had a right to force Protestant morality and belief upon the body politic. . . . Politicians in the churches attempted to secure by public legislation what they were unable to persuade many of their own members was either wise or desirable. In both cases, lacking the authority

of a genuinely disciplined witness, the Protestant reversion to political action was ultimately discredited, and the churches have not to this day recovered their authority in public life. . . . The Fundamentalists won the [Scopes] case but lost the country.[1]

Why "Christian" political action backfires

The world does not understand the true meaning of Christianity. When things like Bible obedience, God's judgment, morality, and faithfulness are mentioned in politics, the terms usually do not mean the same as when Christians use them. Bible verses have repeatedly been twisted and taken out of context to support political efforts and even immoral behavior. This does not change the truth or the sacred character of God's Word. But it does mean that Christians cannot expect the Bible to be respected as the last word in political argument. It never has been considered the final rule in politics, and it occupies a lower position today than several centuries ago.

Perhaps Jesus had a situation like this in mind when He said, "Give not that which is holy unto the dogs, neither cast ye your pearls before swine, lest they trample them under their feet, and turn again and rend you."[2] We live in a time like that of the apostle Paul, when "Christ crucified [was] unto the Jews a stumblingblock, and unto the Greeks foolishness." God chose base, foolish, and weak things to confound the world. True Christians must be willing to be despised and considered foolish if they will have an impact on the world for Christ.[3]

---

1. *From State Church to Pluralism* (Garden City, Ny.: Doubleday & Company, Inc., 1962), pp. 120, 121.
2. Matthew 7:6
3. 1 Corinthians 1:23-29

19 • A Christian View of Political Action: Part 2

So Christians cannot appeal to uninterested unbelievers as if they understood what Christianity means. Indeed, sinners are personally accountable; but after generations of warped religious ideas, they do not have an accurate concept of true godliness.

Before pushing "Christian" policies in the political realm, we should remember that such policies have martyred thousands of sincere Christians through the ages. Rome was the first nation to incorporate Christian doctrine in national law. When its leaders did so in the early 400s, their laws specified the death penalty for people who opposed Catholic doctrine. Throughout most of history, there has been little difference in the way that pagan governments and "Christian" governments treated true Christians.

When Christians enter politics, they become "fair game" in the political fight. Christians tend to enter politics with the purpose of setting things right. But what actually happens is that they enter an arena where every idea and every person—right or wrong, wise or foolish, traditional or radical—competes on a level playing field.

God chose base, foolish, and weak things to confound the world. True Christians must be willing to be despised and considered foolish if they will have an impact on the world for Christ.

Everyone in politics is subject to the rules of politics, which include arrogance, compromise, exaggeration, and personal attacks. The motives, words, actions, and personal history of politicians are all fair game for use and abuse. That is why whenever Christians court political power, blame the government for wrongs, or point out how foolish government policies are, they lose respect and credibility.

Another rule of the political game is that when one makes something a political issue, he is looking for a political solution. Blaming the government for the poor state of national affairs implies that the government has the responsibility and wisdom to make improvements. When a "Christian" politician says such things, he must be ready to accept the solutions that the state offers.

A Christian who wants to avoid becoming political prey has only one option: stay out of the game. He is the most likely to be respected when he does not blame the state or propose solutions that he knows the state cannot provide. In turn, by living above reproach and refusing to become involved in welfare programs and other monetary handouts, he is more likely to be left alone by the state. He is no threat or expense to it, neither has he said what it should do.

The issue of voting

In free countries, voting for political leaders is considered the right and responsibility of every citizen. Even if a person refuses to become involved in political actions like marching to protest war or abortion, he may still vote in local and national elections. Unlike radical political actions like lying on a logging road to keep bulldozers out of a national forest, voting is considered respectable and responsible. In fact, some countries (like Australia) impose a fine on any eligible citizen who does not vote.

The Anabaptists and their descendants have long been ambivalent about voting. In Europe they were considered outlaws, and they never had the opportunity to be involved in government. After many Anabaptists moved to America,

19 • A Christian View of Political Action: Part 2

some of them became involved in voting and even holding office, especially in Pennsylvania. The official position of many Anabaptist groups for most of their history in America was that they discouraged voting and holding office, and in some churches such actions would keep an otherwise qualified man from being considered for ordination. However, voting and holding minor offices did not generally bring church discipline. Only a few small groups in the Anabaptist tradition disciplined members for voting.

Today most conservative Mennonites and Amish take a firmer stand against voting. They do not hold this position because voting is clearly forbidden in the Scriptures, but because it involves direct participation in the political system. Voting gets Christians into situations that they would do better to avoid. It tends to blur the line between the true church and the world.

These may seem like strange conclusions. The following paragraphs explain from the Bible and history why conservative Anabaptists refrain from voting.

They take seriously the New Testament commands not to resist evil by physical force. Most public offices require the use of force, and some are directly involved in war. Conservative Anabaptists do not want to help assign others to do what they believe is wrong for themselves.

They do not support the "chosen nation" and "superior people" ideas that politics represent. People tend to vote for candidates that campaign with a strong, proud, nationalistic spirit. But while Christians appreciate some things about their earthly nation, they also recognize that it has many problems. They should not participate in worldly power struggles such as the conflict between the free world and the Communists or Muslims, and the struggles between Israelis and Palestinians. A Christian loves all men, especially his Christian brothers and sisters everywhere. How can he vote for people who represent proud views of their own nation, and who despise people that oppose their ideals?

They do not want to support people who may be involved in lies, distortions, and personal attacks. These things have characterized American political campaigns as far back as the presidential election of 1800. Humility is replaced by self-glorification, and a candidate may be exalted so highly that the campaign borders on idolatry. There is little place for Christian virtues like honesty, being "kindly affectioned one to another," and "in honour preferring one another."[4] Instead, the candidates and their supporters promote themselves and try to tear down the opposition.

All too often, people caught up in political campaigns get trapped in the same mentality and methods. Even those who choose not to vote may become emotionally affected and await the election results with bated breath, hoping the "right" candidate will win. How can we maintain New Testament attitudes if we get involved, even emotionally, in campaigns or voting?

The Scriptures teach that man has a sinful nature and that worldly systems are essentially evil. We should not charge politicians with lying or accept conspiracy stories about them, but we do believe that "the whole world lieth in wickedness." Also, man without Christ is "carnal, sold under sin," and he cannot by his own strength gain deliverance from "the body of this death." God is the final Judge; but when one considers the works of the flesh and the fruit of the Spirit as described in Galatians 5, the char-

---

4. Romans 12:10

19 • A Christian View of Political Action: Part 2

acter of most candidates becomes clear. Christians cannot put faith in what candidates say about themselves or their abilities.

In spite of the choices that elections seem to offer, strong lobbies and powerful corporations basically control politics. Many individual candidates do not have the power to keep the promises they make or to legislate the values they claim. No one gets anywhere in party politics without official support, and all parties fill their posts with people who are first and foremost able to get and keep power against their rivals in other parties. If good character is an asset in this game it will be exploited. But it is a servant, not a master.

> **How can we maintain New Testament attitudes if we get involved, even emotionally, in campaigns or voting?**

Elected representatives are unable to fully understand, much less control, the powerful elephant they ride. That is why changing the officials usually changes little. Any official is inevitably faced with politics, and politics follows certain patterns over which the politician has little control. Any politician may speak of high goals, noble values, and traditional ethics, but he actually deals only with surface issues and has little power to create the noble things of which he speaks.

To illustrate this, in each of the American presidential elections from Richard Nixon to George H. W. Bush, the winner was the man favored by conservative voters (with the exception of Jimmy Carter, the first American president who claimed to be born again). Yet this period was marked by significant moral decline, which hardly supports the idea that electing the "right" leaders is the way to accomplish lasting good.

"The most High ruleth in the kingdom of men, and giveth it to whomsoever he will, and setteth up over it the basest of men."[5] Here the Bible says plainly that God does not always appoint the man who would seem the most suitable for political office. So how can we ever know, before an election, which man God has chosen? It is better to pray that God's will be accomplished than to vote, when by voting we might be supporting a candidate that is not God's choice.

Regardless of who is elected, Christians never lose an election. We are strangers, pilgrims, and foreigners, not true citizens. We are transients, not residents. We are ambassadors representing a foreign country. Scriptures such as Daniel 4:17 indicate that political elections are God's responsibility, not ours. That is a major reason to avoid political voting, along with talking as if we know which politician should be elected.

In the presidential election of 1896, Ohio Governor William McKinley (Republican) ran against Democrat William Jennings Bryan of Nebraska. This campaign took place during the depression of 1893-1897. Because of the severe economic distress, this campaign generated more interest and participation than any other since the Civil War. The Amish were generally not involved in politics; however, they were suffering financially at this time and became caught up in the excitement of this election and the solutions Bryan was proposing. Bryan was sympathetic toward the workingman and also had a reputation as a fundamental Christian. It is not known how many Amish voted for Bryan; but he was the runaway winner in communities with large Amish populations, such as Holmes County, Ohio. Yet God raised up McKinley in that election.

---

5. Daniel 4:17

19 • A Christian View of Political Action: Part 2

In 1960, the candidates for the presidency were Democrat John Kennedy and Republican Richard Nixon. That year thousands of Amish, Mennonites, and other religious people who had never voted before voted for Nixon to save America from having a Catholic president. But apparently it was God's will to elect Kennedy, and He did so regardless of the many "Christian" votes cast against him. The folly of calling Nixon the better candidate became evident in the early 1970s during the Watergate scandal.

Voting in political elections sets spiritual brethren against each other, while the Scriptures command us to "walk by the same rule" and "mind the same thing."[6] Because the views and principles of political candidates are difficult to evaluate, people in the same family and the same church often vote for opposing candidates. This is another evidence that God has not made clear to Christians how to select worldly leaders.

In the 1865 quote at the beginning of this chapter, Amish Bishop Jacob Swartzendruber pleaded with his brethren to stay aloof from political elections because of how it pitted brethren against each other.

Anabaptist experience with voting in America

Anabaptist participation in politics has always risen in times of peace, but it dropped dramatically in the Revolutionary War, the Civil War, and World War I. During wartime, the church saw political involvement for what it was—a pact with the world that they could not fulfill.

As far back as the struggle with France in the 1750s, Americans told the Anabaptists that if they wanted to vote, they

---
6. Philippians 3:16

needed to be ready to fight. Benjamin Franklin complained that in earlier times the Pennsylvania Germans "modestly declined intermeddling in our Elections, but now they come in droves." These people had refused to volunteer for Pennsylvania's voluntary militia units, he stated, so why should their opinions have any weight?

In 1752, William Smith of Pennsylvania proposed stripping the Quakers and their German supporters (including Anabaptists) of all political rights and offices. He wanted England to enact an oath of office "that they would not refuse to defend their country against His Majesty's enemies." Smith's plan was not carried out at that time, but its basic ideas were implemented during the Revolutionary War.

Anabaptist voters were really brought up short in the Revolution. Many of them had earlier voted extensively for candidates that seemed the most likely to keep the old colonial privileges intact; they feared that they would lose their freedoms under Revolutionary leaders. And their votes made a difference at first. Anabaptists and those of other German sects voted in sufficient numbers to keep the Pennsylvania Assembly under Quaker control, in spite of criticism from a few of their church leaders. There are records of Mennonite meetings in Lancaster County to decide whom to vote for.

Around the 1750s, Bishop Henry Funk (d. 1760) reprimanded his people for their political involvement. Freedom was causing spiritual decay, he said, and using political action to secure this freedom was adopting the ways of the world to escape persecution. Funk disapproved of churches that "make an effort to elect officials or magistrates according to their own wishes and ideas" and members who "seek these

19 • A Christian View of Political Action: Part 2

offices themselves and serve in them in order that they may assure not only those in our own time, but also our children, exemption from the feast of affliction as kept by Jesus."

But the Revolutionary War finally swept away the illusions of using political action to secure freedom, and for over ten years the Anabaptists and Quakers of some areas lost the right to vote or hold office. Thoroughly chastened, most of them abstained from voting for years afterward. Lancaster Mennonite Francis Herr said in 1790, "If we for the gospel and Christ's sake cannot hold any office, how should we be capable to elect others into office?" This expressed the common Mennonite position, though few churches enforced such a stance.

A politician of Franklin County, Pennsylvania, reported the following in 1837.

> The Mennonites, in his part of the state, were numerous, and they were sober, quiet, and industrious citizens. They had nothing to do with public affairs, and it was very difficult to prevail upon them even to exercise the right of suffrage [voting] except at those times when they believed the bulwarks of the Constitution to be assailed, then they will come to its defense.

In the years before the Civil War, this reluctance gradually changed until a significant number of Mennonites were voting again. Daniel Musser of the Reformed Mennonite Church (a group in Lancaster that had adopted a position against voting) gave the following report about some other Anabaptist groups in 1864.

> Last fall a year Thaddeus Stevens was the avowed war candidate for Congress from this county—pledged to support

the Administration in a vigorous prosecution of the war. Great numbers of young men voted for him on this ground. . . . Shortly after the election, the first draft for men to supply the army came off. Now there were numbers of these same young men who had so voted, came forward and affirmed that they were conscientious, and could not fight! Their spiritual teachers and guides testified that they were members of their "church," and that these conscientious scruples are embodied in their tenets. Was this consistent? . . .

[They] cast their [vote] for the President, placed him in office, and put the sword in his hands. . . . How can anyone contend that it is sin for him to use it, and not for them to give him power to do so!

The Mennonites who had voted also raised the ire of some of their non-Mennonite neighbors, as John Ruth wrote in *The Earth is the Lord's*.

Because they voted, they were continually criticized in the local press by those who opposed the Republican party. When the national election came around in 1864, Mennonites caught some of the anger directed toward the men so roundly hated by the Democrats: Abraham Lincoln and his eloquent supporter in Congress, Lancaster's Thaddeus Stevens.

Democrats also felt that the three-hundred-dollar commutation fee [a fee the federal government accepted from conscientious objectors in lieu of military service] was "a blow aimed at the laboring classes," who could not afford it, while "the wealthy German farmers of Lancaster, . . . who happen[ed] to belong to the Mennonitish or similar Christian denominations," could evade the draft by paying what to them was a "paltry sum." They owed this "boon," said one angry political writer in the Intelligencer, to

19 • A Christian View of Political Action: Part 2

"THADDEUS STEVENS who wants their votes . . . to re-elect him to Congress." . . . If the Mennonites "believe that war is just and right," it argued, "then they should be willing to fight in it. If they believe it is wrong, then why do they vote for the candidates [especially Lincoln] pledged to its continuance?"[7]

In the context of World War I, the Franconia Conference recorded the following sentiments on October 4, 1917: "We have learned that the world expects us to be separate. We therefore consider it advisable to abstain from voting." The same thoughts surfaced among the Amish as Old Order Bishop Manasses E. Bontrager (1868-1947) reproved those who had helped to vote President Woodrow Wilson into office.

In Virginia's Shenandoah Valley, the situation in 1917 was typical of that in other areas where many Anabaptists lived.

> The first flurry of enlistment from the Valley rose quickly. All through the summer months, men were registering and leaving for camp . . . Mennonites and Brethren who wanted to register as conscientious objectors were told they had no right to do so. They would have to go to camp and voice their objections there. This was to be a war that ended all wars. All hands were needed to make it so. If they could be involved in politics the previous year to vote against alcohol, why should they not respond to a cause much greater than prohibition?[8] Those who had gone so far as to vote for a President had better be willing to fight for him now.[9]

---

7. (Scottdale, Pa.: Herald Press, 2001), p. 573. Used by permission.
8. In November 1916, Virginia voters had passed a statewide prohibition law. A few Plain People had campaigned for this law, and some had voted for it.
9. Judy Yoder, *Vera's Journey* (Harrisonburg, Va.: Vision Publishers, 2009), p. 156.

In 1918, (Old) Mennonite A. J. Bendle of Johnstown, Pennsylvania, expressed a growing perception when he connected voting with other forms of worldliness. He wrote that he was "grieved at heart to see that wherever Goshen [College] lays their hand *Blight* immediately follows; the head covering begins to shrink until it is only the size of a mushroom; the bangs begin to grow; the jewelry business begins to flourish... their clothes suddenly grow shorter and the shoes longer; the lace and ribbon stores get increased patronage and the County Commissioners have to print more ballots!"

As army officers harangued conscientious objectors in World War I, they often equated the privilege of voting with the responsibility to serve in the armed forces. One CO was Jacob Neuenschwander of Ohio, who had been assigned to Camp Sherman. He was asked, "Why would you help to elect a president and then not support him when war comes?" When Jacob explained that he did not vote, the captain belittled him for not doing his duty as an American. Paul Ebersole of Pennsylvania faced the same question in World War II, as officials grilled him to determine whether his convictions on nonresistance were sincere.[10]

These experiences and many others have convinced most Amish and conservative Mennonites that voting is inconsistent for a nonresistant Christian.

The compromise of identifying with politics

Political involvement compromises the faithfulness needed to raise children for God. Consider the following account from *Building on the Gospel Foundation*.

---

10. *I Couldn't Fight and Other CO Stories* (Ephrata, Pa.: Eastern Mennonite Publications, 2002), pp. 47, 77.

19 • A Christian View of Political Action: Part 2

According to an 1877 newspaper account, "in the days of Henry Clay," Samuel Lehman (1798-1883) was "the wheel horse of the Whig party in the Democratic Township of Letterkenny." He "rarely failed to appear as a delegate from that township in the conventions of the party." Lehman also had served as County Auditor in 1844 and Director of the Poor in 1846 and 1852. At the same time, his obituary in the Herald of Truth attests he was "a member of the Mennonite Brotherhood in Christ, and a regular attendant at the [Upper Strasburg Mennonite] Church near his home." Lehman's political opinions made a great impact on two of his sons. Samuel K. and Elias K. Lehman abandoned their father's nonresistant principles to serve as officers in the Union Army during the Civil War. When they returned, they actively pursued careers in county politics. Their doing so left the older Lehman unchastened. As an old man he continued to take a keen interest in politics and enjoyed regaling his listeners with tales of "the chiefs of the old Whig party."[11]

Political involvement compromises the faithfulness needed for effective Christian witness. The late Mervin J. Baer of McBride, British Columbia, drove into town one day in the 1970s for supplies. In one store, he met several acquaintances who were complaining about politics. Mervin had a few things of his own to say about the situation.

One of the men suddenly stopped him. "Baer," he asked gruffly, "do you vote?"

"No," Mervin replied.

"Then shut up."

---

11. Edsel Burdge, Jr., and Samuel L. Horst (Scottdale, Pa.: Herald Press, 2004), p. 224. Used by permission.

"It was a good lesson for me," Mervin said later. "He was right."

A man of non-Anabaptist background who became attracted to Christ through conservative Mennonite evangelism spent a number of months living with his new friends and becoming acquainted with the church he later joined. Back home with his family, he described his impressions like this: "One thing really puzzles me. Those people are 100 percent Republican, but they refuse to vote!"

In another community, a Republican businessman who had dealings with many conservative Mennonites expressed his frustration in similar terms. "Those people are solid Republicans, but they will not vote. It makes me so angry. They should support what they say they believe in."

A Christian wheat farmer of Canada told of a time when wheat prices were high in the United States and low in Canada, but the Canadian government would not let the farmers truck their wheat into the United States to sell it. Many farmers formed groups such as "Farmers for Justice" to oppose that policy. These groups would mob the border between the United States and Canada, using long lines of loaded wheat trucks to clog the roads. Some farmers were jailed for their involvement in these protests.

One day the Christian's neighbor was talking to him about the unjust rules and how unfair life was for Canadian farmers. The Christian agreed and added a few of his own comments about the situation.

"Well," said the neighbor, "you can do something about it. We are planning another sit-in at the border tomorrow. All you need to do is bring your loaded truck and get in line."

19 • A Christian View of Political Action: Part 2

"No," the Christian replied. "I don't believe it is right to resist the government in that way."

The neighboring farmer became very upset. "You feel the same as we do," he cried angrily, "yet you won't lift a finger to help us!"

The Christian realized that if he was not ready to resist the government's policies, neither did he have the right to voice his feelings in a way that identified him with the worldly farmers around him.

A Christian once accosted another brother who enjoyed discussing politics: "So who are you for this time? The divorced Republican, or the Democrat who is still married to his first wife?" After the Clinton impeachment proceedings, it was discovered that several of the political leaders who had strenuously opposed him on ethical grounds were themselves involved in lying, immorality, or the illegal use of funds.

Do you see how easily the Gospel is perverted by politicizing Christianity or by portraying a certain party or organization as basically Christian? Anything that makes us look, act, or sound politically involved must be put off to maintain a clear witness for Christ. The only way we can fulfill our Christian duties to our families and society is by walking "in simplicity and godly sincerity, not with fleshly wisdom, but by the grace of God."[12] It is not our job to make things turn out right, but to be faithful witnesses for Christ.

---

12. 2 Corinthians 1:12

Showing society God's love

> And Jesus came and spake unto them, saying, All power is given unto me in heaven and in earth. Go ye therefore, and teach all nations, baptizing them in the name of the Father, and of the Son, and of the Holy Ghost: teaching them to observe all things whatsoever I have commanded you: and, lo, I am with you alway, even unto the end of the world. Amen (Matthew 28:18-20).

> To wit, that God was in Christ, reconciling the world unto himself, not imputing their trespasses unto them; and hath committed unto us the word of reconciliation. Now then we are ambassadors for Christ, as though God did beseech you by us: we pray you in Christ's stead, be ye reconciled to God (2 Corinthians 5:19, 20).

The verses above describe the key to having an effect for Christ on the world. Nothing but the life-changing grace of Jesus Christ, through repentance and salvation, has any power to change worldly values. Leading your child or your neighbor to repentance in Jesus Christ is the most powerful of all Christian deeds.

Christian love can go far to change families and communities. The history of God's work in the world has often moved in the background, with unseen actions and unsung heroes. God's work depends on those who wash feet instead of stomping feet; who give cold water instead of blowing hot air; who build character instead of empires. Christian love includes faithfulness at home, honesty in business, adopting needy children, ministering in prisons, and serving the elderly. It also involves caring for accident victims and people facing hard experiences like divorce, financial loss, or death. Christian love will open our eyes to many such opportunities in our communities.

19 • A Christian View of Political Action: Part 2

Actions of love even have the power to change some evil behavior in society in ways that laws can never do. The success of anti-abortion strategies in the 1800s is a good example of this.

Chapter 11 gives the basic history of abortion in the 1800s and early 1900s. In spite of increasingly strict laws against this evil, there was a great increase of abortion in the 1800s. In the Civil War era, the per capita occurrence of abortion in the United States was nearly the same as it is today. The reasons included spiritual apathy, increasing immorality, corruption in law enforcement, and the difficulty of getting prosecution evidence for this secret crime.

After the Civil War, the abortion rate fell steadily. It was greatly reduced by the early 1900s, and it remained relatively low until the 1960s. This was not due to the work of political leaders or mainstream churches. Instead, volunteer people and associations made various creative efforts as described in the following paragraphs.

Conducting public campaigns against abortion. National organizations such as the White Cross Society and the Women's Christian Temperance Union pressured men to control themselves in moral issues as well as strong drink. Young men who fell into immorality at that time could still be accepted in society, but young women who did so often faced lifelong stigma. The national associations pressed men to accept the same standard that society set for women.

In the end, the leaders of these organizations concluded that their pressure was of limited value. They saw more hope in teaching young women to be skeptical of men than in expecting men to change their behavior. Both ideas helped to turn back the tide of abortion, but they fell far short of the leaders' goals.

Offering advice and refuge to newcomers in cities. Thousands of young people, including individuals from rural America and immigrants from Europe, poured into American cities in the 1800s and early 1900s. Many were met by seducers who were trained to allure or force attractive young women into their services, with the result that a person could enter a city like New York or Chicago one day and disappear by the next. Immigrants with little knowledge of English were especially vulnerable.

Concerned citizens started local immigrant protection leagues, which helped immigrants and other inexperienced people to avoid unscrupulous men and places. They taught the newcomers to pursue moral principles and long-term results instead of glowing promises of immediate riches.

Establishing homes for expecting young women. Minneapolis had two or three such homes in 1895, Chicago had twelve of them, and New York City had at least twenty. By the early 1900s, these places of physical, emotional, and spiritual support had helped hundreds of thousands of young women put their lives back together. Some of these young women were restored to their parental homes, many gained enough self-respect and character to marry respectable men, and others found safe employment in productive trades.

Promoting adoption for fatherless children. In those days, single parenthood for mothers was hardly an option. The homes for expecting women encouraged them to place their children in homes that would care well for them. Abortionists painted the picture that an unwanted child was doomed to an unhappy life

19 • A Christian View of Political Action: Part 2

and that abortion was a merciful option. But pro-life people helped the expecting single woman to see that by choosing adoption, she could give her child a normal, happy life. In addition, the mother could avoid the tremendous guilt and sorrow that came with abortion, as well as the physical danger. (Sometimes one out of twenty abortion patients died from infections or poorly performed operations.)

There was rarely a shortage of homes willing to adopt. In Chicago in 1895, children's aid groups reported that children usually remained at refuges for only a few weeks, and that there were more homes requesting children than children available for adoption.

Helping women to avoid prostitution or recover from it. Young women were tempted by this vice because it paid five or six times as much as honest, useful employment. To help these women, thousands of volunteers taught against the evils of immorality and helped newcomers to avoid dangerous places and people. Also, some groups offered rooms with family-style living for low rent, and they watched over the young women who boarded there.

To women already involved in prostitution, volunteers offered help with repentance, forgiveness, and crossing the bridge back into respectable society. Families offered spiritual help and a spare room in their homes to prostitutes desperate to get out of the trap, and evangelists such as Dwight L. Moody carried a list of addresses of such families as they preached in evangelistic meetings.

In many cases, what made the difference for these young women was the love of the volunteers. Concerning the Erring Women's Refuge, which focused on spiritual help for prostitutes, one woman testified that it was the "first place I ever lived that any person cared enough about the salvation of my soul to make it a matter of interest to me."

Helping women to think about the tiny life within them and to consider the spiritual and emotional consequences of abortion. The volunteers did this by describing the features of the little child and by giving the testimonies of women who suffered deep emotional and spiritual scars after an abortion. This helped to turn many women toward better options.

People involved in these rescuing activities generally resisted political attempts to stiffen the penalties for abortion. Every state had anti-abortion laws by the 1870s, yet abortion was not a capital crime, and mothers were hardly ever punished. A few abortionists spent several years in prison or at hard labor, but this was rare. A New York judge in 1871 called for a law to establish abortion as "murder in the first degree, and punishable with death"; but many in the pro-life movement resisted that as unsustainable. They all agreed that abortion was murder and that technically capital punishment was just. The problem was that almost all abortion evidence was secondhand or gossip, and that almost never was there a corpse, an autopsy, or a witness.

Pro-life people in that time were thankful for the laws and the social stigma against abortion, but they did not see those things as significant in dealing with the problem. They gave time and love to the people involved instead of simply seeking a legal solution that would have done little good. Because of that emphasis, they were able to help many people spiritually, as well as significantly reduce the number of abortions. Their work is evidence that real social improvement can come only as a product of God's work in people's hearts.

19 • A Christian View of Political Action: Part 2

The history of abortion in the United States shows us that political efforts alone are not the answer to such problems. It also shows that Christianity today does not need to be rendered helpless by the outcome of court decisions such as *Roe v. Wade*. Much to the contrary, such permissiveness actually gives God's people a wonderful opportunity to show that "what the law could not do," God "sending his own Son" could do.[13]

Real social improvement can come only as a product of God's work in people's hearts.

These examples are not given to endorse all the spiritual concepts of the people involved, nor to suggest that God's people today should try to copy everything the volunteers did. They are intended simply to stimulate new insights into the society of today. We do not need to look at the world with the modern religious-political view. The Bible and history contain plenty of teachings and examples that show us better ways.

Conservative Anabaptists need to develop evangelistic, compassionate methods that help to meet the crying needs in this world, with a focus on gathering souls into the kingdom of God. They will be strategies that are based clearly on the New Testament, that meet the tests of safe fellowship lines, and that demonstrate the strength of united churches and strong families before the world.

---

13. Romans 8:3

We are witnessing for Christ in a way
   we never have before.
We . . . thank . . . God that his followers
   thought it worthwhile to carry
   the gospel of nonresistance down through the ages
   until the present time.

                                  —*Henry M. Baer*

None of us know what might be brought about
   by having the nonresisting people held at these camps
   to show the world what it might mean
   if there would be all or more nonresisting people;
   if there would be such; there could not . . . [be] wars.
But because of sin, these things must exist,
   so we as followers of the prince of peace
   must look to him . . .

                                  —*Hiram Shupp*

*Comments during World War I by Mennonites
of Washington County, Maryland*

20

A Christian View of War

In wartime, Christians are always tested with a basic question: Will you stand with your country's patriotism and military defense, or will you follow the Bible principles of love and nonresistance? In a religious setting, the question may come like this: Will you stand with the God of the Old Testament, King David, and Martin Luther, or will you stand with the God of the New Testament, Jesus Christ, and the Sermon on the Mount?

The answer to that question will decide whether one performs military service, but it should also decide numerous other war-related issues. Christians sometimes do not realize how greatly the New Testament changes the natural view of war. It prohibits the Christian from actual fighting itself, but it also affects how we relate to the war spirit, trusting in war, and trying to eliminate war in the world.

How "just war" ideas formed

It is common for people in a "Christian" society to discuss what constitutes a just war, an acceptable war, or a good war. Since the New Testament teaches being nonresistant and accepting death rather than committing violence against others, how have "Christian" people come to define some wars as just and acceptable?

For the first three hundred years of Christianity, the vast majority of Christians believed that war was wrong. There were some Christians in the Roman military, but some historians believe most of them were converted after promising to serve in the army and were therefore unable to be released. According to Jesus' teaching, such persons should have stopped serving in the army and suffered whatever penalties the Roman government decided; but apparently the church of their time (after A.D. 180) had compromised to the point that it did not require this. It does appear that the church's official position before A.D. 313 was a member who joined the military after he joined the church was to be disciplined.[1]

The church's view of war changed in the 160 years between Constantine's acceptance of Christianity (313) and the fall of Rome (476). During this time, the church gradually lost its New Testament identity and became entwined with the Roman nation. Small remnants of committed Christians separated from the apostatizing church in this time, but the mainstream church felt

---

1. Some historians believe that when Constantine began to promote Christianity instead of paganism, possibly one-third of his army was already "Christian." If that is true, it may be the case that though the official church position was to discipline a member who joined the military, such discipline was often not carried out.

responsible to help the state maintain the economy, stability, and security that Rome provided in the ancient world.

There were many invasions as the Roman Empire declined, and Christians became aware that the political system as they knew might collapse. Frightened by the chaos they saw outside the empire, they decided that their duty was to maintain a "Christian" influence in the world—instead of maintaining a pure church and calling people out of the world. They reasoned that God needed Rome to keep peace in the world, just as He needed the church to save the world. So they tried to be both the church and the state. But in doing so, they were no longer the true church, neither were they able to save the state.

> By the early 400s, every soldier was required to be a Christian, and Christians saw military service as their responsibility.

In the earlier part of this 160-year period, the apostolic teachings against war were still strong. Gradually, however, the church began to allow its members to serve in political and military roles, and by the early 400s the transition was complete. Every soldier was required to be a Christian, and Christians saw military service as their responsibility.

The idea of a "just war" was introduced by Augustine (354-430). Augustine's writings, including his explanation of "Christian" war theology, became the basis for many Catholic doctrines. Christ taught that the world is made up of believers (wheat) and sinners (tares) and that these will exist side by side until the end of the world. Augustine advanced the idea that the *church* is made up of both wheat and tares, and that true Christians are invisible in this conglomeration. He also taught that individual

Christians might operate as wheat or tares, depending on the situation. In this way, Augustine gave the church the right to be involved in the state and the military while still portraying herself as the church.

Since Augustine had dispensed with nonresistance, he needed to define when war was permissible. He did this by borrowing ideas from the Roman statesman Cicero (106-43 B.C.), who in turn had been influenced by Greek philosophies. Cicero had taught that a "good" war must meet the following requirements.
- It must be carried out under the administration of a government.
- It must be fair, as in respecting prisoners and hostages and not involving wanton violence.
- It must be honest with the enemy about the causes of war.
- It must appear to be a winnable war.
- It must have the goal of producing or restoring justice and peace.

To these goals, Augustine added three more ideas.
- The Christian in war must be motivated by love.
- The Christian in war must be sorrowful because of his involvement in killing.
- The injustice of the war must be on the enemies' side so that they would bear the guilt for it.

Islamic ideals were added to these theories as the Muslims influenced western Europe. Islam began in the early 600s, and Muslims were soon fighting to spread their religion. They expanded their territory until they had conquered about half of the former Roman Empire by the mid-700s. At that point the western Europeans were able to hold the line against the Muslims.

But though the advance of Islam had been stopped, some Muslim ideas became part of European thought. *The Subversion of Christianity* makes the case that Islam's idea of "holy war" led "Christianity" even farther away from the New Testament view of war.

> Even when [war was] waged by a Christian emperor it was a dubious business and was assessed unfavorably. . . . In practice Christians would remain critical of war until the flamboyant image of holy war came on the scene. In other words, . . . war has always been in essential contradiction to the gospel. Christians have always been more or less aware of this. They have judged war and questioned it.
>
> In Islam, on the contrary, war was always just and constituted a sacred duty. . . . To spread the faith, it is necessary to destroy false religions. This war, then, is always a religious war, a holy war. . . .
>
> The famous story of Charlemagne forcing the Saxons to be converted on pain of death simply presents us with an imitation of what Islam had been doing for two centuries. But if war now has conversions to Christianity as its goal, we can see that very quickly it takes on the aspect of a holy war. It is a war waged against unbelievers and heretics. . . . But the idea of a holy war is a direct product of the Muslim jihad. If the latter is a holy war, then obviously the fight against Muslims to defend or save Christianity has also to be a holy war. The idea of a holy war is not of Christian origin. Emperors never advanced the idea prior to the appearance of Islam. . . .
>
> The Crusade is an imitation of the jihad. Thus the Crusade includes a guarantee of salvation. The one who dies in a holy war goes straight to Paradise, and the same applies to the one who takes part in a Crusade. This is no coincidence; it is an exact equivalent...

We find here a terrible consequence and confirmation of a vice that was eating into Christianity already, namely, that of violence and the desire for power and domination. To fight against a wicked foe with the same means and arms is unavoidably to be identified with this foe. Evil means inevitably corrupt a just cause.... Here we have one of the chief perversions of faith in Jesus Christ and of the Christian life.[2]

By the year 1000, the Catholic Church had accepted war as a useful tool to advance God's kingdom. Some resistance to war lived on in the form of holy days during which fighting was not allowed, and in monasteries where people followed Bible principles more fully than in the "real" world. The leading reformers in the 1500s, such as Luther, Zwingli, and Calvin, accepted the Catholic view of war, so these wrong ideas became firmly entrenched in the mainline Reformation churches.

Only among scattered remnants did the radical idea survive that all war is wrong. Such people often paid for their beliefs with their blood. Refusing to hate and kill was considered heresy after hatred and killing were "Christianized" by the mainstream churches.

Christianity and violence

The concept of "Christian" wars helped to produce a world of violence and bloodshed. As explorers came to the New World for God, gold, and glory, they felt justified in any violence they used against the "unrighteous" natives. Similar sentiments drove the religious fervor for the Revolutionary War. Ministers in that time said that Jesus did not teach

---

2. Jacques Ellul (Grand Rapids, Mi.: William B. Eerdmans Publishing Company, 1986), pp. 101-103. Used by permission.

nonresistance in the case of self-defense; that the Christian soldiers of America must conduct the war in a just, lawful, and righteous manner; and that nature, the Bible, and the example of Christ all proved the foolishness of nonresistance.

Writing against the nonresistant Mennonites during the Civil War, the editor of a Lancaster newspaper called the war "a righteous struggle." Religious people all over the nation felt the same way, whether Northerners or Southerners. In World War I, people demonized the Germans as devils impersonated, and they represented the Allied forces as the defenders of Christianity, true civilization, and democracy. World War II, "the good war," was cast in the same light.

In all these conflicts, there are many hints that people still felt a sharp contradiction between calling themselves Christians and going to war. In the peaceful periods before World Wars I and II, almost all mainline denominations in America were firmly committed to peaceful solutions. But when the wars actually started, the peace emphasis quickly disappeared. Some religious leaders said that regrettably, since all other options had been exhausted, the nation must now go to war. In World War II, some people admitted that the war was sinful, but they said it was less sinful than any other option.

To pacify tender consciences, war theologians reiterate that Christianity is founded not only on the Gospel but also on powers and rights that naturally belong to countries. So Christians should not feel compelled to make their military exploits align with the New Testament.

But all these attempts to justify military action are only so much rhetoric. No war has ever been fought that achieved Augustine's ideals for a "just war." It has been noted that when so-called Christians wage war, they seem to magnify instead of minimize revenge and hatred. The Bishop of London said in World War I,

> Kill Germans—to kill them, not for the sake of killing, but to save the world, to kill the good as well as the bad, to kill the young men as well as the old, to kill those who have shown kindness to our wounded as well as those fiends who crucified the Canadian Sergeant. . . . As I have said a thousand times, I look upon it as a war for purity, I look upon everyone who dies in it as a martyr.[3]

Because of these facts, some historians have suggested that "Christian" societies, just like ancient societies, seem to need occasional wars in order to prove that they are the "right" kind of civilization and that they have real purpose and virtue. Many people looking at Christianity have wondered why people who claim the name are so violent, when the New Testament clearly teaches the opposite. Someone asked Mohandas Ghandi, the famous Indian promoter of nonviolent resistance, why he did not become a Christian. He replied that he appreciated Jesus and His teachings, but that he could not identify with Christendom because it did not follow Jesus' teachings. Ghandi went on to say, "The only people on earth who do not see Christ and His teachings as nonviolent are Christians." Muslims often express

"Just war" may have a place in the world, where Greek and Roman philosophies rule, but it has no place in the kingdom of God, where the New Testament rules.

---
3. Roland Bainton, *Christian Attitudes Toward War and Peace*, p. 207.

amazement at the way "Christians" hate their enemies yet claim to follow Jesus.

C. S. Lewis, though he himself was no champion of nonresistance, was reflecting on this contradiction in mainstream Christianity when he said,

> Patriotism often borrows the terms and claims of the heavenly kingdom and uses them to justify the most abominable earthly actions. Christendom should confess their specific contribution to the sum of human cruelty and treachery. Large areas of the world will not hear us till we have publicly disowned much of our past. Why should they? We have shouted the name of Christ and enacted the service of Moloch.

"Just war" may have a place in the world, where Greek and Roman philosophies rule, but it has no place in the kingdom of God, where the New Testament rules. Because the Christian is authorized to relate to the world only by New Testament standards, he has nothing to say about whether a "just war" is possible, nor does he try to classify wars. Using *Christian* to describe wars and war theories is simply a misuse of the term.

In the New Testament view, all wars are waged between sinners. Adolf Hitler and Winston Churchill did not have the same ideals of justice. But they both served the carnal, transitory kingdom of the world.

The great divide between the sentiments of a "Christian" nation at war and those of a true Christian are illustrated in the book *Report for Duty*.[4] This is the story of John Witmer, a Mennonite conscientious objector of Columbiana, Ohio, who was drafted into World War I in 1918. As John and a Brethren

---

4. Lily A. Bear (Harrisonburg, Va.: Christian Light Publications, Inc., 2003).

friend traveled by train from Youngstown to Camp Sherman near Chillicothe, their traveling companions tried to attract the attention of every girl the train passed. They also made fun of prayer and mocked the young men as cowards.

At the camp, John was kicked, had his personal belongings stolen, was cursed in vile language, and was given the choice of wearing the army uniform or going without clothes. His head was shaved bare, and some of the strokes took both skin and hair. He was threatened with death and was forced to read the Bible while surrounded by mocking soldiers using vile language. Once a leering soldier ran toward him with a bayonet, yelling, "Death to slackers!"—and John ducked just in time as the bayonet grazed his head. John became sick with a cold and chest congestion; and one evening as he took a walk in that condition, five soldiers caught him and drenched him with cold water. He had to sleep in damp clothes that night. In this weakened state, John became sick with Spanish influenza and died after he had been in camp for only thirty-two days.

When his family took his body off the train in Columbiana, they removed the flag that covered his casket. His father, unaware of the codes for handling the flag, folded it in an ordinary manner. Enraged by this insensitivity to their national symbol, the watching crowd called the father a traitor, and several people threw stones at the family.

The experiences of John Witmer and of hundreds of other Christians in America amply prove the fallacy of "just war" ideas. In wartime, the average "Christian" American shamelessly despises any fellow citizen who does not fall in step with his ideals. Much less would he try to treat his national enemies according to "just war" theories. Americans in wartime clearly reveal which kingdom the majority of them are supporting, along with its ungodly morals and its contempt for the Word of God.

Contrasting the War Views of Christendom and Anabaptism

In the Revolutionary War

Christendom: [Defenselessness] is monstrous and unnatural. The ox has his horns, and the horse his teeth and hoofs. The deer her feet for flight, and the fowls their wings to escape danger, and to preserve themselves. And shall man, the noblest creature in the lower world, be destitute of this necessary principle! which we see engraved by instinct on the irrational creation? [New Testament peace teachings] must be understood in a consistency with this great law of nature. (*Excerpt from sermon preached in May 1775 by Presbyterian John Carmichael, Chester County, Pa.*)

Anabaptism: [We] are not at liberty in Conscience to take up Arms to conquer our Enemies, but rather to pray to God . . . for US and THEM. . . . We have dedicated ourselves to serve all Men in every Thing that can be helpful to the Preservation of Men's Lives, but we find no Freedom in giving, or doing, or assisting in any Thing by which Men's lives are destroyed or hurt. We beg the Patience of all those who believe we err in this Point. (*Excerpt from letter written in November 1777 by Mennonite bishop Bentz Hirschi to the Pennsylvania Assembly*)

In the Civil War

Christendom: The Union feeling pervading this entire community is most unanimous and enthusiastic. There is but one sentiment—one purpose—one determination among men of all political parties, and that is, to stand up for the Government and sustain it in all efforts to put down rebellion and reestablish the Union. (*Excerpt from article published on April 19, 1861, in* Valley Spirit, *a newspaper of Chambersburg, Pa.*)

Anabaptism: The political condition of our country is very dark at present, even this day [Sunday] is disturbed with rumors of war and armed men on the march. . . . Our poor country is in a very wretched condition. (*Excerpts from entries for April 17 and May 4, 1861, in the diary of Reformed Mennonite Jacob Stouffer, Stoufferstown, Pa.*)

Christendom: Worse than all, we have been deeply pained at the wavering faith of some of our fellow citizens in the righteousness of our cause, and the noisy clamors of others for the speedy termination of our sufferings by a dishonorable and ignominious peace. A compromise with rebellion is treason against God. (*Excerpt from the minutes of the 1864 annual conference of the Methodist Episcopal Church*)

Anabaptism: Further, the Lord and Savior Jesus Christ says how one people shall rise up against another, and there has been war for many years about religious matters and about the Spiritual kingdom, but how many struggle and fight to enter the narrow gate onto the way of the cross? There are so few that find it but there are many who go about seeing how they can get in through some other way. . . . We should all be subject one to another and hold fast onto humility because God abhors everything the world exalts. (*Excerpt from letter written in April 1862 by Mennonite bishop Peter Eshleman of Washington County, Maryland to Mennonite leader Jacob Nold of Columbiana, Ohio*)

Christendom: No more slavery in these United States. . . . And that Christianity has been the great agent in the extirpation of this evil, is a fact so clear, that it cannot fail to impress the mind of every candid and unprejudiced thinker. (*Excerpt from the minutes of the 1865 annual conference of the Methodist Episcopal Church*)

Anabaptism: Who will be responsible for the much blood which has been shed in the war and finally the President's blood? Here is sin piled upon sin. (*Excerpt from letter written in 1865 by Amish bishop Jacob Swartzendruber of Johnson County, Iowa, to the annual Amish ministers' meeting*)

In World War I

Christendom: Nonresistance is acting like a baby. Loving your enemy is something to be done in the millennium, when Christ reigns on the earth. God helps him who helps himself. (*Conversation of a local man in Washington County, Maryland with his Mennonite neighbor, December 1917.*)

Anabaptism: If all the people humbled themselves as the king of Nineveh did, the war would close today. (*Comment by Mennonite bishop George Keener of Washington County, Maryland in December 1917*)

Christendom: Are they [nonresistant people] willing to turn the world over to the Huns [Germans] and the rulers of the Huns? Are they willing when the Huns are seeking to conquer the world, that they be permitted to murder little children, cut their throats, cut off their arms and legs? . . . Are they willing that murder and rapine and arson and all God's ten commandments shall be broken in order that the Kaiser may rule the world? Are they willing to turn their backs upon the religion of Jesus Christ which they had practiced so simply and has been the inspiration of their church? (*Excerpt from letter written in June 1918 by Robert Cain, state director of the Maryland War Saving Stamps campaign*)

Anabaptism: I said the scriptures acknowledge governments and gives us instruction what attitude to take toward such. Then that Christ's kingdom is not of this world . . . I pointed out to him the character of both Kingdoms, the works of each. I stated

> what the work of the flesh is and the works of the spirit as stated in Galatians. I told him that if I tho't that the scriptures sanctioned war, I would want to be at the place where I could do the most good for the country and would not be afraid of anything. But I said, the Bible forbids war. (*Excerpt from letter written on October 30, 1917, by Mennonite CO Isaac Baer of Washington County, Maryland to his sister Martha.*)

Christians accept the fact of war.

Christians note that "just war" theories can never be carried out, that every war kills more innocent people than guilty ones, and that hatred poisons the spirits of everyone involved in war. What should they do about these things? Should they urge the government never to wage war? Should they advance the position that there are always peaceable ways to settle worldly conflicts?

According to the Old Testament, God permits war for His own reasons. Consider these Scriptures.

> And they [Israelites] made war with the Hagarites, with Jetur, and Nephish, and Nodab. . . . For there fell down many slain, because the war was of God. . . . And they transgressed against the God of their fathers. . . . And the God of Israel stirred up the spirit of Pul king of Assyria, and the spirit of Tilgathpilneser king of Assyria, and he carried them away (1 Chronicles 5:19, 22, 25, 26).

> And in those times there was no peace to him that went out, nor to him that came in, but great vexations were upon all the inhabitants of the countries. And nation was destroyed of nation, and city of city: for God did vex them with all adversity (2 Chronicles 15:5, 6).

> He maketh wars to cease unto the end of the earth; he breaketh the bow, and cutteth the spear in sunder; he burneth the chariot in the fire (Psalm 46:9).

O Assyrian, the rod of mine anger, and the staff in their hand is mine indignation. I will send him against an hypocritical nation, and against the people of my wrath will I give him a charge, to take the spoil, and to take the prey, and to tread them down like the mire of the streets (Isaiah 10:5, 6).

I have also called my mighty ones for mine anger. . . . The Lord of hosts mustereth the host of the battle. They come from a far country, from the end of heaven, even the Lord, and the weapons of his indignation, to destroy the whole land (Isaiah 13:3-5).

Because of the day that cometh to spoil all the Philistines, . . . for the Lord will spoil the Philistines, the remnant of the country of Caphtor. Baldness is come upon Gaza; Ashkelon is cut off with the remnant of their valley: how long wilt thou cut thyself? O thou sword of the Lord, how long will it be ere thou be quiet? . . . How can it be quiet, seeing the Lord hath given it a charge against Ashkelon, and against the sea shore? there hath he appointed it (Jeremiah 47:4-7).

Behold ye among the heathen, and regard, and wonder marvellously: for I will work a work in your days, which ye will not believe, though it be told you. For, lo, I raise up the Chaldeans, that bitter and hasty nation, which shall march through the breadth of the land, to possess the dwelling places that are not their's (Habakkuk 1:5, 6).

In the New Testament, Christ told His followers to expect war and carnal strife to increase as time passes.

And ye shall hear of wars and rumours of wars: see that ye be not troubled: for all these things must come to pass, but the end is not yet.

> For nation shall rise against nation, and kingdom against kingdom: and there shall be famines, and pestilences, and earthquakes, in divers places (Matthew 24:6, 7).
>
> But when ye shall hear of wars and commotions, be not terrified: for these things must first come to pass; but the end is not by and by (Luke 21:9).

The Scriptures indicate that God uses war to judge sin. However, that does not mean the sin is only on the losing side. The world wars of the twentieth century certainly judged the nations that started the wars. But they also judged those who fought to defend themselves. For example, both world wars proved to the Allies that their ideas about solving the world's problems were not valid.

At the beginning of the 1900s, especially in America, society believed that man had conquered many ancient problems through science, medicine, and the development of industry. They believed that the 1900s would be a bright century of unparalleled progress in every field. The efforts leading to Prohibition are just one example of how people believed that by enlightened cooperation, modern society would solve mankind's problems. After World War I, some leaders believed that world peace through cooperation was just around the corner and could easily be achieved through human effort. All those ideas were judged and disproved in the turmoil of that century.

The evils of war are part of the devil's earthly triumph. But the controlling hand of God limits the devil's victory. God does not erase sin and all its consequences, but He controls the progress of sin to keep man from total self-destruction. He allows sin to bear ample fruit so that man is continually confronted with sin's dark, bitter, and hopeless results. "The wages of sin is death"; and God gives men a thousand partial paydays, including war, to demonstrate that they are working for the wrong employer and that they need to repent to avoid the final paycheck.

Because of the carnal nature of mankind, people will never be able to abolish war. When Jesus told us to expect war He was simply telling us a fact about the fallen world. The many people who refuse to enter the narrow way will often choose to fight out their differences. That does not make us callous about war and its terrible effects; we still rejoice when a worldly conflict can be resolved, even temporarily, without bloodshed. But we expect war and its suffering because carnal man cannot lift himself above the final resort to arms, no matter how "enlightened" he becomes. If man by himself could solve the many problems of his sinful nature, of which war is part, then and only then could he abolish war.

The Bible teaches that the only people who can abolish war among themselves are the followers of Jesus Christ. Only Christians can absorb injustice, forgive wrongs, and give up hatred. Only Christians can uproot the sprouts of war when they first appear in the human heart. Christians love their fellow men unconditionally, and they work to relieve the suffering caused by sin, but they do not pin their hopes on a war-free world. Instead, they look for a sin-free heaven.

The state "beareth not the sword in vain" (Romans 13:4). In keeping with its carnal, worldly character, it will use the sword. Christians simply need to accept that truth. God uses the state to control people who live by their evil desires rather than by the Holy Spirit. "People sleep peaceably in their beds at night," one man pointed out, "only because rough men stand ready to do violence on their behalf."

Christians sleep peaceably because of their trust in God, but they are also glad if they can live where civil order is enforced. They do not trust in the police, but neither do they pretend that the sinful world could be governed entirely by nonviolent means. Expecting the state to act nonviolently is a denial of the state's character, just as expecting a child to behave without discipline is a denial of the child's character.

After the Amish extended personal forgiveness to the family of the murderer at the Nickel Mines school, a commentator suggested that if President Bush had been the Christian he claims to be, the world would have been spared the awful contradiction of a nation of "believers" driven insane by the uncontrollable urge to kill in the Name of an all-loving God. Another suggested that the Amish should be invited to administrate the Department of Homeland Security. She asked these questions: What if Americans had offered Osama bin Laden forgiveness on September 12, 2001? What if the families of the terrorists had been invited to the funerals of the victims of September 11? What if people always lived in forgiveness instead of perpetual fear?

Expecting the state to act nonviolently is a denial of the state's character.

These commentators had some wrong perspectives. They did not seem to understand that only the Spirit of God can enable anyone to personally forgive an enemy. Retaliation is a trait that is practically unchangeable outside of true conversion.

The true Christian is thankful when the world takes seriously the witness of an incident like that at Nickel Mines, but he does not expect the billions outside of Christ to apply such lessons in world-changing ways.

Christians are much more likely to be respected by the state if they recognize the place that God has given it in the world. If they try to control the state or to deprive it of its arms, they can expect the state to control them and deny them many privileges. Christians need to accept the ill treatment that comes from serving a higher King, without trying to make the state over into the image of a King it does not consciously serve.

Nonresistant Christians do not identify with the world by accepting guilt for the world's wars. No true Christian of Germany need apologize to the world. No true Christian of America need apologize to Germany, Japan, North Korea, Vietnam, Afghanistan, Iraq, or any other country for the horrors that America inflicted on those nations. True Christians were not a part of those horrors. To insist that all people (or at least all "Christians") of the world take responsibility for the wars of the world is simply to refuse to live in the way Christ taught, here and now. No one has explained this better than Jacques Ellul in *The Political Illusion*.

> To consider oneself responsible for the tortures in Algeria while actually being a professor in Bordeaux, or for all the hunger in the world, or for racist excesses in various countries, is exactly the same thing as to reject all responsibility.... To say that we are all murderers means, translated, that nobody is individually a murderer, i.e., that I am not a murderer. To admit that I am co-responsible for all the evil in the world means to assure a good

conscience for myself even if I do not do the good within my own reach. To admit that I am a dirty dog because, being French, I am involved in the acts of all Frenchmen in Algeria, means to free myself of the slightest effort to cease being a dirty dog personally and to do so, moreover, at the cheapest price, namely by joining a political party or shouting in the streets; in addition, I am assured of being on the right side of those who want "the French" to cease being dirty dogs.[5]

Christians realize the horror of war.

True Christians do not admire the "game" of war. In recent wars, as some people relaxed in their homes far from the scenes of conflict, they admired the high-precision artillery and "smart" missiles of modern nations, and they seemed to view war almost as a game. People tend to think only about their national interests and forget war's incalculable costs in human suffering. In every conflict, more innocent people are killed than guilty ones, and often the pursuit of the guilty causes thousands or millions of innocent men, women, and children to be maimed, diseased, directly killed, or starved to death.

What Christians should do is not to assume guilt for the conflict or try to make nations act in godly ways, but to avoid being caught up in war hysteria themselves. In the war in Iraq that began in 2003, for example, true Christians were more likely to be found weeping over the killing and destruction than praying that the coalition forces would bring Saddam Hussein to justice. The true Christian cannot act as though his country is God's earthly agent in the fight against evil; for no matter

---

5. (New York, Ny.: Alfred A. Knopf, 1967), pp. 188, 189.

which nation is his home, he knows that it is sinful, essentially the same as all other nations.

These perspectives were keen among nonresistant Christians in earlier American wars. But they seem to have weakened in recent years, for the CO status seems well established, and for the moment the draft appears to be a thing of the past. Too many American Christians have easily accepted government propaganda about the terrorist conflicts, not realizing that all propaganda contains elements of falsehood. We are in danger of losing the keen perception of earlier generations on such matters. It appears that nonresistant Christians have become too quick to judge worldly events, bless national aims, and take sides in conflicts.

More than nonresistance

In some Anabaptist churches, there was a disturbing amount of support for war with Iraq that began in 2003. When an Anabaptist believer in Australia noted this, he said, "I can't believe it. Aren't they nonresistant?" Another confused young man in a conservative Anabaptist church at the time wrote the following in a letter.

> As a young person, [nonresistance] was very confusing for me. On one hand, I heard the teaching on the subject. On the other hand I watched the older generation getting excited around election time and eagerly watching the papers over the time of Bush's pre-Iraq invasion hype. I heard them say, "We don't vote," but it was obvious even to children who didn't know what was going on who was the "good guy" and who was the "bad guy." I heard in words that war is wrong, but it was obvious that middle-

aged businessmen and fathers in my church really did believe that war made a difference in this world for good and moved history forward. The result was a natural conclusion that our nonresistant doctrine was irrelevant, something to be ashamed of. I occasionally heard stories of Anabaptist martyrs, but it was obviously not representative of the reality that my community held to. The reaction of some of my peers—to vote and talk of joining the Marines—made sense to me. And yet I was somehow repulsed by that.[6]

Enthusiasm over national goals in war can easily lead young people to question the doctrine of nonresistance, as this letter indicates. The resulting confusion can lead to another error—misguided people believing that their role in the world is to persuade governments to abandon war or to accept the tactics of nonviolent resistance.

I too saw some of the things described in the letter above, but I was encouraged by the immediate response of some churches. They emphasized teaching on nonresistance and worked to bring young people up to date with the experiences of conscientious objectors in the past.

In my experience, what was lacking was teaching on such subjects as why true Christians cannot thrill to patriotism, believe propaganda, adopt the government's view of foreign peoples, or accept their nation as having righteous goals. If we fail in this teaching, our Christian youth may not be able to face the severe grilling that conscientious objectors have endured in the past. The result may also be an inconsistent witness that

---

6. Personal letter from Javan Lapp to Stephen Russell, November 2006. Used by permission.

destroys the church's testimony, such as the comment of an Anabaptist during the Korean war: "I am thankful that our people have an exemption from fighting in this war, but I am sure glad that somebody can go over there and fight to keep the Communists from taking over the world."

It would be good to hear more voices like those that warned the nonresistant Moravian community at Lititz, Pennsylvania, during the Revolutionary War. The leaders there reprimanded their congregation because two parties had developed among them: those who supported the king, and those who supported the fledgling American government. They said that God did not approve such factions among His people. Both the people who slandered the British king and those who opposed the American government, they said, were failing to wait patiently until the will of God was revealed. The leaders firmly rebuked the older boys for being too interested in the war, pointing out that this worked against the purposes of Christian people.

The incongruity of war

Some of the most contradictory and terrible things that ever happen take place in wartime. *Small Man of Nanataki* tells the story of Kiyoshi Watanabe, a Japanese Lutheran pastor who was assigned to work as an interpreter in a Japanese army camp in Hong Kong during World War II. Kiyoshi loved Japan and was eager to see the British prisoners of war at the camp. But when he saw them, he was filled with pity. They were ragged, dirty, and emaciated. Kiyoshi felt terrible about the way his fellow Japanese treated the prisoners, especially how they beat the ones accused of petty misdemeanors. He spoke about it to Inouye, a fellow interpreter. But Inouye's response surprised him.

'My dear Watanabe, your pity is misplaced. Pity them! It serves the pigs right. They are treated far too well for my liking, but then I hate them. All of them. I hate them.'

The Christian and the pastor in Kiyoshi recoiled at this word 'hate'. This was the first time he had ever heard a man use it about some other human beings and really mean it. He had to say something about it now, but all that came out was an embarrassed laugh and an apologetic: 'I don't think it is necessary to hate anyone.'

'Well, I hate them, and so should every good Japanese. What's wrong with you, Watanabe? Is it that you are not a good Japanese?'

Kiyoshi Watanabe was frightened. He was also indignant. He was frightened at the sight of someone so consumed with hatred. He was indignant that anyone should doubt that he, Kiyoshi Watanabe, was a good Japanese. He was proud of and loyal to his country. His mind fought for words to say to Inouye, but the words remained unvoiced. Inouye's eyes narrowed and took on a faraway look as if he was remembering.

Then he said: 'Yes, I shall get my revenge, every single day and night's worth. I shall treat them like the filthy animals they are and deserve to be.'

'That is not the way of God,' Kiyoshi said, and he said it without thinking, involuntarily, because it was an instinctive thing for him to say.

Inouye bent down to him.

'God? So you are a Christian, are you?'

'Yes,' Kiyoshi said, 'I am a Christian.' He picked up his pen and began to write something, anything, on the piece of paper in front of him. Other people, the remainder of the office staff, were coming in. He wished Inouye would go away now and leave him alone. He was sorry he had started the conversation, and just hoped against hope Inouye would let the matter drop. But Inouye stayed sitting at the table.

Inouye said, after a little while, 'Let me tell you this, Mr. Christian Watanabe, I too have lived amongst them, in Canada, and they despised me. I knew it. I could feel it. They humiliated me. I was just another dirty little Jap to them. But two can play that game, and now they are the pigs and I am the master. The pendulum always swings the other way too. It has already been their way, now it has come to my side.'

Inouye left when he saw that Watanabe was not going to be drawn any further into this conversation. For two whole hours Kiyoshi sat unseeing at his desk. He was thinking about this awful hate which was seething in his fellow interpreter. This wasn't typical of all Japanese. But was this going to be the face of Japan which the whole world would grow to know?[7]

The same day, Kiyoshi was forced to watch Inouye beat a British prisoner who was accused of stealing rice. The experience made him sick with shame, revulsion, and despair, and in this awful moment he was driven to his knees.

Oh God, was this what war did to men? Was it for this that Christ, the Son of God, became Man and died on a cross? Wata-

---

7. Liam Nolan, *Small Man of Nanataki* (New York, Ny.: E.P. Dutton & Co., Inc., 1966), pp. 29, 30. Used by permission.

nabe could find no answer, and in his black despair he wondered if he wasn't losing his faith in God.

He got down on his knees in the confined and smelling space and prayed until the words became more than mere repeated sounds, until they started to mean something, until they began to blot out the scenes and doubts, until he was actually talking to his God and pleading desperately for help. He asked for many things—strength and help and understanding. And faith.

He finished by saying: 'Forgive me Father, forgive me for my weakness and frailty. Forgive Inouye his cruelty even as Thou forgave the thief on the Cross. And take me, unworthy and frail as I am, and do with me what you will. Make me the tool of Thy goodness. Not my will, but Thy will be done.'

He knelt in reverence and humility. When he stood up a calmness was already flowing into his veins, and with it an as yet undefined determination. The future, he knew, was going to be hard. He would have to walk carefully, risk his life, perhaps even lose it. But the only thing he feared was physical pain. I am a coward, he told himself, I am a coward and I am afraid of pain. I am a coward, O God, so please help me.

As he slipped back the bolt and walked out again into the sunlight, he had the certainty of knowing that no matter what he did or suffered, he would be watched over by Him to whom he had just offered his life.

For a few days after the beating incident, Watanabe kept to himself. The reaction to what he had seen hadn't set in properly yet, and indeed it was twenty-four hours before the full brunt of it hit him. When it did, it was in the form of a staggering attack on his mental faculties and sensitivities. Then all the thoughts and emotions which made a turmoil of his mind precipitated him into a state of confusion in which he was afraid to speak. He did not want a repetition of the Inouye business, though he knew full well that at some time or other in the future he might have to face far worse. There were other conflicts that had to be solved too. He asked himself a thousand times if his instinctive desire to help the prisoners of war wasn't traitorous. Japan, his mother country, was very dear to him, and he loved her far too much ever to entertain any real thoughts of treason.

But, during the long nights, and up to the grey hours before dawn, he lay sleepless, his mind a torment. At the end of each day he felt exhausted, and yet too tensed up to sleep. Questions whirled maddeningly inside his head until he craved a few brief hours' sleep as a respite. He wished Mitsuko were near at hand so that he could tell her the things that worried him; dear gentle Mitsuko who could listen so patiently and often resolve his problems in her own quiet simple fashion.

But Mitsuko was far away in Hiroshima, oblivious of Kiyoshi's mental stresses. When he wrote to her, as he did often, he never mentioned what he had found in Hong Kong, nor what the discovery was doing to him. Instead he told her of the beauty of the place and described painstakingly the simpler things in his life, like what food he was eating, what the weather was like and the condition in which his shirts came back from the laundry.

Writing these simple letters to his wife was for him like going into rare little oases where misery was unknown. At each writing he prized his consciousness away from the happenings and thoughts which distressed him. He projected himself into the atmosphere of his home at Takasho Street, and asked simple searching questions about Kimi and Kei. He enquired about the older children also, Miwa and the two boys Shinya and Shigawo.

But once the letters were written, and their answers read, his mind once more seethed with doubts and fears and total confusion.

And then, after a period of mental anguish, the soul-searching crystallised out into a clear-cut question. The facts stood out startlingly clear to him, ranged as they were on opposite sides. Which was it to be—God or Country?

For Kiyoshi Watanabe there could be only one answer to that. He made his decision. "For the least you do unto one of these, my children, you do also unto me." The words he knew so well, and quoted so often, would be his guide from now on.[8]

Kiyoshi risked his life many times by helping the British prisoners with food, medicine, and other needs. The Lord led him as he tried to understand how a Christian should act in each situation he faced. As the war went on, Kiyoshi felt a sense of impending doom. One night early in August 1945 he despaired of ever seeing his wife again.

He turned his head into the pillow and wept without shame or restraint. There was nobody who could help him or help Mitsuko. There was only the Almighty. When he regained his composure, he chided himself for thinking of God as 'only.'

He got up and, remembering that he was a Lutheran Pastor, prayed for strength and guidance; he prayed for his family, particularly for his wife and two daughters in Hiroshima. He asked that they be allowed to get away from the city, to get clear outside Hiroshima, or to Hatsukaichi in the Southwest. Lastly he prayed

---

8. Ibid., pp. 32, 33, 34.

for anyone else who might need prayers this night and on the day that was coming.

In a hut on the Pacific Island of Tinian, a young chaplain was standing before a group of men. In less than a couple of hours from now these men would be flying off the coral runway and into the night sky. Their planes had other names, apart from the maker's classification.

There was the 'Great Artiste' and the 'Full House' and 'Jabbit III' and the 'Straight Flush.' And there was another plane, the most important of the lot, and she was called 'Enola Gay.' In Enola Gay's bomb bay was a fat stumpy bomb called 'Little Boy.'

The crews of these aeroplanes, and of No. 91, the photography plane that was to go on their mission with them, were listening to the chaplain. He was praying. He said: 'We pray Thee that the end of the war may come soon, and that once more we may know peace on earth. May the men who fly this night be kept safe in Thy care, and may they be returned safely to us. We shall go forward trusting in Thee, knowing that we are in Thy care now and forever. In the name of Jesus Christ, Amen.'

The chaplain's name was William B. Downey. Like Kiyoshi Watanabe, he too was a Lutheran. The date was August 5, 1945.

In Hiroshima, Mitsuko Watanabe's school in Takasho Street had been affected only slightly by the evacuation. She was waiting for clearance for herself and Kimi and Kei to get to Kyushu, but she was worried about Kei having to work over in Kure. A naval depot, that was sure to be one of the first targets when the bombing began. Mitsuko would be glad when she could shut down the school and get away to Hidezi's place.

There had been no word now from Kiyoshi for some weeks. Perhaps tomorrow would bring a letter.

At 7:17 a.m. on Monday, August 6th 1945, one of the aircraft from Tinian was six miles over Hiroshima. It was "Straight Flush."

Her wireless operator sent out a weather report to the plane carrying the stumpy fat bomb "Little Boy."

Aboard "Enola Gay," it was the last part of the message which, in a way, was the most important. It said: "Advice: Bomb Primary."

And so, precisely 61 minutes later, from a height of 31,600 feet, and from a position 3 miles East of the city, the fat stumpy bomb, "Little Boy," fell from the underbelly of "Enola Gay" and dropped in free flight towards Hiroshima. At that moment, hardly any of the city's population were in air raid shelters. This was an atomic bomb attack, the first one ever.[9]

And so it was that while Lutheran Kiyoshi Watanabe was in Hong Kong, praying desperately for help for himself and his family, Lutheran William Downey was on Tinian praying that the bombers involved in dropping Little Boy on the Watanabe family and thousands of other Hiroshima residents would be kept safe in the Lord's care.[10]

This is one of the most striking historical examples of the incongruity of war. According to the New Testament, Wata-

---

9. Ibid., pp. 142, 143, 144.
10. On August 6, 1945, Kiyoshi's wife and daughter were preparing to leave Hiroshima when they were burned to dust in the Little Boy blast.

nabe and Downey should have had more in common with each other than they had with the aims and cultures of their respective countries. But the stark reality is that in wartime, people of the same religious tradition will shamelessly shoot each other down and destroy each other's families. This has taken place many times since "Christians" invented the theory of a "just war."

The incongruity does not start with blessing the carriers of atomic bombs. It starts with adopting nationalist aims, passing judgment on other cultures, seeing a certain nation as better than others, and interpreting history selectively to support nominal Christendom's view of the world. It includes trying to make the world a better place through political involvement and legislation—a process in which the saving Gospel of Jesus Christ becomes adulterated and finally obliterated. It looks so right but ends so horribly, just like all the works of darkness.

Who then is willing?

If God's standards of peace, political noninvolvement, and acceptance of suffering are the right way for Christians to live, they are right all the time, not just in peaceful times. But thousands of Christians who knew better have become involved in political action and war when the crisis became so great that they could no longer resist the pressure. It was no longer great enough or heroic enough to live according to the Bible. It did not seem to make enough difference to be worth their time. When the crisis became critical enough, New Testament nonresistance seemed like fiddling while Rome burned.

During World War II, C. S. Lewis reminded his students that a crisis such as war is merely an aggravation of the situation in which believers always find themselves. Christians in Communist Russia faced essentially the same situation as Christians in Nazi Germany, in the Catholic Philippines, or in "Christian" America. Political and military crises do not change the essential world in which all Christians live, so they should not change a Christian's simple obedience to God's Word.

> **Political and military crises do not change the essential world in which all Christians live, so they should not change a Christian's simple obedience to God's Word.**

In order to be faithful Christians, we must leave politics behind. That does not mean we have no interest in the lives of people around us. On the contrary, freedom from politics enables us to truly care about people in the New Testament way. It enables us to come to grips with the world's problems in the way Jesus Christ intended. It allows us to engage with society deeply and decisively, not merely to dabble with surface issues.

These are concepts that we must never forget as the end of time draws closer. We are going to be thrown into yet greater crises. If history is any indicator, many Christians will finally give up the New Testament stance in order to make a difference for "good" in the world as truth appears to lie dead in the streets and cultures collapse in a moral vacuum. When it seems that nothing but political action will set the world straight, we will need the calm, solid foundation pictured in Revelation 13:10. "He that leadeth into captivity shall go into captivity: he that killeth with the sword must be killed with the sword. Here is the patience and the faith of the saints."

No matter what people do, no matter what crises come our way, we need to patiently plow on in the pattern Jesus left for us. Looking back will only make us unfit for the kingdom of God.

Only God knows when the time will come that Revelation 22:12 speaks of: "And, behold, I come quickly; and my reward is with me, to give every man according as his work shall be." What is our work? What is our focus? If it is to improve the kingdoms of this world, we will be rewarded with the judgment awaiting those kingdoms. But if we focus on living and spreading the truth of God's Word, we will be worthy through the blood of Jesus to receive the blissful reward of God's eternal, heavenly kingdom.

> "And in the days of these kings shall the God of heaven set up a kingdom, which shall never be destroyed: and the kingdom shall not be left to other people, but it shall break in pieces and consume all these kingdoms, and it shall stand forever" (Daniel 2:44).

> "And let us not be weary in well doing: for in due season we shall reap, if we faint not. As we have therefore opportunity, let us do good unto all men, especially unto them who are of the household of faith" (Galatians 6:9, 10).

> "But ye, beloved, building up yourselves on your most holy faith, praying in the Holy Ghost, keep yourselves in the love of God, looking for the mercy of our Lord Jesus Christ unto eternal life. And of some have compassion, making a difference: and others save with fear, pulling them out of the fire; hating even the garment spotted by the flesh. Now unto him that is able to keep you from falling, and to present you faultless before the presence of his glory with exceeding joy, To the only wise God our Saviour, be glory

and majesty, dominion and power, both now and ever. Amen" (Jude 20-25)

Magnificat anima mea Dominum!

For Further Reading

Andrew, Brother and Al Janssen. *Light Force*. Grand Rapids, Mi.: Fleming H. Revell, 2004.

Artz, Frederick B. *The Mind of the Middle Ages*. Chicago, Il.: The University of Chicago Press, 1953.

Augsburger, Myron S. *The Robe of God*. Scottdale, Pa.: Herald Press, 2000.

Barclay, William. *Letters to the Seven Churches*. New York, Ny.: Abingdon Press, 1957.

Barna, George. *What Americans Believe*. Ventura, Ca.: Regal Books, 1991.

Bear, Lily A. *Report for Duty*. Harrisonburg, Va.: Christian Light Publications, 2003.

Bender, Wilbur J. *Nonresistance in Colonial Pennsylvania*. Ephrata, Pa.: Eastern Mennonite Publications, 2001. (Reprint of 1949 edition).

Brown, Dale W. *Biblical Pacifism*. Nappanee, In.: Evangel Publishing House, 1986.

Burdge, Edsel Jr. and Samuel L. Horst. *Building on the Gospel Foundation*. Scottdale, Pa.: Herald Press, 2004.

Camp, Lee C. *Mere Discipleship*. Grand Rapids, Mi.: Brazos Press, 2008.

Contenau, Georges. *Everyday Life in Babylon and Assyria*. London, England: Edward Arnold Publishers Ltd, 1954.

Chacour, Elias. *Blood Brothers*. Grand Rapids, Mi.: Chosen Books, 2003.

Cullmann, Oscar. *The State in the New Testament*. New York, Ny.: Charles Scribner's Sons, 1956.

Davids, Richard C. *The Man Who Moved a Mountain*. Philadelphia, Pa.: Fortress Press, 1970.

Durant, Will. *Caesar and Christ*. New York, Ny.: Simon and Schuster, 1944.

------. *Our Oriental Heritage,* New York, Ny.: Simon and Schuster, 1954.

Ellul, Jacques. *The Political Illusion*. New York, Ny.: Alfred A. Knopf, 1967.

------. *The Subversion of Christianity*. Grand Rapids, Mi.: Eerdmans, 1986.

Gaustad, Edwin and Leigh Schmidt, *The Religious History of America*. New York, Ny.: HarperCollins Publishers, 2004.

Glover, T. R. *The Conflict of Religions in the Early Roman Empire*. Boston, Ma.: Beacon Press, 1960.

Guinness, Os. *The American Hour*. New York, Ny.: The Free Press, 1993.

Hislop, Alexander. *The Two Babylons.* Neptune, Nj.: Loizeaux Brothers, 1959.

Hornus, Jean-Michel. *It Is Not Lawful for Me to Fight.* Scottdale, Pa.: Herald Press, 1980.

Hunter, James Davison. *Before the Shooting Begins.* New York, Ny.: The Free Press, 1994.

I Couldn't Fight and Other CO Stories. Ephrata, Pa.: Eastern Mennonite Publications, 2002.

Ingram, Robert T. *Government Schools versus Free Schools.* Chicago, Il.: Christian Schools Service, Inc., 1961.

Juhnke, James C. *Vision, Doctrine, War.* Scottdale, Pa.: Herald Press, 1989.

Kraybill, Donald B. ed. *The Amish and the State.* Baltimore, Md.: The Johns Hopkins University Press, 1993.

------, Steven M. Nolt, and David L. Weaver-Zercher. *Amish Grace.* San Francisco, Ca.: John Wiley and Sons, 2007.

Lind, Millard. *Answer to War.* Scottdale, Pa.: Mennonite Publishing House, 1952.

Littell, Franklin Hamlin. *From State Church to Pluralism.* Garden City, Nj.: Anchor Books, 1962.

MacMaster, Richard K. *Land, Piety, Peoplehood.* Scottdale, Pa.: Herald Press, 1985.

------, Samuel L. Horst and Robert F. Ulle. *Conscience in Crisis.* Scottdale, Pa.: Herald Press, 1979.

Marty, Martin E. *Protestantism in the United States.* New York, Ny.: Charles Scribner's Sons, 1986.

May, Henry F. *The Enlightenment in America.* New York, Ny.: Oxford University Press, 1976.

Miller, William Lee. *Piety along the Potomac.* Boston, Ma.: Houghton Mifflin Company, 1964.

Morgan, Edmund S., ed. *Puritan Political Ideas.* Indianapolis, In.: The Bobbs-Merrill Company, Inc., 1965.

Murray, Margaret A. *The Splendor that was Egypt.* Mineola, Ny.: Dover Publications, 2004 (revised edition).

Nolan, Liam. *Small Man of Nanataki.* New York, Ny.: E. P. Dutton and Co., 1966

Noll, Mark A., Nathan O. Hatch, and George M. Marsden. *The Search For Christian America.* Westchester, Il.: Crossway Books, 1983.

Nolt, Steven M. *A History of the Amish.* Intercourse, Pa.: Good Books, 1992.

Olasky, Marvin. *Abortion Rites.* Wheaton, Il.: Crossway Books, 1992.

Osbeck, Kenneth. *101 More Hymn Stories.* Grand Rapids, Mi.: Kregel Publications, 1985.

Rahner, Hugo. *Church and State in Early Christianity.* San Francisco, Ca.: Ignatius Press, 1992.

Rohrer, Fred. *Saloon Fight at Berne, Ind. Berne, In.*: The Berne Witness Company, 1913.

Russell, Stephen. *Overcoming Evil God's Way.* Guys Mills, Pa.: Faith Builders Resource Group, 2008.

Ruth, John L. *The Earth Is the Lord's.* Scottdale, Pa.: Herald Press, 2001.

------. *Twas Seeding Time.* Scottdale, Pa.: Herald Press, 1976.

Saggs, H. W. F. *The Greatness That Was Babylon.* New York, Ny.: The New American Library, 1962.

------. *The Might That Was Assyria.* London, England: Sidgwick & Jackson, 1984.

Schlabach, Theron F. *Peace, Faith, Nation.* Scottdale, Pa.: Herald Press, 1988.

Showalter, Lester. *The History of Christian Education: A Mennonite Perspective.* Crockett, Ky.: Rod and Staff Publishers, Inc., 1997

Spiritual Life in Anabaptism. Translated and edited by Cornelius J. Dyck. Scottdale, Pa.: Herald Press, 1995.

Thomas, Cal, and Ed Dobson. *Blinded By Might.* Grand Rapids, Mi.: Zondervan Publishing House, 1999.

Toews, Paul. *Mennonites in American Society, 1930-1970.* Scottdale, Pa.: Herald Press, 1996.

Wertenbaker, Thomas Jefferson. *The Puritan Oligarchy.* New York, Ny.: Charles Scribner's Sons, 1947.

Yoder, John Howard. *Discipleship as Political Responsibility.* Scottdale, Pa.: Herald Press, 2003.

------, *The Christian Witness to the State.* Scottdale, Pa.: Herald Press, 2002.

Yoder, Paton. *Tradition and Transition.* Scottdale, Pa.: Herald Press, 1991.